Brown and Black Communication

**Recent Titles in Contributions to the
Study of Mass Media and Communications**

Brown and Black Communication

*Latino and African American
Conflict and Convergence in
Mass Media*

Edited by Diana I. Rios and A. N. Mohamed

Foreword by Clint C. Wilson and Felix Gutierrez

*Contributions to the Study of Mass Media and Communications,
Number 65*

PRAEGER

**Westport, Connecticut
London**

Library of Congress Cataloging-in-Publication Data

Brown and Black communication : Latino and African American conflict and
convergence in mass media / edited by Diana I. Rios and A. N. Mohamed ; foreword by
Clint C. Wilson and Felix Gutierrez.
    p. cm.—(Contributions to the study of mass media and communications, ISSN
   0732–4456 ; no. 65)
  Includes bibliographical references and index.
  ISBN 0–313–31650–3 (alk. paper)
    1. Hispanic Americans in mass media.   2. African Americans in mass media.   3. Mass
media and minorities—United States.   4. United States—Ethnic relations.   I. Rios, Diana
Isabel Arredondo, 1962–   II. Mohamed, A. N. (Ali N.), 1958–   III.   Series.
P94.5.H58 B76 2003
302.23′089′68073—dc21   2002072850

British Library Cataloguing in Publication Data is available.

Library of Congress Catalog Card Number: 2002072850
ISBN: 0–313–31650–3
ISSN: 0732–4456

First published in 2003

Praeger Publishers, 88 Post Road West, Westport, CT 06881
An imprint of Greenwood Publishing Group, Inc.
www.praeger.com

Printed in the United States of America

The paper used in this book complies with the
Permanent Paper Standard issued by the National
Information Standards Organization (Z39.48–1984).

10 9 8 7 6 5 4 3 2 1

Copyright Acknowledgment

The editors and publisher gratefully acknowledge permission to quote from the following:

Chapter 10 is condensed from Domke, D., McCoy, K., & Torres, M. (1999). News media, racial perceptions, and political cognition. *Communication Research, 26,* 570–607. Copyright © 1999 by Sage
Publications, Inc. Reprinted by permission of Sage Publications, Inc.

Contents

Foreword

Clint C. Wilson and Felix Gutierrez

As recently as the mid-1980s there was a very small body of scholarly literature on the relationship between American cultural/racial "minority" groups and popular mass communications media. Moreover, although the wave of multicultural demography had long since begun to wash across the social landscape of the United States, most scholars were focusing attention on the perceived omnipotence of a mass communications system that they believed effectively brought all cultural groups under its socioeconomic umbrella.

Implicit in this notion was the idea that the media treated all Americans alike and that all Americans-even those with prefixes, like African and Latino—would respond alike to the mass messages.

This approach persisted despite revelations made nearly 20 years earlier by the Kerner Commission and other government agencies that vast discrepancies in communications media content, portrayal, employment opportunity, and perspective smacked strongly of racism and threatened the very fabric of American democracy. And, while media industries moved at a snail's pace to correct their inequities, higher education institutions moved even more slowly toward encouraging scholarship and developing curricula that would demonstrate leadership in a vital discipline of the social science academy.

When we began our work in this field in the late 1960s it was immediately evident that much of the groundwork was uneven. For example, much more research had been done on black press history than on Latino press history in the United States. This circumstance largely resulted from the fact that black Americans were numerically the largest nonwhite racial group in the United and their long civil rights struggle had captured the national and international consciousness for decades. Our approach, however, was rooted in the idea that although there were—and remain—many differences between and among African Americans and Latinos, there are commonalties in the way both groups have historically been treated by mainstream communications media.

Yet, except for the work of a few barrier-breaking scholars such as Sharon Murphy and Alexis Tan in the mid-1970s, no researchers were consistently examining the similarities and differences in communication behavior between African Americans and Latinos. With the field of cross-cultural media diversity research not yet established by scholars or understood by publishers and journal editors, the opportunities for research and publication in the field were quite limited through the mid-1980s. This, no doubt, had a chilling effect on faculty members who saw little publication opportunity for work in this area of growing importance.

Now comes the present anthology that takes a multifaceted approach to the consequence of the dynamics of demographic change as Latinos begin to surpass blacks for the dubious honor as the largest cultural "minority" group in the United States. It goes beyond the common interests shared by the two groups and instead focuses on areas that portend conflicts that may arise as Latinos flex their demographic muscles and assume a larger share of media attention.

Some may apply an adage we recall from our past incarnation as soldiers in President Lyndon B. Johnson's War on Poverty, which cautioned blacks and browns against fighting over crumbs that remained after the majority had eaten the pie. With that caveat in mind, we applaud this volume in the spirit of its contribution to continued exploration and dialogue that will hopefully lead to better understanding of how media impact on both groups and affect their relationships with each other. The contributors and editors who made this volume possible have broken new ground in building an understanding of similarities and differences in communication media issues affecting the nation's two largest communities of color. We encourage you to read their works and hope it will inspire others to further develop this important field of scholarship.

Preface

What will United States communities and their accompanying communication issues be like after the turn of the millennium? Social scientists agree that a "browning" phenomenon is now more prominent than ever in major cities where non-white ethnic and racial groups have established households, businesses and significant social, cultural and political presence. Part of the "browning" process of our country is the proportional growth of Spanish-speaking heritage peoples. It was long predicted that Latinos would eventually become the nation's largest ethnic group, a position long held by African Americans. This demographic shift is sure to heighten both processes of conflict and convergence in cross-cultural and mass communication realms. Disjunction and cooperation will exist between ethnic and racial minorities and European Americans as well as among ethnic and racial groups themselves.

The goal of this book is to focus on the two largest ethnic minority groups. Past research across the disciplines have focused on black and white or white and brown relations. The two largest ethnic groups in the United States have rarely been studied together. In the spirit of cultural, ethnic and racial convergence, this interdisciplinary collection brings to the forefront cultural and racial themes that have been discussed in closed meetings and behind closed doors. Now is the key time to acknowledge problems in our communities and to wrestle with the solutions to these problems. Our anthology contains four parts, each containing insightful contributions from scholars grounded in brown, black, and other ethnic and racial experiences and expertise:

Part I: Cross-Cultural Relations

Part II: News

Part III: Advertising

Part IV: Education and Community Relations

This volume is valuable as a research, classroom, and professional tool in understanding the basis for cooperation and misunderstanding among Latinos and African Americans.

ACKNOWLEDGMENTS

The co-editors wish to thank many people and organizations for assistance and support of this endeavor.

The Puerto Rican and Latino Studies Institute at the University of Connecticut and the Edinboro University of Pennsylvania provided research support necessary for conducting this work. We are especially indebted to Jim Whiteman of the Technology and Communications Center at Edinboro University for his patience and selfless assistance with technical aspects of editing this text. Angela L. Walker from the Department of Psychology at the University of Connecticut was a star research assistant on this project from beginning to end. Colleagues in the Minorities and Communication Division of the Association for Education in Journalism and Mass Communication, other AEJMC divisions, and the Commission on the Status of Minorities and Commission on the Status of Women provided us with key advice. We are grateful to our families for their patience and high spirits throughout the conception, editing, and finalization of this project.

Finally, we are indebted to people in our communities in the United States and around the globe for nurturing tolerance and understanding in multiethnic/racial and multicultural societies.

Introduction

Diana I. Rios

CULTURAL UNDERSTANDING AND COMMUNICATION, THE BROWN AND BLACK WAY

I was introduced to blackness in Fresno, California at Edison High School in the early sixties. My father had chosen to teach at a predominantly black high school and when my mother and we small children went to pick up papa after school, I recall pretty girls waving and cooing at us, saying how cute we were and could we tell them our names. I assumed they were Mexican just like I was, and that when I became older, I would look and act just like them. I understood the high school students to be culturally similar to "us," having no contradictory information from my parents that led me to conclude otherwise. Their verbal responses to our presence was the same as that which I and other siblings received from relatives and close friends of the family, who were by and large of Mexican heritage.

I became more aware of the world of Chicano-black relations in the late sixties in Tucson, Arizona and in the early seventies in Oakland, California. In my majority Mexican American elementary school in Tucson, a play yard conflict arose between two girls, one of whom was much darker in skin tone than all the others. Childish insults were traded and then physical conflict followed when one Mexican American girl, notorious for abrasive communication style, used the "n" word in her ultimate verbal attack. A team of self-appointed Mexican American girls pulled both fighters from the ground and held onto both of them. A yard-lady came across the field to escort them to the principal's office. As the yard-lady arrived, several voices advised her, "She used the 'n' word." Other voices confirmed "Ohhhhh, she's in trouble, she used the 'n' word." After the incident, we all con-

ferred with each other about how many black students went to our school. We then
continued to discuss how bad it was to use the "n" word.

In the early 1970s, my family moved to Oakland, California, and settled into a
predominantly black neighborhood. My parochial school classmates appeared to
be about half black and half Mexican to me. I identified the "smartest" girl in class
to be Shirley, a chubby black girl with glasses, a big curl resting on her forehead
and a smartly pressed uniform. One of my favorite programs was "Julia," which I
believed was the kind of family that Shirley and half the school must have come
from—it was the only black family on television. These were some of the early
foundational experiences in my developing internal perspectives about
brown-black conflicts and convergences.

At various times Latinos and African Americans have found themselves as one
of the few in a predominantly Latino or black site. Latinos and African Americans
have also lived with minority status among European Americans. Growing up in
communities where Chicanos and blacks had the opportunity to know a great deal
about one another, I was later surprised when I found this cross-cultural knowledge not to be the norm. This became especially obvious to me when befriending
students of color attending my predominantly white high school and later, in predominantly white universities.

It is clear that as Latinos and African Americans continue to move into higher levels of work and study we have more opportunities to engage and learn about the
things that bind us together. African Americans and Latinos are the two largest eth-
nic/racial groups. We all have experienced losses, challenges, and gains with regard
to our languages, cultural systems, and voting rights; our educational, work, and advancement opportunities; and more favorable media representation and more fair and
balanced news. We cannot rely on the myths propagated by general market media
about each other. We must critique media and train our students to eliminate cultural
bias. We must make efforts to learn more about each other, and encourage, and support diplomatic communication efforts. Many problems and treasures bind us and
will continue to do so more intensely than ever before in the twenty-first century. Let
us use this book as one place to begin reaching toward one another. It is through cultural understanding and discerning human and mediated communication that we can
better contribute to our communities and our society.

Part I: Cross-Cultural Relations

Chapter 1

Communication in Brown-Black Personal Relationships

Stanley O. Gaines, Jr., and Stella D. Garcia-Lopez

INTRODUCTION

The Spike Lee-directed film, *Jungle Fever*, caused quite a stir when it was released in 1991. *Jungle Fever* depicted a romantic liaison between an African American man (Flipper) and an Italian American woman (Angie) and, at times, seemed to derive as much of its controversy from the anti-miscegenationist views of its director as it did from its storyline (see Guerrero, 1993). In some circles, the term "jungle fever" became synonymous with romantic relationships that crossed ethnic (and, especially, racial) boundaries (Mills, 1996).

As it turns out, *Jungle Fever* was not the first Spike Lee film that dealt with interethnic romance. Two years earlier, Spike Lee's *Do the Right Thing* (1989) featured a romantic relationship between an African American man (Mookie) and a Puerto Rican woman (Tina) that already had produced a son (Hector). However, neither the director nor his critics spent much time commenting on the interethnic aspect of the relationship between Mookie and Tina (see Guerrero, 1993). Apparently, a black-brown romantic relationship either was not considered as "deviant" or was not as anxiety-provoking in the minds of many relationship outsiders as was a black-white romantic relationship (see Root, 1992).

Despite the presumed lack of alarm accompanying the brown-black romance in *Do the Right Thing*, personal relationships between Latinas/os and African Americans—especially romantic relationships—are relatively rare in occurrence, even when compared with other types of interethnic relationships (e.g., Latino-Anglo, Asian American-Anglo; Baptiste, 1991). Perhaps because of the rarity of their occurrence, brown-black romantic relationships seldom have been objects of discussion within the field of personal relationships. In this chapter, we shall examine communication in personal relationships between members of the two largest groups of persons of color in the United States. Due to space constraints, we will limit our focus to heterosexual romantic relationships between Latinas/os and African Americans. We shall consider (1) relationships involving Latinas/os in general, (2) relationships involving African Americans in general, and (3) relationships specifically involving Latinas/os paired with African Americans. Moreover, within each section, we will compare and contrast the perspectives of "outsiders" (i.e., persons other than the relationship partners) versus "insiders" (i.e., the relationship partners), consistent with the necessity for adopting both perspectives when studying interracial relationships (Gaines & Ickes, 1997).

Relationships Involving Non-Black Latinas and Latinos in General

As a whole, Latinas/os are poised to become the largest ethnic minority group in the United States shortly after the dawn of the twenty-first century (Fox, 1996). Most Latinas/os can trace their ancestry to nations other than (or in addition to) the United States, although much of what is known today as the western United States once belonged to Mexico (the nation of origin for ancestors of most Latinas/os in the United States; Chilman, 1993). More than 70% of all married Hispanics in the United States are paired with other Hispanics; the spouses frequently (though not always) share a common nation of origin (e.g., Cuba, Puerto Rico; Baptiste, 1987).

According to Gaines et al. (1997), much of the social science literature on Hispanic male-female relationship processes historically has adopted and reinforced negative stereotypes regarding "macho" men and "submissive" women. In contrast, Gaines et al. (1997) argued that a more culturally sensitive and factually accurate portrayal of relationship processes between Hispanic men and women must take the influence of a cultural value termed familism (i.e., an orientation toward the welfare of one's immediate and extended family) into account. Gaines et al. (1997) reasoned that the degree to which Latinas and Latinos internalize a familistic orientation is likely to be related positively and significantly to individuals' reciprocity or give-and-take of socioemotional support (i.e., communication of affection and respect; Foa & Foa, 1974).

Outsiders' perspective. In an experimental, large-scale study of outsiders' perceptions of presumed relationships involving persons of color, Garcia and Rivera (1999) found that Latina-Latino couples were viewed as relatively high in stability, compatibility in general, sexual compatibility in particular, and attractiveness. Conversely, relationship outsiders generally viewed Latina-Latino couples as relatively unlikely to argue or to dissolve their relationships. Overall, relationship outsiders viewed Latina-Latino couples as relatively unlikely to experience communication problems.

In another experimental, large-scale study, favorable perceptions by outsiders regarding perceived Hispanic-Hispanic couples were reported by Garcia-Lopez, Dzindolet, and Rivera (2000). In general, perceivers of Hispanic-Hispanic and other racially similar couples believed that such pairings would receive approval from the friends and parents of male as well as female partners. These positive perceptions were evident for brown-brown pairs who ostensibly had reached either the friendship stage or the "in love" stage of their relationships.

Insiders' perspective. Some correlational, large-scale research, relying on self-reported data from participants, has focused on particular similarities and differences in the communication of relational issues or concepts among Latinas/os. For example, according to Castaneda (1993), the qualities that Mexican Americans associate with romantic love include trust, communication/sharing (e.g., self-disclosure), mutual respect (which was hypothesized to have a vital role in Hispanic culture), and shared attitudes and values (which referred to individuals' understanding, but not necessarily acceptance, of partners' beliefs). Castaneda's (1993) findings suggest that in order for marital therapy to be effective among heterosexual Hispanic couples, mental health professionals should incorporate the qualities that partners associate with romantic love into clinical and counseling sessions. In another correlational study, Negy and Snyder (1997) found that Mexican American couples tended to score higher in marital distress than did Anglo couples. However, ethnicity was not a significant predictor of partners' efforts at problem-solving communication. Unfortunately, the studies by Negy and Snyder (1997) and Castaneda (1993) did not examine the impact of stereotypes, familism, or discrimination on the daily lives of Hispanic couples.

In a qualitative, clinical study of Spanish-heritage immigrant families, Baptiste (1987) observed that not all newly arrived Latina/o couples in the United States embrace familism to the same degree. Nevertheless, regardless of the spouses' nation of origin, nearly all Latina/o couples in the United States have been subjected to cultural discrimination and to societal pressure to internalize the cultural value of *individualism* (i.e., an orientation toward the welfare of oneself; Gaines et al., 1997). Both discrimination and individualism can undermine Latina/o couples' attempts to maintain satisfying, stable relationships via mutual socioemotional support. One consequence of relationship instability is a decrease in the proportion of children living with two parents in Latina/o households over time (i.e., from 80% in the 1970s to 65% in the 1990s; Fine, 2000). Thus, one challenge facing Latina/o couples is the establishment of communication patterns (e.g., reciprocity of affection and respect) that foster relationship satisfaction and stability.

Relationships Involving Non-Hispanic African Americans in General

African Americans comprised the largest so-called ethnic minority group in the United States (Fox, 1996). Unlike Latinas and Latinos, most African Americans cannot trace their ancestry outside the United States; and most African Americans have ancestors who lived and died in the southern United States (see McAdoo, 1997). More than 90% of all married blacks in the United States are paired with other blacks (Glick, 1997); even among blacks who were born outside the United States, the spouses frequently (though not always) share a common nation of origin (e.g., Haiti, Jamaica; Baptiste, Hardy, & Lewis, 1997).

According to Gaines et al. (1997), much of the social science literature on black male-female relationship processes historically has adopted and reinforced negative stereotypes regarding "ineffectual" men and "domineering" women. Thus, the stereotypes concerning female and male African Americans paired with each other are markedly different from the stereotypes concerning Latinas and Latinos paired with each other. In contrast, Gaines et al. (1997) argued that a more culturally sensitive and factually accurate portrayal of relationship processes between black men and women must take the influence of a cultural value termed collectivism (i.e., an orientation toward the welfare of one's larger community, regardless of how one defines that community) into account. Gaines et al. (1997) reasoned that the degree to which blacks internalize a collectivistic orientation is likely to be related positively and significantly to individuals' reciprocity or mutual giving of socioemotional support (i.e., communication of affection and respect).

Outsiders' perspective. In the aforementioned experiment on outsiders' perceptions of presumed relationships involving persons of color, Garcia and Rivera (1999) found that African American couples were viewed as relatively high in compatibility in general, sexual compatibility in particular, and likelihood to marry. Conversely, relationship outsiders generally viewed African American couples as relatively low in stability and as high in likelihood to argue. Overall, relationship outsiders viewed African American couples as relatively likely to encounter difficulties in communication.

In the aforementioned experiment by Garcia-Lopez, Dzindolet, and Rivera (2000), black-black couples who were presented either as friends or as lovers were viewed by outsiders as having the approval of the partners' friends and parents. Summarizing across the studies by Garcia-Lopez, Dzindolet, and Rivera (2000) and by Garcia and Rivera (1999), relationship outsiders tended to view African American men and women as physically "belonging" together (although not necessarily happy together). Such a viewpoint on the part of outsiders concerning who does or does not "belong" together may reflect a basic cognitive organizing principle of similarity (Gaines & Ickes, 1997).

Insiders' perspective. Some large-scale research on African American couples directly addresses societal stereotypes about, and cultural values among, African American couples. For example, in a quantitative study, Taylor and Zhang (1992) found that maritally distressed black couples were more likely to have internalized negative stereotypes about African Americans than were martially nondistressed black couples. Also, in a qualitative study, Thomas (1990) reported that dual-career, professional black couples consciously sought to impart black (i.e., collectivistic) cultural values to their offspring but felt stymied to some extent by the pervasiveness of white (i.e., individualistic) values in American society. Finally, both studies revealed that racism weighs heavily on the minds of African American spouses (Thomas, 1990), especially husbands (Taylor & Zhang, 1992).

In a qualitative, clinical study of English-speaking Caribbean immigrant families, Baptiste, Hardy, and Lewis (1997) observed that newly arrived African-descent couples in the United States are far from monolithic concerning African (i.e., collectivistic) cultural values. By the same token, regardless of where the spouses were born, virtually all African-descent couples in the United States have been subjected to racial discrimination and to societal pressure to internalize the cultural value of individualism. As is the case with Latina/o couples, both discrimination and individualism can undermine African American couples' attempts to maintain satisfying, stable relationships via mutual communication of socioemotional support. One consequence of relationship instability is a decrease in the proportion of children living with two parents in African American households over time (i.e., from 60% in the 1970s to 33% in the 1990s; Fine, 2000). Therefore, as was true for Latina/o couples, one challenge facing African American couples is the establishment of communication patterns (e.g., reciprocity of affection and respect) that foster relationship satisfaction and stability.

Relationships Involving Non-Black Latinas and Latinos Paired with Non-Hispanic African Americans

Within the United States, fewer than 5% of all marriages can be classified as "interracial" (Gaines & Ickes, 1997). In turn, fewer than 25% of all "interracial" marriages involve African Americans. Finally, fewer than 15% of all "interracial" marriages involving African Americans are with non-black Latinas/os, Asian Americans, or members of other ethnic minority groups (Pinkney, 1993). Compared to the literatures on Latina/o romantic relationships and African American romantic relationships, respectively, the literature on romantic relationships between non-black Latinas/os and non-Hispanic African Americans is virtually nonexistent (Baptiste, 1991).

According to Gaines et al. (1997), much of the social science literature on interethnic male-female relationship processes historically has adopted and reinforced negative stereotypes regarding "depraved" men and "accessible" women. Other reviews of the literature have hypothesized potential structural and nonstructural influences on individuals' willingness to date or marry outside their racial or ethnic group. Structural influences may include social class (e.g., Kouri & Lasswell, 1993) and equity in the exchange of social and monetary assets (e.g., Wade, 1991). Conversely, nonstructural influences may include individuals' perception of their field of eligibles (e.g., Tucker & Mitchell-Kernan, 1995), self-esteem (e.g., Gurung & Duong, 1999), sexual and other-race curiosity (e.g., Shibazaki & Brennan, 1998), and rebellion/liberation from their own racial heritage (e.g., Porterfield, 1978, 1982).

The stereotypes concerning women and men in interracial relationships are similar to the stereotypes concerning Latinas and Latinos paired with each other but are dissimilar to the stereotypes concerning female and male African Americans paired with each other. In contrast, Gaines et al. (1997) argued that a more culturally sensitive and factually accurate portrayal of relationship processes between men and women from different ethnic groups must take the influence of a cultural value termed romanticism (i.e., an orientation toward the welfare of one's romantic relationship) into account. Gaines et al. (1997) reasoned that the degree to which women and men in interethnic relationships internalize a romantic orientation is likely to be related positively and significantly to individuals' reciprocity of socioemotional support.

Outsiders' perspective. In the aforementioned experiment on outsiders' perceptions of presumed relationships involving persons of color, Garcia and Rivera (1999) found that Hispanic male-black female couples were viewed as relatively low in stability, compatibility in general, sexual compatibility in particular, attractiveness, and likelihood of marriage. Conversely, relationship outsiders generally viewed Hispanic male-black female couples as relatively unlikely to argue.

Interestingly, Garcia and Rivera (1999) found that relationship outsiders' perceptions of black male-Hispanic female couples were not viewed as negatively as were Hispanic male-black female couples. For example, black male-Hispanic female couples were viewed as higher in compatibility in general, sexual compatibility in particular, attractiveness, and likelihood to marry than were Hispanic male-black female couples. Nevertheless, black male-Hispanic female couples were viewed as less stable than were intraracial black couples (who, in turn, were viewed as less stable than were intraracial Hispanic couples). Despite the negativity that relationship outsiders apparently felt toward brown-black couples in general, it is noteworthy that relationship outsiders did *not* view brown-black couples as saddled with communication problems per se.

Insiders' perspective. On one hand, the romantic model of interracial relationship processes as proposed by Gaines et al. (1997) explicitly suggests a cultural basis for similarity between Hispanic and black partners. On the other hand, the familistic model of Latina/o relationship processes and the collectivistic model of African American relationship processes implicitly (though not explicitly) suggest cultural bases for *dis*similarity between Hispanic and black partners. Results of a qualitative, clinical study of interracial and/or intercultural families by Baptiste (1984) suggest that a genuine dynamic tension often arises between similarity in interethnic spouses' romanticism and dissimilarity in the spouses' other cultural values (e.g., familism, collectivism). Such dynamic tension may be manifested in spouses' agreement that they must shield themselves and each other from the verbal and physical slings and arrows directed toward them by outsiders (a romantic belief), coexisting with spouses' disagreements concerning the moral imperative to formally adopt nieces and nephews (a familistic belief) versus friends of offspring (a collectivistic belief). Furthermore, even if the spouses themselves do not hold competing views regarding collectivism, familism, or romanticism, relationship outsiders might try to persuade both partners to choose one value system over the other (see Baptiste, 1991).

Conceptually speaking, Gaines et al. (1997) resolved the apparent paradox between interethnic spouses' value similarity and value dissimilarity by proposing a "we-oriented," inclusive model of relationship processes that transcends husbands' and wives' racial and cultural backgrounds. According to the inclusive model, collectivism, familism, and romanticism—all of which are intercorrelated positively and significantly (Gaines et al., 1999)—may be embraced to varying degrees by individuals within any ethnic group; and all three cultural values are likely to be reflected positively and significantly in individuals' reciprocity of socioemotional support. Empirically speaking, partners in brown-black romantic relationships can surmount cultural barriers by developing appreciation for each other's heritage. Some brown-black couples might achieve such mutual appreciation through their own efforts; whereas other brown-black couples might achieve mutual appreciation through the intervention of mental health professionals (Baptiste, 1984, 1991).

Given that the divorce rate for "interracial" couples in general is well above the national average of 50% (Gaines & Liu, 2000), brown-black couples may experience special difficulties in maintaining satisfying, stable relationships. brown-black couples are likely to encounter racial as well as cultural discrimination, along with pressures toward the "me-orientation" of individualism, from society at large (Baptiste, 1991). The establishment of communication patterns that foster relationship satisfaction and stability, such as the reciprocity of affection and respect, may be especially crucial for the long-term survival of brown-black couples.

CONCLUSION

As we have seen in this chapter, communication problems are not inevitable in brown-black personal relationships. Among interethnic couples in general, differences between husbands' and wives' verbal and nonverbal forms of communication can be identified and addressed successfully in therapy, especially when mental health professionals who work with those couples have been trained to adopt multicultural perspectives (Baptiste, 1984, 1991). In fact, according to Tannen (1990), *any* male-female romantic relationship—whether they cross ethnic boundaries or not—can be considered "cross-cultural" in that, at least within the United States, women and men are socialized to communicate in ways that society deems to be appropriate for their particular gender. All in all, relationship outsiders' stereotypes notwithstanding, results of empirical studies on relationship insiders indicate that brown-black heterosexual couples are just as capable of engaging in pro-relationship patterns of communication as are other heterosexual couples.

In closing, we return to the images of interethnic relationships that appear in director Spike Lee's films, such as *Jungle Fever* and *Do the Right Thing*. In one of the more memorable scenes of *Jungle Fever*, two white racist police officers—in fact, the same two officers who had killed a black man (Radio Raheem) during a fight outside Sal's Pizzeria (and who, it seems, were transferred to another division in New York City, rather than fired or placed on suspension)—misinterpret play-fighting between Flipper and Angie as attempted rape on Flipper's part and ultimately pull their weapons on Flipper. How would the police officers have responded if, in *Do the Right Thing*, Mookie and Tina had been play-fighting on a public street? Would the police officers have misinterpreted the situation as badly (or reacted as aggressively) if they had seen a Puerto Rican woman (Tina), rather than a white woman (Angie), entangled physically and emotionally with a black man? The fact that such questions are left unanswered attests to the "out of sight, out of mind" attitude toward brown-black personal relationships that, unfortunately, characterizes much of academia and popular culture alike.

REFERENCES

Baptiste, D. A., Jr. (1984). Marital and family therapy with racially/culturally intermarried stepfamilies: Issues and guidelines. *Family Relations*, 33, 373–380.

Baptiste, D. A., Jr. (1987). Family therapy with Spanish-heritage immigrant families in cultural transition. *Contemporary Family Therapy*, 9, 229–251.

Baptiste, D. A., Jr. (1991). Therapeutic strategies with Black-Hispanic families: Identity problems of a neglected minority. *Journal of Family Psychotherapy*, 1, 15–38.

Baptiste, D. A., Jr., Hardy, K. V., & Lewis, L. (1997). Family therapy with English Caribbean immigrant families in the United States: Issues of emigration, culture, and race. *Contemporary Family Therapy*, 19, 337–359.

Castaneda, D. M. (1993). The meaning of romantic love among Mexican-Americans. *Journal of Social Behavior and Personality*, 8, 257–272.

Chilman, C. S. (1993). Hispanic families in the United States: Research perspectives. In H. P. McAdoo (Ed.), *Family ethnicity: Strength in diversity* (pp. 141–163). Newbury Park, CA: Sage.

Fine, M. A. (2000). Divorce and single parenting. In C. Hendrick, & S. S. Hendrick (Eds.), *Close relationships: A sourcebook* (pp. 139–152). Thousand Oaks, CA: Sage.

Foa, U. G., & Foa, E. B. (1974). *Societal structures of the mind*. Springfield, IL: Thomas.

Fox, G. (1996). *Hispanic nation: Culture, politics, and the constructing of identity*. Tucson: University of Arizona Press.

Gaines, S. O., Jr., with Buriel, R., Liu, J. H., & Rios, D. I. (1997). *Culture, ethnicity, and personal relationship processes*. New York: Routledge.

Gaines, S. O., Jr., Gilstrap, S., Kim, M., Yi, J., Rusbult, C. E., Holcomb, D., Gaertner, L., & Lee, J. (June, 1999). Cultural value orientations: Measurement and manifestation in responses to accommodative dilemmas. Paper presented at the 1999 joint conference of the International Network on Personal Relationships and the International Society for the Study of Personal Relationships, University of Louisville, Louisville, KY.

Gaines, S. O., Jr., & Ickes, W. (1997). Perspectives on interracial relationships. In S. Duck (Ed.), *Handbook of personal relationships* (2 ed., pp. 197–220). Chichester, UK: Wiley.

Gaines, S. O., Jr., & Liu, J. H. (2000). Multicultural/multiracial relationships. In C. Hendrick, & S. S. Hendrick (Eds.), *Close relationships: A sourcebook* (pp. 97–108). Thousand Oaks, CA: Sage.

Garcia, S. D., & Rivera, S. M. (1999). Perceptions of Hispanic and African-American couples at the friendship or engagement stage of a relationship. *Journal of Social and Personal Relationships*, 16, 65–86.

Garcia-Lopez, S. D., Dzindolet, M., & Rivera, S. (2000). Viewed from a different angle: Perceptions of same and mixed race couples. Unpublished manuscript.

Glick, P. C. (1997). Demographic pictures of African American families. In H. P. McAdoo (Ed.), *Black families* (3 ed., pp. 118–138). Thousand Oaks, CA: Sage.

Guerrero, E. (1993). *Framing Blackness: The African American image in film*. Philadelphia: Temple University Press.

Gurung, R. A. R., & Duong, T. (1999). Mixing and matching: Assessing the concomitants of mixed-ethnic relationships. *Journal of Social and Personal Relationships, 16,* 639–657.

Kouri, K. M., & Lasswell, M. (1993). Black-White marriages: Social change and intergenerational mobility. *Marriage and Family Review,* 19, 241–255.

McAdoo, H. P. (1997). Upward mobility across generations in African American families. In H. P. McAdoo (Ed.), *Black families* (3 ed., pp. 139–162). Thousand Oaks, CA: Sage.

Mills, C. (1996). Interracial marriage is identical to same-race marriage. In B. Szumski (Ed.), *Interracial America* (pp. 210–215). San Diego: Greenhaven Press.

Negy, C., & Snyder, D. K. (1997). Ethnicity and acculturation: Assessing Mexican American couples' relationships using the Marital Satisfaction Inventory—Revised. *Psychological Assessment, 9,* 414–421.

Pinkney, A. (1993). *Black Americans* (4 ed.). Englewood Cliffs, NJ: Prentice-Hall.

Porterfield, E. (1978). *Black and white mixed marriages: An ethnographic study of black-white families.* Chicago: Nelson-Hall.

Porterfield, E. (1982). Black-American intermarriage in the United States. *Marriage and Family Review, 5,* 17–34.

Root, M.P.P. (1992). Within, between, and beyond race. In M.P.P. Root (Ed.), *Racially mixed people in America* (pp. 3–11). Newbury Park, CA: Sage.

Shibazaki, K., & Brennan, K. A. (1998). When birds of a feather flock together: A preliminary comparison of intra-ethnic and inter-ethnic dating relationships. *Journal of Social and Personal Relationships*, 15, 248–256.

Tannen, D. (1990). *You just don't understand: Women and men in communication.* New York: Morrow.

Taylor, J., & Zhang, X. (1992). Cultural identity in maritally distressed and nondistressed black couples. *Western Journal of Black Studies*, 14, 205–213.

Thomas, V. G. (1990). Problems of dual-career black couples: Identification and implications for family interventions. *Journal of Multicultural Counseling and Development,* 18, 58–67.

Tucker, M. B., & Mitchell-Kernan, C. (1995). Social structural and psychological correlates of interethnic dating. *Journal of Social and Personal Relationships*, 12, 341–361.

Wade, J. T. (1991). Marketplace economy: The evaluation of interracial couples. *Basic and Applied Social Psychology*, 12, 405–422.

Chapter 2

Perceiving Conflict: Similarities and Differences between and among Latino/as, African Americans, and European Americans

*Kiesha T. Warren, Mark P. Orbe, and
Nancy Greer-Williams*

INTRODUCTION

The field of communication has considerable resources in terms of research that explores the different ways in which African Americans and European Americans communicate (e.g., Dsilva & Whyte, 1998; Hecht, Ribeau, & Alberts, 1989; Martin, Hecht, & Larkey, 1994). A smaller amount of research has focused on the communication of Latino/as (i.e., Bradford, Meyer, & Kane, 1999; Hecht & Ribeau, 1984; Hecht, Ribeau, & Sedano, 1990). However, very few studies have looked at conflict styles, or the perceptions of conflict, of these different racial/ethnic groups (Kochman, 1981; Ting-Toomey, 1986). While this type of research is helpful in gaining preliminary insight into the general differences between different groups, they tend to make other salient cultural markers such as gender invisible (Orbe, 1995). Recently, some communication scholars have begun focusing their research on interactions of race and gender (Bell, Orbe, Drummond, & Camara, 2000; Flores, 1996; Houston, 2000; Orbe, 1994; Shuter & Turner, 1997); this development has produced scholarship that does not solely privilege men or European Americans as the "norm." For instance, scholarly inquiry that focuses on Latinas or African American women specifically (see Flores, 1996 and Bell et al., 2000, respectively) provides greater insight not possible through research on Latinos or African Americans generally.

Consistent with this growing line of inquiry, we combine gender and race to explore the differences and similarities in how groups perceive communication episodes. Specifically, we explore how U.S. women and men of Latino, African, and European descent perceive a particular example of conflict. In this regard, we suggest that by looking at intersections of both gender *and* race scholars are better apt to discover communication patterns that are not detectable when simply focusing on gender *or* race.

Along with the need for the study of how different groups communicate about conflict, there are also calls for more qualitative work in this area of research. Perceptions of conflict are situated within a particular standpoint (Collins, 1986; Orbe & Warren, 2000; Wood, 1992) and most appropriately explored through qualitative methodologies. Orbe (1995) contends that quantitative research offers insight into the phenomenon of culture and communication, but is largely ineffective—in and by itself—in providing a comprehensive understanding to the complex ways that culture and communication intersect in our everyday lives. Like others (Asante, 1987; Gonzalez, Houston, & Chen, 2000; Hecht, Collier, & Ribeau, 1993), we believe that qualitative work holds great promise in advancing existing knowledge in terms of the inextricable relationship(s) between cultural group identity and communication practice. To this end, this chapter reports on research that utilized a phenomenological approach to explore the following question: How do different racialized/gendered groups perceive conflict?

METHODS

Since our study sought to use a videoclip excerpt from a television program to facilitate discussion, we looked to existing studies that also used this method to examine the perceptions that diverse groups of people had in terms of specific mass media images of race, culture, and communication (Cooks & Orbe, 1993; Orbe, Seymour, & Kang, 1998). These studies provided clear direction for the ways in which we organized the recruitment and organization of participants, implementation of focus group discussions, and subsequent analysis of transcripts.

Participants

Participants for this study were recruited primarily from two different sources: (1) undergraduate classes (from Departments of Communication and Sociology) and student organizations at a mid-sized state university; and (2) community-based organizations (sorority graduate chapters, support groups, special interest groups, etc.). Data collection occurred in two different cities (one mid-sized and the other large) in the Midwest. Volunteers from undergraduate classes received extra credit for their participation; other university and community volunteers received no compensation.

Initial participants were recruited through personal contacts during spring 1999. Following the preliminary stages of data collection, additional participants were recruited during spring, 2000. In all, these persons (57 in total) represented a set of diverse standpoints in terms of age (18–51 years), sex (38 women and 19 men), and racial/ethnicity identity (22 European Americans, 17 African Americans, 16 Latino/as, 3 Asians, and 1 Native American).[1] Although obtaining a random sampling of participants is not within the values of qualitative work, the diversity of our participants is important in terms of the procedures of our study. Following the strategies of early studies (Cooks & Orbe, 1993; Orbe, Seymour, & Kang, 1998) these participants were organized by their sex and/or racial/ethnic identity into 10 different focus groups. While most of the focus groups were created among cultural peers (e.g., a group of European American men or African American women), a few were organized across cultural differences (e.g., Latinos and Latinas together or European American and African American women together). One focus group was comprised of a cross section of individuals. This strategy was employed in order to tap into discussions that occur during in-group and out-group conversations (Morgan, 1988). In short, the variety of focus group formations represents the most productive method to achieve a balanced assortment of open discussions (see, e.g., Morgan, 1988; Patton, 1990).

A total of 10 focus groups, ranging in size from three to 10 participants, were facilitated. Following the explanation and distribution of consent forms, a 15-minute videoclip of MTV's "The Real World" (Season #1; New York cast) was shown to the group. This clip featured a "real-life" conflict situation captured on film in 1991 between an 18-year-old European American woman from a small town in Alabama (Julie) and an 24-year-old African American man from Jersey City, New Jersey (Kevin). Once the group had finished viewing the clip, the researcher facilitated a discussion by using several open-ended questions; including: "Can you describe what you saw taking place in the clip?"; "What did you think the conflict was about?"; Can you describe your perceptions of each person's conflict style?"; "What are your thoughts about the appropriateness of how each person conflict style?"; "Who do you perceive to be the aggressor in this conflict?"; and "Can you describe a similar situation that has happened in your life?" These questions served as an effective means to prompt discussion in terms of how participants perceived the conflict displayed in the videoclip; specific follow-up questions were also posed when participants' comments explored additional issues not explicitly identified in the initial set of questions. Each focus group discussion lasted between 40 and 70 minutes and was audiotaped.

THEMATIC ANALYSIS

The ten focus-group discussions, when transcribed verbatim by the particular facilitator who led the group, resulted in 66 pages of single-spaced text. Our analysis process began with each researcher conducting her/his own preliminary review of each transcript. Once initial themes were identified, researchers met face-to-face to share their insights. Over time, each set of preliminary themes—which had a great deal of overlap in their initial form—were merged into a collaborative analysis of the diverse perceptions of the conflict on MTV's "The Real World."

As expected, the different compositions of the focus groups seemed to foster different perspectives in discussing the conflict between Kevin and Julie. However, at this juncture, it is important to recognize that our interpretations of these discussions represent a fusion of the researcher's expectations and the participant's actual meaning (Cooks & Orbe, 1993).[2] Therefore, it should not necessarily be seen as the only interpretation of themes (Polkinghorne, 1983). With these caveats in mind, the following sections are designed to explain the perceptions that European American women, African American women, Latinas, European American men, African American men, and Latinos expressed in terms of the conflicts that they viewed.

European American Women

As European American women discussed the conflict between Kevin and Julie, several issues were covered. The most significant marker within European American women's perspectives, however, was that the conflict was primarily about the issue of gender, not race. Although one or two European American women did acknowledge the possibility that racial differences impacted Julie and Kevin's conflict, most voiced doubt as to what extent the discourse between Kevin and Julie was culturally related. One European American stated:

I think that if it was a white male, she would have probably would have probably said the same thing. But if it was a female, she wouldn't have. The stereotype isn't that black men don't hit girls, the stereotype is that men don't hit women. . . . And it was never black or white, from my personal experience.

This idea was shared by another European American woman who was in a different focus group. In her comments, she also marked gender (and not race) as the most salient issue in the conflict pointing to specific differences in how women and men communicate (e.g., "the way men and women use space").

While most of the European American women did not view the differences in conflict style as culturally related, they did perceive Kevin as the aggressor. However, the stereotype that African American men are aggressive and people should fear them (as compared to men in general) is something that only one European American woman addressed. (This is significantly different from those discussions among people of color as presented in subsequent sections.) In fact, she shared how coming to college and interacting with African Americans for the first time forced her to question how she had been socialized:

Unfortunately, I grew up in probably a similar situation with [Julie]. I grew up on the other side of the state and my little community would not allow an African American family to move in. . . . So, my only exposure to [an] African American was when I went to [another larger town] to shop. I didn't have any African Americans in my high school . . . all through my schooling. I rarely saw one in my hometown. If I did, they passed through. And when I came here, unfortunately, it was my first extended contact with African Americans. It was very hard for me to try and get past the things that I had been socially taught through living in the town that I did. . . . I remember even going to bed crying one night because I was so scared because there was an African American man that lived down the hall from me. He [was known to] be aggressive—physically. And I went to bed crying freshmen year because . . . I knew that I didn't have to [be so] scared and I knew that there was no reason why I should be worried. I had never seen him being aggressive. It was this perceived thing that people had told me.

African American Women

Like the European American women, a pattern emerged in the ways that the African American women involved in this research project defined and discussed the conflict between Kevin and Julie. Many (not all, though) African American women questioned why others in the focus group or on the videoclip automatically saw Kevin as the aggressor and Julie the victim. Instead, many of these women saw both as "mutually aggressive." Interestingly, several African American women voiced anger because they believed that Julie had "played up" the role of victim by crying and "acting as if she needed protection." In fact, several pointed to how existing stereotypes concerning black men also contributed to her success in bringing others to her defense.

This perception leads to the major thematic difference between the ways that European American men and women defined the conflict and the ways that African American women did not. Both European American women and men (almost without exception) did *not* define the conflict in terms of race. For African American women (as well most African American men and Latinos/as, which will be discussed in subsequent sections), "Race is always an issue—whether you want to acknowledge it or not, it always plays a part." The differences in perceptions were clearly defined: For European American women the conflict was about gender; African American saw race as a salient issue. This perceptual difference is best captured in a series of comments from one group discussion between European American and African American women:

African American woman #1: People think stuff [have stereotypes] about black people in general. . . . There is a general stereotype of the black man or black woman. That they are going to get in your face and they are going to hit you. . . . I think that that might have played a factor in her saying, "What are you going to do, hit me?" Because if it was a white guy in her face, I can't see her saying [it].

European American woman #1: I can.

European American woman #2: I can.

European American woman #3: I can, too. Just because . . . the thing is when we feel intimidated it is because the other person is bigger, stronger, or coming at you. I think that it's more of a gender issue.

African American woman #2: I think that the "big black guy" perception did play a part. And he wasn't even physically big, so the stereotype was there.

Immediately following this exchange, both of the African American women shared experiences where they had witnessed firsthand how stereotypes affect the ways that European Americans generally, and European American women specifically, interact with African American men. (Similar examples of what brothers, friends, and sons have to deal with were offered by other African American women in other groups.) After a pause, an interesting exchange occurred where a European American woman questioned the African American women in the group if they would be afraid if a "taller, white male" confronted them? One of African American woman responded "yes," which the European American woman took as further evidence that gender was more of an issue than race. African American women, however, continued to disagree.

Latina Women

As illustrated by this interracial exchange, European American and African American women appeared to disagree as to the role that race played in Julie and Kevin's conflict. Like European American women, Latinas understood the role that gender differences—and issues of power—played in the conflict. However, they were also able to simultaneously see the important role that personal and racial differences also played. This tendency to see Kevin and Julie's conflict through a "both/and" perspective (about race, gender, and personality) instead of an "either/or" perspective (choosing one issue as the defining element) best characterizes their general perceptions.

For instance, some of the comments from the Latinas who participated in our study reflected a keen sense of awareness of the role that racial stereotypes play in interracial interactions. Several examples were provided, including one that pointed to a prevailing stereotype that Mexican American females are aggressive and potentially violent. One focus group participant, for instance, recounted a time when others had assumed that she would turn violent during an argument—despite the fact that she had "never gotten in a fight with anyone!" This example, as well as others provided by Latina/os, pointed to a number of societal stereotypes that heightened conflict between different racial groups. This dominant perception was similar to that which was discussed among African American focus groups. However, what was particularly interesting were other discussions about stereotypes—including one set of comments in which a Latina acknowledged how the media have shaped her perceptions of African American men.

Stereotypes played a big role for her [Julie]. I was thinking about how she may have taken it [Kevin's expressiveness and close proximity] a different way. If they had never said anything to each other . . . right away she was probably thinking that he was dangerous. In the media, that's all you see with black men . . . showing them as criminals or attackers. . . . I would have sort of thought that, too.

This set of comments notwithstanding, the role that racial stereotypes (either *of* Latinas or *held by* Latinas) was not the only major issue discussed. In fact, Latina participants in our study spent fairly distributed amounts of time talking about how a number of factors possibly were at the center of the conflict. For instance, when a facilitator asked Latinas (who were sitting in a circle) to share how they defined the conflict, each highlighted a different defining element. One talked about the difference that gender played: "It was a gender thing. She was getting in an argument with a guy, but if it had been a girl, it would have been totally different. It wouldn't have gotten out of hand." The very next woman "thought it was about personality because both were acting the very same way." The next Latina to speak reflected, "I don't know I guess from experience, I think that when you have two different races, race plays a role."

Some comments may have highlighted one element, but they also mentioned the probable role that other cultural markers also played. Consequently, their comments included qualifiers like, "I do not think it was just about gender, probably gender and personality," and "it was due to different personalities, but gender and race made it even worse." As one Latina participant articulated, the conflict between Kevin and Julie was caused by "personality differences, and at the same time, cultural differences like those based on race and gender."

European American Men

As demonstrated in previous sections, different perceptual patterns emerged across different racialized and gendered groups. European American women primarily saw the conflict in terms of gender, African American women predominately saw race as a salient marker for the conflict. Latinas, it appears, were able to discuss the conflict in terms of both aspects. In comparison, European American men defined the conflict in terms of personal problems not associated with gender or race.

Interestingly, attention to gender and race differences was something typically not raised by European American men. Their focus was more on trying to understand the causes of the behaviors, and subsequently analyzing what should have been done by both participants in order to resolve their conflict. Attempts to see how gender and/or race played a part in the conflict appeared to be of little significance. Only one European American man commented on how Kevin had been stereotyped by others in the house. However, this stereotype was based not on Kevin's race and/or gender, but on his past actions. The consensus was that race was not an issue in the conflict. When brought up by the focus group facilitator, European American men responded in this way:

Well, the whole issue of race, I knew that it was going to get brought up. . . . But it really had nothing to do with the issue of race at all. I mean there was zero race relevance to that.

Because the predominant perception of European American men was that race was not an issue, they saw Kevin's attempt to explain how race was a factor as irrelevant, unproductive, and manipulative. In fact, several European American men perceived Kevin as "blaming the conflict on race" or "using race as an excuse." Similar comments about how they perceived Kevin as "playing the race card" emerged in other more diverse focus groups as well. However, they were not as forceful as those shared in the one focus group that only included European American men.

The comments of European American men highlighted thus far reflect a specific perspective of the conflict between Julie and Kevin. However, one (and only one) European American man did share his attempt to see the conflict from a "minority" viewpoint:

The whole time I was watching this [the particular episode of "Real World"—and I've seen it lots of time—I was trying to reverse it and watch it as if it was a house of blacks with one Caucasian male living there. Would I be having the same perceptions of these behaviors? And I'm not racist, I never have been. . . . So, I tried to hone in on the anger that was being placed there, and not on the race issue. But it is realty hard not to do that.

His comments suggest that the perceptions of European Americans might be filtered by a standpoint that disallows them to see their own privileged position based on gender and race. In other words, they see race and gender, but find it difficult to understand how these markers are as important as personal (individual) differences. The pattern of European American men not defining the conflict as racialized and gendered, then, may be more of an issue of (in)ability than simply (un)willingness.

Latino Men

The perceptions of Latino men, like those of their Latina counterparts, were diverse. Many discussed the difficulty of attempting to pinpoint one defining element of the conflict. Instead, they spent considerable time in their focus groups talking about how personality, race/ethnicity, and gender issues were all part of the conflict. Like African American men (to be discussed later), many of the Latinos involved in our study acknowledged the pervasive nature of race in the United States. As one Latino participant concluded, "I think that whenever you have two different races, race is a factor."

One primary issue, societal stereotypes, was discussed at great length. Like many of the other people of color, Latino men articulated their heightened consciousness of how others—mostly European Americans but some African Americans—interacted with them based on negative stereotypes. In this regard, focus group discussions contained a number of personal examples when they had been stereotyped by others. Some of these were based on vivid childhood memories (e.g., being called a "taco" and harassed by "red necks with big hats driving by in BIG trucks"). Others were more recent:

People are always stereotyping Mexicans. Like last year I ran cross country for [a college team]. Every time I would go to practice, they would call me "hard-core" . . . you know assuming that all [Mexican Americans] are gangsters. I guess because of my physical appearance—having a little goatee—or the type of jacket I wore. They would call me hard-core, thinking that . . . every Mexican is like a gangster or something.

However, race was not the only issue discussed regarding Julie and Kevin's conflict (and their own experiences related to conflict). For instance, Latino participants talked about how personal differences can be the major source of conflict. Examples of both interracial and intraracial conflict were provided illustrating how personality conflicts sometimes are more hard to negotiate than racial ones. This aspect appeared to reflect some of the comments shared by European American men. In this regard, both Latinos and European American men spent some time in their focus-group discussions highlighting the problematic communication styles of both Kevin and Julie and then offering specific solutions for their problems.

Within a focus group of both Latinos and Latinas, gender differences took center stage in an abbreviated discussion of male/female conflict. Gender was not addressed as much as race and personal differences. However, of particular interest to our study was a discussion of how "machismo" affects communication between Latinos (men) and Latinas (women). Described as an increased sense of masculinity where men must be in control, machismo was discussed by participants who pointed to similar values in other cultures. When asked if those values affected how women and men communicate—generally in their own experiences, and specifically in the example of Kevin and Julie's interaction—Latinos perceptions varied. A few discussed how machismo affected their own interactions, but most pointed to a number of factors including how traditional their families were, if they were raised in the United States or not, and their age. In fact, these exchanges typify the ways in which Latino/as discussed Kevin and Julie's conflict: Race/ethnicity, gender, and other individual differences contributed to their problems; attempting to separate one issue as the most important was difficult, if not impossible.

African American Men

As the group of African American men viewed the clip, they had many different ideas as to why the conflict occurred. Some defined the conflict as an "interracial disagreement." In this regard, they—like most of the other people of color involved in this study—recognized that "race is always in effect." However, other factors were given equal attention in their discussions of Kevin and Julie's conflict. In other words, many of the African American males who viewed the clip did not feel that the differences in conflict styles were solely based on culture/race. Instead, several pointed to other issues that might have been just as, if not more important than, racial differences.

Several African American, for example, specifically mentioned the role that socioeconomic status, age, and region played in terms of how individuals react to each other. This point became apparent throughout an African American male focus group. Many of these participants agreed that the way a person reacts to conflict is not solely because of his/her race/ethnicity. So, when asked if he agreed with Kevin's explanation that certain behaviors are part of the African American culture, he responded by saying:

Oh no, that is absurd. I think that it is about lots of issues. Say you've got two black men in a room and one is a passive, he is not going to be in this person's face. It all depends on how and where you've been raised.

Like the Latino and Latina focus groups, discussions among African American men were quite diverse in terms of how they described the conflict between Kevin and Julie. For instance, while a significant number of African American men pointed to issues of race/culture, just as many believed the conflict was the result of individual differences. Interestingly, this perception appeared to be more prevalent among younger participants. There were a few older African American men who did feel that the differences were cultural. However, they felt that other cultural differences were also a factor. They did not seem to agree over to what extent it was cultural because of race or because of other cultural factors. One older man stated:

I don't know if I think that it is a learned behavior because I don't know what it is but I don't think that you learn it. Maybe it is a fear reaction. I know that whenever I am in a situation and feel a little fearful I react by becoming more aggressive.

In short, most African American men acknowledged the subtle ways in which race permeates different interpersonal interactions. However, as illustrated by the diverse responses included in this section, the extent to which this is perceived to be true varied among African American men. In other words, African American men simultaneously share common and divergent perspectives. Based on the small sampling of African American men included in our study, notable distinctions appeared to occur based on age differences. Older men seem to see cultural differences between the two as the cause of their conflict. In comparison, younger men seem to have various opinions as to the differences in the two reaction. Some young men attributed the difference between the two to difference in just individual personalities. Others seem to feel that the difference is caused by a "lack of good communication."

DISCUSSION

As expected, the different compositions of the focus groups seemed to foster different perspectives in discussing the conflict between Kevin and Julie. However, at this juncture, it is important to recognize that our interpretations are based on a small number of Latino/as, African Americans, and Europeans. Given the relatively limited number of participants, additional research steps are needed to gain feedback for our interpretations from those that they seek to represent. Consequently, additional data collection is needed to hear more voices and subsequently gain feedback on our interpretations. Still, our analysis provides a preliminary interpretation of the issues discussed. With these limitations in mind, we offer the following brief discussion.

As alluded to earlier, standpoint epistemology (e.g., Hartsock, 1987) provides a productive lens to understand our findings. According to standpoint theorists (Collins, 1986; Wood, 1992), life is not experienced the same for all persons. Instead, individuals' life experiences are similar and different depending on group membership(s). In explicit and implicit ways, our standpoints affect how we communicate as well as how we perceive the communication of others. Part of acknowledging diverse standpoints involves recognizing that different persons will perceive the world differently based on their experiences living in a racialized and gendered society. This became apparent within our thematization process.

For example, the comments from people of color in our study were situated within an understanding that racial issues are interwoven into the past, present, and future of the United States. The common thread, therefore, among African American women and men, and Latino/as was the recognition that "race was always in effect"—either at, or just below, the surface level. As one African American woman explained,

So, it's always there. It's something that you can't say is NOT there. Race is always an issue. Whether you want to acknowledge it or not it always is there.

Many of the people of color involved in our study—especially African American men, Latinas, and Latinos—understand, however, that race was not the only factor in communication episodes. However, for most European Americans, it seemed like the issue of race was brought into situations unnecessarily. From their perspective, many conflicts between people of different races (like the one between Kevin and Julie) had little to do with race. Personality and gender issues were most salient. In this regard, standpoint epistemology helps to explain our findings both in terms of how racialized and gendered standpoints prompted different interpretations of the same conflict.

Standpoint theories are most productive when they are utilized to reveal both the *similarities* and *differences* within and among cultural groups (Wood, 1992). While persons share a core of experiences based on group memberships (e.g., by race and/or gender), this does not negate the presence of differences within any singular group or the possibilities of similarities across groups. This is an important point given the findings of our study. Clear patterns of how different groups perceived conflict emerged; however, these patterns were not universal. For instance, a small (but distinct) number of European Americans did speak to the role that race played in the conflict between Kevin and Julie. Within their comments, these persons related experiences (e.g., living in a diverse neighborhood or taking a black studies class) that encouraged an acknowledgment with, if not an understanding of, an alternative standpoint. Furthermore, we might argue that involvement in interracial discussions—like those facilitated within our focus groups—assists in increasing awareness of different perspectives. One European American man, who was initially convinced that Kevin and Julie's conflict was solely about personality differences, concluded at the end of the focus group discussion "If another person had been involved, I don't know what would have hap-

pened. . . . It would have been the *same situation* but it would have been *different*."
To us, this indicates the beginning of an awareness as to the role that difference
(based on race, gender, and the like) plays within communication episodes. Given
the increasing significance of diversity with the United States, such a heightened
awareness is needed for effective communication across and within different cultural groups.

NOTES

1. Given the focus of this book chapter, only the responses of the European Americans,
African Americans, and Latino/as will be discussed.

2. See Bauer and Orbe (2001), who describe the importance of including a
"post-syntagmatic spiral" (returning researchers' interpretations back to the participants in
order to include them at every stage of the research process) within phenomenological inquiry.

REFERENCES

Asante, M. (1987). Social interaction of black and white college students. *Journal of Black
    Studies*, 14, 517–516.
Bauer, K., & Orbe, M. (2001). Networking, coping, and communicating about a medical
    crisis: A phenomenological inquiry of transplant recipient communication. *Health
    Communication*, 13 (2), 141–161.
Bell, K. E, Orbe, M., Drummond, D. K., & Camara, S. K. (2000). Accepting the challenge
    of centralizing without essentializing: Black feminist thought and African Ameri-
    can women's communicative experiences. *Women's Studies in Communication*, *23*,
    41–62.
Bradford, L., Meyer, R. A., & Kane, K. A. (1999). Latino expectations of communication
    competence: A focus group interview study. *Communication Quarterly*, 47,
    98–117.
Collins, P. H. (1986). Learning from the outsider within: The sociological significance of
    black feminist thought. *Social Problems*, 33, S14–S23.
Cooks, L. M., & Orbe, M. (1993). Beyond the satire: Selective exposure and selective per-
    ception in "In Living Color." *Howard Journal of Communications*, *4*, 217–233.
Dsilva, M., & Whyte, L. (1998). Cultural differences in conflict styles: Vietnamese refu-
    gees and established residents. *Howard Journal of Communications*, 9, 57–68.
Flores, L. A. (1996). Creating discursive space through a rhetoric of difference: Chicana
    feminists craft a homeland. *Quarterly Journal of Speech,* 82, 142–156.
Gonzalez, A., Houston, M., & Chen, V. (Eds.) (2000). *Our voices: Essays in culture, ethnic-
    ity, and communication.* Los Angeles, CA: Roxbury.
Hartsock, S. (Ed.). (1987). *Feminism and methodology.* Bloomington: Indiana University
    Press.
Hecht, M. L., Collier, M. J., & Ribeau, S. (1993). *African American communication: Ethnic
    identity and cultural interpretation.* Thousand Oaks, CA: Sage.
Hecht, M. L., & Ribeau, S. (1984). Ethnic communication: A comparative analysis of satis-
    fying communication. *International Journal of Intercultural Relations, 8*, 135–151.

Hecht, M. L., Ribeau, S., & Alberts, J. K. (1989). An Afro-American perspective on interethnic communication. *Communication Monographs*, 56, 385–408.

Hecht, M. L., Ribeau, S., & Sedano, M. V. (1990). A Mexican American perspective on interethnic communication. *International Journal of Intercultural Relations*, 14, 31–55.

Houston, M. (2000). When black women talk with white women: Why dialogues are difficult. In A. Gonzalez, M. Houston, & V. Chen (Eds.), *Our voices: Essays in culture, ethnicity, and communication* (pp. 98–104). Los Angeles: Roxbury.

Kochman, T. (1981). *Black and white styles in conflict*. Chicago: University of Chicago Press.

Lloyd, S. A. (1987). Conflict in premarital relationships: Differential perceptions of males and females. *Family Relations*, 36, 290–294.

Martin, J. N., Hecht, M. L., & Larkey, L. K. (1994). Conversation improvement strategies for interethnic communication: African American and European American perspectives. *Communication Monograph*, 61, 236–255.

Morgan, D. L. (1988). *Focus groups as qualitative research*. Newbury Park, CA: Sage.

Orbe, M. (1994). "Remember, it's always whites' ball": Descriptions of African American male communication. *Communication Quarterly*, 42, 287–300.

Orbe, M. (1995). African American communication research: Toward a deeper understanding of interethnic communication. *Western Journal of Communication*, *56*, 6–78.

Orbe, M., Seymour, K., & Kang, M. E. (1998). "Ethnic humor" and ingroup/outgroup positioning: Explicating perceptions of "All-American Girl." In Y. R., Kamalipour & T. Carilli (Eds.), *Cultural diversity in the U.S. media* (pp. 125–136). Albany: State University of New York Press.

Orbe, M., & Warren, K. T. (2000). Different standpoints, different realities: Race, gender, and perceptions of intercultural conflict. *Qualitative Research Reports in Communication,* 1(3).

Patton, M. (1980). *Qualitative evaluation methods*. Beverly Hills, CA: Sage.

Polkinghorne, D. (1983). *Methodology for the human sciences*. Albany: State University of New York Press.

Shuter, R., & Turner, L. (1997). African American and European American women in workplace: Perceptions of conflict communication. *Management Communication Quarterly*, 11, 74–96.

Ting-Toomey, S. (1986). Conflict communication styles in black and white subjective cultures. In Y. Y. Kim (Ed.), *Interethnic communication* (pp. 75–88). Newbury Park, CA: Sage.

Wood, J. T. (1992). Gender and moral voice: Moving from women's nature to standpoint epistemology. *Women's Studies in Communication, 15*, 1–24.

Chapter 3

Brown and Black Women in Nancy Savoca's *The 24-Hour Woman*: A Critical Analysis of Multicultural Imagery

Meta G. Carstarphen and Diana I. Rios

INTRODUCTION

The presence of Latina and African American women in film and video is an increasingly important phenomenon to examine across the academic disciplines, given large growth among ethnic and racial consumer audiences and the evolving cultural landscape in the United States. Academic research that critically examines the presence of women of color in mediated communication has not been able to keep up with the need for careful and deliberate discussion. The Hollywood industry, the long-held bastion of cultural production, has not only been unable to keep up with the nation's cultural and ethnic mosaic, it has consistently fallen short in the quality of images that it creates and disseminates.

The traditions of people of color within Hollywood-produced movies have been fragmented. Ethnic and racial minorities have enjoyed periods of artistic opportunity and creative expression in Hollywood, but this has occurred in fits and starts. Improved artistic opportunity and expression have followed the whims of film corporations that discover opportunities for commercial markets. In past decades film and broadcast companies have demonstrated wavering acquiescence to social pressures by showcasing members of certain ethnic and racial groups, such as American Indians, Asian Americans, African Americans or Latinos on screen and television. Regarding certain historical eras, such as post-civil rights and World Wars I and II, the Hollywood machine has demonstrated some acquiescence to community demands, U.S. government policies, and international mandates for more congenial international relations with some peoples of color. There are still gains to be made in Hollywood with regard to fair representation of people of color and women. Because of the long road ahead, some directors and producers have turned to small-budget projects. Independent films by nature are not wed to standard narrative formulas, story themes, or big film-star box office names. Independents have permission to take more chances with film topics and content. Most importantly, small films have the space for heightened realism and fairer representations of women of color. It is the goal of this chapter to critically examine women of color in Nancy Savoca's *The 24-Hour Woman* starring actors Rosie Perez, a woman of Puerto Rican heritage (Puertorriqueña) and Marianne Jean-Baptiste, a British woman playing an African American. We will examine how the film reconstructs images of women of color and critique the extent to which the film breaks new ground. Our analytic approach includes ideas from multicultural "womanism" (Walker, 1983), which could be understood as versions of "hembrismo" or "mujerismo," (see overviews in Mirande & Enriquez, 1981) but is parallel to U.S. third world feminist criticism, or "mestiza" perspectives (Sandoval, 1998). The womanist/mestiza perspectives are appropriate for this film analysis since they lend insight into woman character thinking and decision-making throughout the film narrative.

ISSUES OF WOMEN OF COLOR IN FILM

Scholars agree that women of color have not fared well in quality of film roles. Bogle (2001) describes that while the roles for African American actors, in general, have been severely limited, the positive roles for African American women have been particularly dismal. Bobo (1991) characterizes the roles of black women as being historically limited to four types: the mammy, the sexpot, the shrew, and the domestic. Perhaps the best known mammy and domestic is Hattie McDaniel, playing "Mammy" in Selznick's *Gone with the Wind* (1939). Dorothy Dandridge, out of financial necessity played a blend of sexpot and shrew roles such as those in *Carmen Jones* (1954), *Tamango* (1959), and *Porgy and Bess* (1959). The quality of exoticism made Dorothy Dandridge the actress and Dandridge's characters slightly more palatable to general market audiences, as in the mixed blood characters she played in *Tamango* and *Island in the Sun* (1957). Burks (1996) cautions that though films with improved African American female imagery have been created over the years, unflattering images can also be found in new independent films and Hollywood films directed by African Americans. She points out that new stereotypes of black females have arisen and black women are often relegated to the periphery. Extending Bobo's audience research (1995), we would see current African American women still hard pressed to gain cultural fulfillment from most of today's films.

As we look at the common role types for Latinas and African American women we see that the role limitations for these groups have much in common. Fregoso (1993) draws our attention to various films that hold improved Chicana-Latina imagery but also points out that Chicano productions do not guarantee sensitive, well-rounded portrayals. Rios's (1996; 1999; 2000) fieldwork in several Latino communities in the Southwest and Northeast describes how female audiences may struggle to find cultural gratifications in Hollywood and Spanish-language media productions. Berg (1990) explains that negative typing of people of color such as Latinos in film can be traced to the social construction of cultural Others in our society. We might say that negative typing of ethnic and racial groups demonstrates society's repressed desires and denial of its own undesirable tendencies. Society's repression and denial causes it to assign the negative to out-groups such as those of American Indian, Arab, Asian, African, and Latino heritage. Common Chicana types, which can be applied to "Puertorriqueñas" and other Latinas include: the half-breed harlot, the female clown, the Latin lover, and the dark lady (Berg, 1990). Keller's (1994) list includes: cantina girls, the faithful, moral, or self-sacrificing señorita, and the vamp or temptress, among many others.

Wilson and Gutierrez (1995) note that movies featuring Latinas during the 1930s and 1940s promoted the brown female ideal as "sensuous" and "tempestuous" (p. 80), in line with the stereotype of the "irrational Latino temperament." A legendary Hispanic actress in Hollywood film was subject to ethnic erasure and presented to the general market as an anglicized Rita Hayworth (Hadley-Garcia, 1993). Margarita Carmen Cansino was physically remade in Hollywood as a lighter, thinner, red-haired Anglo siren (McLean, 1992–93). Her reign as one of Hollywood's legendary sexpots, more famous than the original "spitfire" named Lupe Velez, was certainly part of the industry's practice of female objectification. However, history notes that her most prevalent casting as an exotic beauty evokes an unspoken hint of her hidden cultural heritage. Like all celluloid rites of passage, more contemporary Latina actresses such as Rita Moreno (*West Side Story*, 1961), Sonia Braga (*Moon over Parador*, 1988) Salma Hayek (*Desperado*, 1995) Rosie Perez (*White Men Can't Jump*, 1992; *It Could Happen to You*, 1994), and Jennifer Lopez (*Blood and Wine*, 1997; *Out of Sight*, 1999) have all had to portray tempestuous Latinas during their careers regardless of their wide-ranging talents.

In the 1999 film, *The 24-Hour Woman* starring Rosie Perez, one of the striking aspects of this narrative is how Perez is cast in a decidedly unexotic role—that of career woman, wife, and stressed-out mom. Actor Marianne Jean-Baptiste complements Perez's role by also living a multifaceted life as a modern working woman. Quite distinctive from the big-budget movie *Baby Boom* (1987) starring Diane Keaton, Perez and Jean-Baptiste speak for many women who are not members of the economic European American upper class. Women like Grace and Madeline do not inherit properties and money nor do they have the luxury of monetary savings and social class currency to make the maneuvers we see Diane Keaton's character make. Grace and Madeline's moves are on a much smaller scale, making their experiences to women in general and women of color more accessible. The making, release, and distribution of the film in major markets is a triumph of filmmaker Nancy Savoca and her supporters. She is recognized as a director with a commitment to exploring real people's lives. She is part of a faction of directors and producers, like Darnell Martin (*I Like It Like That*, 1994) and Jonathan Demme (*Beloved*, 1998), who have successfully worked outside of blockbuster formulas. Their heroines deviate from cookie-cutter prototypes and customary film standards.

FEMINISM, MULTICULTURAL WOMANISM, U.S. THIRD WORLD FEMINISM, AND MESTIZA WORLD VIEWS

In its consideration of woman and her relationship to the family, feminism as it emerged in the 1970s raised essential questions about her role. Although no uniform feminist ideology may exist exploring woman's role within the family, feminist scholarship has argued well that "family forms are socially and historically constructed" (Zinn, 2000) and that roles are not universally, or biologically, subscribed by gender. However, while mainstream feminism, defined by a social experiences of Anglo women, identified patriarchy as the site of women's oppression (Zinn, 2000, p. 4), such thinking left little room for feminists of color, who, from their world view, related to oppressions of race and class structures. In a practical way, feminists of color needed to sort out the effect of patriarchy upon their lives, along with the influence of social class and pervasive racism on their lives. Separating out the oppression of male dominance from the experience of racism was not an option for most.

Perhaps in no other arena was the contrast of world views more sharply felt than in the work arena. While Anglo feminists focused much of their concern upon entering a male-dominated workplace and achieving economic parity with men for comparable (usually professional) types of jobs, such a view ignored the very different workplace concerns of many women of color. In contrast to a tradition where women of a certain class and economic status became homemakers for some period of time after marriage, women of color followed this tradition with much less frequency. By contrast, workplace statistics and studies demonstrate that for African American women, especially, work outside of the home was part of a long tradition (Zinn, 2000). Among Latinas, Puerto Rican women in particular, who have often been heads of households on the mainland, have experienced high economic pressures for workforce participation (see Morales & Bonilla, 1993; Torres, 1995).

Working outside the home became a necessary tradition as a response to the social restrictions in place by law and custom against men of color, binding women's commitment to work as part of family survival strategies. Complicating the relationships between Anglo women and women of color in the post-World War II era when more women of all ethnicities entered the workplace, were the stark differences in paid work opportunities for these women, especially when "many professional lifestyles in dual-career families depend on race and class privileges to hire immigrants and other women of color as child care and domestic workers" (Zinn, 2000, p. 5).

Thus, as a consequence of this paradox, feminists of color looked for ways to explore their condition as women within the contexts of their cultural and familial experiences. Through the lenses of collectivism and familism women saw their embrace of empowerment aligned with their commitment to support all members of their communities be they male, young or old, to survive against the persistent patterns of prejudice and racial discrimination that assaulted them. Furthermore, as minorities functioning within social systems dominated by others, such women had skills, as a part of their practical experiences, in functioning within culturally diverse contexts.

Out of these sensibilities women of color across the spectrum define, and continue to refine, a cross-disciplinary international feminist movement that takes into account the "isms" of human oppression. African American author Alice Walker articulated a way of knowing feminine power called "womanism." In Walker's original framework, she identifies "womanism" as a different kind of feminist activism. Some of the qualities that distinguish a "womanist" was her appreciation of all things female, a love for herself, commitment to the survival and wholeness of all in her community, and a universal embrace of all cultures (Walker, 1983). This perspective parallels U.S. third world feminist praxis, and "mestiza" (from the Latina and world experience of "mixed blood") streams of thought. The significance of having "mixed blood" is that one does not attempt to make classist, racist claims of racial purity or superiority. Acknowledging "mestizaje," the state of mixed blood, begins a kind of freedom from "isms" and embraces the heritage all peoples. These world views offer a theoretical and methodological compass by which women and women of color can work toward egalitarianism in their lives and social justice in their communities (Lunsford, 1998; Sandoval, 1998; Anzaldua, 1987).

FILM NARRATIVE ELEMENTS: OPPOSITIONS AND CHOICES

In *The 24-Hour Woman*, director Nancy Savoca creates a film world revolving around the lives of modern women. "The 24-Hour-Woman" of the film's title is the name of a daily television show whose thrust is to showcase news and features on every aspect of a woman's busy life. The program, with its fragmented perspective on the "real" lives of women, juxtaposed against the lives of the "real" women who work for the show, establishes a clever counterpoint for sorting out the everyday world from this idealized one. With its steady streams of cheery experts and knowledgeable talking heads, this fictional morning show aptly mimics the world of daytime informative TV. Appearing authoritative, the televised set of "The 24-Hour Woman" assumes the legitimacy of the larger society. Thus, the first basic oppositional question looms: how and where does a "real" woman fit within the projected ideal of "The 24-Hour Woman" woman, a televised ideal paragon who can keep all aspects of her personal and professional life in balance?

Into this basic conundrum enters the movie's main protagonist, Grace Santos, played by Rosie Perez. The film opens with the yet-unidentified heroine as she studies a line appearing slowly across the diagnostic bridge of a home pregnancy kit. As the visual confirmation of her pregnancy unmistakably emerges, a quickly moving montage of shots showing a promotional spot for "The 24-Hour Woman" television show begins on a television set in the background.

Meanwhile, in another household, "The 24-Hour Woman" television show holds the attention of another important character in the movie, Madeline Labelle, played by Marianne Jean-Baptiste. We learn that she has a job interview pending as an assistant producer for this show, and she is studying the show intently with her husband. Soon, she is called away by the sounds of a child in the background.

Now, another set of oppositional relationships is set. Grace, with her pending motherhood, faces juggling the probability of a child against what we will learn is a successful professional career. On the other hand, Madeline, already ensconced in motherhood with three children, has to measure the tradeoffs of reestablishing her career against the demands of her already existent brood.

Together Grace and Madeline pose a cultural opposition, as women of color, to the question, what and who is the 24-Hour Woman? Grace and Madeline are destined to meet, and each will grapple with lifestyle questions in their individual lives within the context of their own cultural markers. As representational modern women of color, though, even as they emerge from different cultural contexts, they are more alike than different. For both, the real oppositional relationship comes between them and a lifestyle standard best represented by the Anglo executive producer, Joan Marshall, played by Patty LuPone.

On the very morning that Grace Santos and her husband, Eddie Diaz, played by Diego Serranto, discover that they are expecting, the news becomes part of the morning banter between Eddie and Margo, who are the on-camera co-hosts of "The 24-Hour Woman." Reluctantly, Grace is forced out from the anonymity of the producer's chair to the front of the camera where the whole audience shares in the news. At first, Grace and Eddie's top boss, Joan, is furious over this impromptu departure from the script. But as she learns that Grace's due date is during sweeps month in November, Joan decides to capitalize on what she calls "baby madness." Thus, regular segments are planned centering around the pregnancy and childbirth topics, while Grace herself is constantly on view as the audience keeps track of her progress.

Joan's insistence that Grace's pregnancy is a programming opportunity obscures any misgivings Grace herself has; her feelings and reservations are irrelevant, subservient to the work. Joan's single-minded purpose in producing a successful show and driving the ratings up prevails as she asks for assurances from Grace that the she will not stay out long after the baby is born.

Later, when Grace and Madeline meet for their planned interview, Joan's ethos surfaces through Grace. When Madeline explains the four-year gap on her resume by explaining that she was raising three children, Grace immediately reacts with wonder and concern: "Wow! It's not going to interfere with your job?" she asks anxiously, as Madeline calmly explains how she and her husband have worked out childcare arrangements. Grace shares her ambivalence by admitting that while she really needs an assistant, Madeline is overqualified for the job. Still, despite the low pay, the long hours, and the stress the assistant's job promises, Madeline is eager to "get [back] in somehow" and happily accepts the job.

Finally, when Grace reviews her hiring decision with Joan, she reminds her boss that the assistant will come in handy during her planned maternity leave. Noticing Joan's immediate displeasure and surprise at the thought of such a break from work, Grace apologizes for needing a maternity leave, assuring her boss that it "will only be a few weeks." At the end of this scene, Joan problematizes motherhood, with a harangue about the complications that lay waiting to sabotage working moms like Madeline and expectant mom Grace: "sick kids, parent-teacher conferences, nannies that quit." To allay her boss' fears that Madeline, and Grace herself, will fall prey to the named hazards, Grace offers that Madeline has a husband who will help. To this, Joan boisterously declares, "Her husband? Hah! She better hire some real help. I been there honey. I was a single mother long before I divorced [throaty vomit noise] Jeffrey!" She communicates to all women across the offices that husbands are no help at all to professional women with children.

If Grace and Madeline represent contemporary women trying to have it all, then Joan is a more linear role model of the career woman who knows she cannot have it all and chooses accordingly. Joan is a symbol of a rigid kind of feminism taken to its furthest point. She is a lonely, manic, workaholic. She could be raising children on the side or have given them up entirely. In Joan's world view career is queen and personal options giving weight to the family are irrelevant. The dichotomies between Joan and Madeline offer the starkest contrast since Joan is vacant of domesticity and Madeline cooperatively maintains a household and marriage. Madeline appears to have found her multicultural, mestiza, womanist path, and moves forward refining her path day by day. Meanwhile, we see Grace as the character who navigates between career and family and must come to weighty decisions about the course of her life. Will she fashion herself after Joan, after all? Will personal and cultural demands of the family win her over as they did with Madeline in the past? Grace is in a "borderlands" where she must define a path best for her. Overall, these three characters offer examples of the tensions between a type of feminism where children and spouse have no place and where work offers a primary identity, and other ways of seeing and constructing life.

FILM NARRATIVE ELEMENTS THROUGH WOMANIST/MESTIZA FRAMEWORKS

Over the last three decades the contributions of feminist thought in media studies have proliferated, giving rise to a considerable body of work dedicated to feminist media studies (see Watkins & Emerson, 2000). One view considers the film medium itself to be a technological outgrowth of the male's desire to "gaze" at the female, thereby proscribing her role to that which is socially, physically, psychologically pleasing to males (see Kaplan, 1997; Watkins & Emerson, 2000). Working women, as one subset of the feminine experience in film, reflect some of the social ambivalence that has existed about women in the workplace. For Anglo women actors, playing in distinctly middle-class career roles during Hollywood's heyday in the 1940s, such images first gave rise to the notion of a "superwoman" who had it all long before late twentieth-century century feminism anguished over similar questions. But these World War II-inspired depictions evolved after earlier, socially defined women's roles had run their course, from the "young, carefree flappers" of the 1920s, to the "sacrificial mothers and downtrodden working girls" of the 1930s (Walsh, 1984).

But such broad categories did not reflect the cinematic images of women of color, who as a whole were either barely visible, or limited to clearly stereotypical roles. Consequently, the depiction of women of color in working class or middle class roles, and in professional jobs, were late in arriving on film, as seen in such movies as *The Joy Luck Club* (1993), *I Like It Like That* (1994), and *Waiting to Exhale* (1995). In a womanist interpretation of *Waiting to Exhale*, the four African American female protagonists are seen as negotiating their way through personal relationship issues in a communal way that both validates the individual while drawing strength from social and cultural relationships (Carstarphen, 1999). Similarly, the "career versus family dilemma" that Grace faces in *The 24-Hour Woman* finds its resolution through womanist/mestiza-defined strategies.

Nine months after the news of her pregnancy becomes a feature on the television show she produces, Grace Santos anxiously awaits delivery. Over the months, the strategy of capitalizing on the Diaz-Santos baby experience has netted the benefits that executive producer Joan has sought, and that is a huge increase in Neilsen ratings. A baby shower hosted by her office mates, though, causes Grace to sob secretly in the ladies' room. And, when she is two days late past her due date, she feels that everyone is blaming her. When Grace does deliver her daughter, the cameras are in the hospital to capture her dutiful smiles. But, when the crew leaves, she finds that her desire to rest is thwarted by an officious nurse who, as she refuses to take the crying newborn to a nursery, insists that Grace needs to "keep her so they can bond."

At home, Grace surrounds herself with her mother, mother-in-law, and grandmother, all of whom have differing views on whether she should continue to work and raise a family. Her husband, Eddie Diaz, who pledged his full partnership early in the pregnancy, has nevertheless accepted a film role in California in addition to his television show. Attempting to keep up with her producing duties from home while tending to her newborn proves to be overwhelming, as Grace explodes to her husband during one stressful night that she "can understand child abuse." But, just as Grace feels bonded to her daughter, Lilly, she has to return to work as the show is propelled by its newfound ratings boost and contemplates a jump to network stardom.

Grace's juggling comes to a head one year later, after a crisis at work and a series of mishaps causes her to miss Lilly's first birthday party. Eddie is busy in California shooting a film and cannot make it home. Madeline assists as much as Grace allows. Her wanting to help Grace is earnest, not to be mistaken with the back-biting character Eve Harrington who tries to overtake Margo Channing's career in *All About Eve* (1950). Neither is Madeline trying to push out from under an unethical boss as we see in *Working Girl* (1988) where an industrious and empathetic secretary, Tess McGill, implements several maneuvers to get ahead. Madeline is in a supportive relationship with Grace. We see Grace, trying to maintain professional control and frantically trying to obtain a highly desirable guest for her show the next morning, find a certain brand of doll at a toy store, make it home during rush hour traffic, and locate a "comadre" (females in kinship or fictive kinship network) to pick up the special birthday cake. Grace's mother and "comadres" carry forth the party for little Lilly and help her with her first steps. In a desperate attempt to gain back the moments she lost with Lilly and to assuage her guilt, she goes through the trouble of staging home video baby birthday party scenes with Lilly and soon after that she plans to include these through the magic of editing. It is the crisis with Lilly's birthday party that pushes Grace to reconsider her full-time professional commitments.

When Grace resolves to quit her job, or take a break, she sounds out Joan's opinion in the control room. But if she expected sympathy or empathy, she is sorely disappointed, embarrassed, and shamed. Taunting Grace for "being off her game all year," Joan accuses her subordinate of suffering from a bad case of "mommy-itis." As a counterpoint to this dramatic off-camera scene, Grace's husband, Eddie, is on camera, describing how much he has shared in his daughter's upraising. Galvanized by Eddie's inaccurate remarks, Grace confronts her husband on television with a revolver, left over from a previous show, that she discovers while angrily cleaning out her office. Ever the opportunist, Joan decides to call CNN instead of 911 to garner publicity for the unexpected crisis she labels "a hostage situation." After several tense moments of sensationalist TV-style, on-camera confrontation between Grace and Eddy, Grace is handcuffed and arrested by police. We note that throughout Grace's crisis at the TV station, Madeline maintains their friendship and aids her as much as she is able. Even as police are arriving on the set, Madeline declares to them that she is her friend.

Until the point in the narrative where Grace confronts her husband on camera, the film clearly reveals the work and family tensions that have exacerbated over the decades for contemporary women. Grace's reactions and high emotions might be understood in the context of unreasonable professional and domestic demands placed upon her. Women audiences, in particular, are drawn to empathize with her struggles and even recall her struggles as those of their mothers. From a womanist, U.S. third world feminist, and "mestiza" perspective, Grace has every right to behave as an expectant woman, pregnant woman, and postpartum woman, complete with variations in emotions and verbal expressions. Furthermore, Grace is a "Puertorriqueña" who, like many "Puertorriqueñas" before her on the mainland, has to live with cultural, individual, and practical tensions (Korrol, 1994; Torres, 1995; Hero, 1992). She, as a Puerto Rican woman, experiences internal conflicts of obligation to her family and the need to contribute financially and have a personally fulfilling job (see accounts in Flores, 1993; Glasser, 1997; Suro, 1999). The women in her extended family, plus a nanny and excellent co-worker Madeline, work collectively to help her in her new role. Womanist strategies are developed among their characters and a womanist analysis is easily imparted.

It is Grace's confrontation with her husband with a pistol, her firing of the pistol, and her humiliating on-camera arrest that raises questions as to the womanist quality of the film. Grace's rage is shown to be out of control. We see outlandish melodrama evoking archetypal images of Latinas past. She is a hot-tempered fiery Latin mama out to do someone harm. And that someone is her loving but no-help, media star husband. The surprising turn of events in the narrative was dismissed as post-partum depression within the film dialogue. However, this narrative climax cannot be ignored in analysis of the film given the common Latina archetypes. In the broader context of womanist media studies is Grace's outrage to be understood as a kind of destructive, yet somehow understandable behavior as in the double girlfriend suicide in *Thelma and Louise* (1991)? Does Grace's behavior fit alongside the behavior vividly illustrated in *The Burning Bed* (1984) and *Extremeties* (1986)? Does the outrage that Grace express fit with the womanist, U.S. third world feminist, and "mestiza" agenda? Issues regarding violence against women and women's response to all forms of abuse are topics that feminists and the general public continue to debate today.

Given certain situations, critics and publics may say that women's violent defenses against their oppressors can be necessary. How we see Grace's case may not be clear if we are to consider the many aspects of her situation. These authors wish that the film would have used a different way to bring the film to a climax. The second author showed the film to a University of Connecticut undergraduate class of 13 women and one man as part of the course curriculum during the spring of 2001. About half of the students were Latino/a or African American and the others were European Americans. Several students described "the gun part" as "cheesy," "silly," and "stupid" during discussion. They more fully expressed themselves in written comments that they prepared before we discussed the film together. The following are some observations from a Latina, a European American and an African American woman, respectively:

I think her reactions were extreme to go in front of cameras and point a gun at her husband. Anybody in her case would have shouted, screamed, etc. but not bring a gun into the picture. There were I think other ways to get her message through even though he was lying. I think it was a representation of how women usually feel and think when they feel helpless or in a conflicting situation with their husbands who don't understand where they come from.

I can understand Grace being over-pressured and unsure of the decisions she was making. I also feel for her not getting sympathy from her family and husband. However, her breaking out a gun and the interruption of the show was an extreme reaction.

It is appropriate when you're on the job market and society is telling you, you have to stay home to be the ideal mother and the other half is telling you, well you have to earn a living and become a woman of the times. When that great of a response is placed on you, without any help from the child's father, one becomes frustrated. Any drastic actions are sometimes needed to bring consciousness to the people around you for them to realize you can't do it all.

The second author noted that students seemed cautious about putting too much blame on Grace. On one hand they may see her behaviors as too extreme, but on the other hand they may also want to be understanding toward Grace and the pressures she has in her life. They sympathize with Grace's not getting all the support she needed and not being able to "do it all."

Madeline is Grace's sister in arms, her compatriot in the family-job struggle. She appears to be roughly the same age as Grace but is older in family experience.

She is wiser, having left a job in media and gone through four years of child-rearing. Grace knew upon hiring her new assistant that Madeline represented a point in life that she herself could be in, given four or five more years. Therefore, Madeline holds the keys to experiences that Grace herself does not yet have. Madeline usually meets the pressures of family with physical and vocal calm, with brief moments of high emotion expressing anger or frustration. Overall, her behaviors do not beckon past images of black female archetypes. She meets TV-producing demands with subdued excitement and consistency, something that seems to frustrate at least one female African American co-worker whose reactions tend to be more high-strung like those of Grace, Margo (Eddie's co-host), Crystal (the show's resident psychic), and boss-lady Joan. Her even temperament reveals to us that she has been through trials of life and job glitches or life setbacks will not push her over the edge. She is an excellent role model for Grace, and Grace is fortunate to have this centered woman as a friend and co-worker.

HAPPY ENDING: BUILDING THE WOMANIST/MESTIZA AGENDA OR SELLING OUT?

The neat happy ending of the film might be considered by some to be necessary because it inspires and nurtures hope among so many women audiences in struggle. The film may be saying that Grace found her way, it wasn't easy but she found her way after all and has a job, a husband, children, and a best friend named Madeline. Perhaps one can say that Grace found her place by finally embracing herself and finding her inner power; she used womanist/mestiza strategies and is on a productive path. Another perspective on the ending of the film is that it is illogical, given Grace's extreme emotional turmoil and the degree of career and spousal relationship damage she has committed. Some students in the University of Connecticut seminar expressed that the neat happy ending of the film was "unbelievable" and that is was an old "happily ever after" ending. It seems that the "cheesy" gun scenes and the too-neat ending may be viewed as a sell-out to standard Hollywood techniques of action and closure. Grace may be seen as failing to work through her difficulties using womanist/mestiza strategies to their fullest. The ending, then, could be considered a false one.

Applying the womanist/mestiza approach idealistically, we could also say that Grace finds her way back to wholeness after gathering her individual parts on a long journey. A Latino student commented, "It was very enjoyable . . . it focused more, detailing a woman's life, one that does encompass a variety of roles." A European American student said "I think the video exposes what it truly is to be a female. It depicts the life of a woman as it truly is. Grace is the average female in the U.S." At the end we see that she is mother, wife, daughter, friend, and careerist all at once. She probably respects the experiences of her mothers, but accepts that she is free to decide her own path. As a wife reconciled with her husband, she negotiates with him a more truthful understanding of their roles in their marital crisis, and a re-dedication to their union. And as "The 24-Hour Woman" takes off into network affiliation without her, Grace pitches a concept for a new show on a women's television network that reflects her newfound commitment to look at the lives of "everyday people" with "everyday problems." When we see Grace and Madeline take off in a taxi together to begin their new show, we know that Grace and Madeline are strong womanists, working in mutual cooperation and support. With the centered Madeline as a partner, and Eddie taking charge of the baby, we may feel success is in the air. To complicate matters, however, and lend material for a sequel, Grace ends the film with the surprise of another pregnancy. How will Grace negotiate the needs of yet another baby and a new show? We expect that she will be successful once again.

Though clearly a subordinate story to Grace's trials, Madeline also has her share of challenges balancing her reentry into a career with her family's needs. Her husband, Roy (played by Wendell Pierce), moves from being stay-at-home dad to returning back to work with a discernible appreciation for how hard the domestic sphere can be. At points throughout the film, Grace and Madeline's experiences seem to be reverse images of the same dilemmas. For instance, while Grace sorts out her new responsibilities as a mother, Madeline copes with office politics. Madeline's role, and the roles of her husband and family are excellent complements. They are characters in a sub-theme that gives depth to the film and breadth to the question of negotiating career and family.

Overall, black and brown female experience becomes linked by similar sensibilities about family and work, serving as a unified opposition to the old traditional feminist binary of work versus home. In *The 24-Hour Woman*, which filmmaker Savoca dedicates to her mother ("para mi mama"), the question about whether a woman can have it all is not answered simplistically. Exposing the idea of a superwoman as a myth through the lens of its aptly named fictional show, "The 24-Hour Woman," Grace and Madeline can be viewed as redefining career and family on their own womanist and mestiza terms. This independent film, despite inconsistencies revealed in a womanist/meztiza framework, is a valuable contribution to popular culture. It underscores cooperative and supportive relationships between Latina and African American women and expands the multifaceted and positive ways in which women of color can be understood.

REFERENCES

Anzaldua, G. (1987). *Borderlands: The new mestiza.* San Francisco: Spinsters/Aunt Lute.

Applebome, P. (February 14, 1999). Trying to shake a stereotype but keep on being Rosie Perez. (Review of the film *The 24 Hour Woman*). In the *New York Times* (Online), Section 2, p.11. Available: Newspaper Source/AN: 1569378.

Berg, C. R. (Summer, 1990). Stereotyping in film in general with Hispanics in particular. *Howard Journal of Communication, 2,* (3), 286–300.

Bobo, J. (July–October, 1991). Black women in fiction and nonfiction: Images of power and powerlessness. *Wide Angle,* 13, (3 and 4), 72–81.

Bobo, J. (1991). Black women in fiction and nonfiction: Images of power and powerlessness. *Wide Angle,* 13, (3), 72–81.

Bobo, J. (1995). *Black women as cultural readers.* New York: Columbia University Press.

Bogle, D. (1988). *Blacks in American film and television: An encyclopedia.* New York: Simon & Schuster.

Bogle, D. (2001). *Toms, coons, mulattoes, mammies and bucks: An interpretive history of blacks in American Films.* New York: Continuum

Brummett, B. (1994). *Rhetoric in popular culture.* Boston: Bedford/St.Martin's.

Burks, R. E. (1996). Intimations of invisibility. In V. T. Berry & and C. L. Manning-Miller (Eds.) *Mediated messages and African American culture: Contemporary issues.* Thousand Oaks, CA: Sage.

Carstarphen, M. G. (1999). Getting real love: *Waiting to Exhale* and film representations of womanist identity. In M. Meyers (Ed.), *Mediated Women* (pp. 369–382). Cresskill, NJ: Hampton Press.

Carstarphen, M.G. & Zavoina, S. (Eds.) (1999). *Sexual rhetoric: Media perspectives on sexuality, gender and identity.* Westport, CT: Greenwood Press.

Doane, M. A. (1991). *Femmes fatales: Feminism, film theory, and psychoanalysis.* New York: Routledge.

Flores, J. (1993). *Divided borders: Essays on Puerto Rican identity.* Houston: Arte Publico.

Fregoso, R. L. (1993). *The bronze screen: Chicana and Chicano film culture.* Minneapolis: University of Minnesota.

Glasser, R. (1997). *Aqui me quedo: Puerto Ricans in Connecticut.* Hartford: Connecticut Humanities Council.

Hadley-Garcia, G. (1993). *Hispanic Hollywood: The Latins in motion pictures.* New York: Citadel.

Hero, R. E. (1992). *Latinos and the U.S. political system: Two-tiered pluralism.* Philadelphia: Temple University Press.

Hoffman, J. (October 9, 1994). Mom always said, don't take the first $2 million offer. In the *New York Times* (Online), p. H28. Available: Newspaper Source/AN: 9412285258.

hooks, b. (1981). *Ain't I a woman: Black women and feminism. by bell hooks.* Boston: South End Press.

Jones, G. W. (1991). *Black cinema treasures: Lost and found.* Foreword by Ossie Davis. Denton: University of North Texas Press.

Kaplan, E. A. (1997). *Looking for the other: Feminism, film, and the imperial gaze.* New York: Routledge.

Keller, G. D. (1994). *Hispanics and United States film: An overview and handbook.* Tempe, AR: Bilingual/Review Press.

Korrol, V. E. S. (1994). *From colonia to community: The history of Puerto Ricans in New York City.* Berkeley: University of California Press.

Lunsford, A.A. (1998). Toward a mestiza rhetoric. *JAC: A Journal of Composition Theory,* 18, 1–27.

Maslin, J. (October 14, 1994). A Bronx charmer with problems and all the answers. [Review of the film *I Like It Like That*]. In the *New York Times* (Online), p. C23. Available: Newspaper Source/AN: 9412290105.

McLean, A. L. (1992–1993). "I'm a cansino": Transformation, ethnicity, and authenticity in the construction of Rita Hayworth, American love goddess. *Journal of Film and Video,* 44, (3–4), 8–26.

Mellencamp, P. (1995). *A fine romance: Five ages of film feminism.* Philadelphia: Temple University Press.

Miles, J. (1992). Blacks vs. browns: A struggle for the bottom rung. *The Atlantic Monthly,* 270, 41–68.

Millner, D. (2000, April 19). How the woman behind "love and basketball" fulfilled her hoop dream. In the *New York Daily News*. (Online). Available: Newspaper Source/AN: 4N21302592395381.

Mirande, A. & Enriquez, E. (1981). *La Chicana: The Mexican American woman*. Chicago: University of Chicago.

Morales, R. & Bonilla, F. (1993). *Latinos in a changing U.S. economy*. Newbury Park, CA: Sage.

Mordden, E. (1983). Movie star: the women who made Hollywood. New York: St. Martin's Press.

Natale, R. (July 15, 2000). Singing a different tune. In the *Los Angeles Times*. (Online). Available: Newspaper Source/AN: 000066333531852000.

Rios, D. I. (1996). Chicano cultural resistance with mass media, in R. De Anda (Ed.), *Chicanas and Chicanos in contemporary society*. Boston: Allyn and Bacon.

Rios, D. I. (1999). Latina/o experiences with mediated communication. In A. Gonzalez, M. Houston & V. Chen (Eds.), *Our voices*. Los Angeles: Roxbury.

Rios, D. I. (2000). Chicana/o and Latina/o gazing: Audiences of the mass media. In D. R. Maciel, I. D. Ortiz & M. Herrera-Sobek (Eds.), *Chicano renaissance: Contemporary cultural trends*, pp. 169–190. Tucson: University of Arizona.

Rita Hayworth. (1975). In *A biographical dictionary of film*. (Vol. 1, pp. 238–289). New York: William Morrow & Co.

Sandoval, C. (1998). Mestizaje as method: Feminists-of-color challenge the canon. In C. Trujillo (Ed.), *Living Chicana theory,* Berkeley, CA: Third Woman Press.

Seiler, A. (January 29, 1999). On the fly with super "woman." (Review of the film The 24-Hour Woman). In *USA Today* (Online), p. 9E. Available: Newspaper Source/AN: 1532803.

Steinhauer, J. (December 28, 1997). A director who films what she knows best. (Profile of film director Nancy Savoca). In the *New York Times* (Online), Section 2, p. 7. Available: Newspaper Source/AN: 76957.

Stockton, S. (1995). "Blacks vs. browns": Questioning the white ground. *College English,* 57, 166–181.

Suro, R. (1999). *Strangers among us*. New York: Vintage.

Tasker, Y. (1998). *Working girls: Gender and sexuality in popular cinema*. New York: Routledge.

Thomas, L. E. [2000, September 15]. Womanist theology, epistemology, and a new anthropological paradigm. In *Cross Currents* (Online), 48(4), p. 488–449. (Available: Academic Search Elite/AN: 1474246.

Torres, A. (1995). *Between melting pot and mosaic: African Americans and Puerto Ricans in the New York political economy*. Philadelphia: Temple University Press.

The 24-Hour Woman. (1999). Video. Dir. Nancy Savoca. Artisan Entertainment. 92 mins.

Vargas, J.A.G. (1999). Who is the Puerto Rican woman and how is she?: Shall Hollywood respond? In M. Meyers, (Ed.), *Mediated women* (pp. 111–132). Cresskill, NJ: Hampton Press.

Vargas, J. A. G. (1996). A case study of Hollywood's constructed puertorriqueña identity. *Studies in Latin American Popular Culture,* 15, 2–19.

Walker, A. (1983) *In search of our mothers' gardens*. New York: Harcourt Brace Jovanovich.

Walsh, A. S. (1984). *Women's film and female experience, 1940–1950*. New York: Praeger Publishers.

Watkins, C. S. & Emerson, R. A. (September 15, 2000). Feminist media criticism and feminist media practices. In *Annals of the American Academy of Political & Social Science* (Online), 571, pp. 151–166. Available: Academic Search Elite/AN: 3449255.

Wilson, C. & Gutierrez, F. (1995). *Race, multiculturalism, and the media.* Newbury Park, CA: Sage.

Zinn, M. B. (September 15, 2000). Feminism and family studies for a new century. In *Annals of the American Academy of Political & Social Science* (Online), 571, pp. 42–56. Available: Academic Search Elite/AN: 3449233.

Chapter 4

Polarization of Minorities: Projecting Trends in the New Media Environment

Don Umphrey and Alan B. Albarran

INTRODUCTION

During the 1970s and 1980s the answer to "What is television doing to American society?" centered around a homogenization effect. Veteran broadcaster Eric Severeid said television had counteracted the country's tendency toward fragmentation (Mann, 1982). In reviewing literature on television effects, Comstock (1978) noted that television provided "an unprecedented sharing of the same experience" (p. 19), which may have served to reduce differences between various strata of society.

Some two decades later the question has changed to "How will media convergence affect American society?"

Just as the question has changed, so has the answer—dramatically. According to Vacker (2000), it includes a fragmentation of consensus. "The vision of a homogenous or universal cultural ideal can no longer dominate the media landscape" (p. 232).

Researchers agree that convergence of the television, telephone, and computer will provide for multitudinous choices, where an audience member may construct a media environment specifically to meet his or her own interests (Letwin, 1994; Owen, 1999; Vacker, 2000). According to Webster and Phalen (1997), this will lead toward audience polarization, "the tendency of individuals to move to the extremes of either consuming or avoiding some class of media content" (p. 110).

Since this new media environment is evolving, potential audience effects cannot be based solely on data. But existing audience information may be used to shed some light on the question. To see how this is possible, it is instructive to consider Owen's (1999) classification of four types of present and future television, including: (1) conventional TV that was dominated by the three major networks; (2) cable TV, similar to conventional TV but with many more channels and more specialized programming; (3) interactive TV, where the viewer decides in advance what to watch, including videotape rentals and video on demand (VOD) and near video on demand (NVOD) available through cable, satellite or over the air; and (4) Internet TV, where one accesses the world wide web via broadband or wireless services.

Each step includes greater viewer choice than the one preceding it. Therefore, observations made about cable television in relationship to broadcast may be helpful in shedding some light on what will happen when even more choices are available.

As noted by Heeter and Greenberg (1988), differences between traditional broadcast television and the multichannel cable environment included the following, all of which would also be true in the new media environment: (1) greater number of choices; (2) channels offering specialized fare; (3) broadcasting perceived as "free," while customers had to pay for cable.

Because of these differences, Heeter and Greenberg (1985) posited that cable offered "the potential to improve predictions of selective exposure" (p. 220). The same researchers suggested in 1988 that the choices made on cable should be a more accurate reflection of viewers' content preferences. Thus, with the opportunity, it was expected that people would select specialized programming.

In focusing mostly on cable television audiences, Webster (1986) speculated there would be increasing polarization as viewers would be "in a position to construct media environments that may be quite different from those of their neighbors" (p. 77). The same idea is repeated by Webster and Phalen (1997) in relationship to a media environment that would offer unlimited choices at a timetable of the viewer's choosing.

Some studies have focused on specialized cable channels and may be helpful to shed light on audience behavior in the new media environment. Greenberg, Sipes, and McDonough (1988) found demographic differences between Playboy subscribers and subscribers to other pay services. There was also evidence among the Playboy viewers of exposure to other media content that was similar to what they would receive on the Playboy Channel (greater exposure to adult magazines and R-rated movies) and differences in beliefs about premarital sex and male domination of women.

In addition to demographic differences among heavy MTV viewers, Paugh (1988) found them to be less culturally oriented, more materialistic, and less conservative.

Differences in viewing styles between program types mostly offered on specialized cable channels (e.g., MTV, pay movie services, ESPN, and CNN) were examined by Heeter and Baldwin (1988). An example of described differences included the extent to which people plan ahead to watch programs or whether they run across them when changing channels. The researchers also speculated that viewers to premium channels engaged in instrumental, as opposed to ritualistic, viewing. This observation opens larger questions pertaining to different viewing orientations in a multichannel environment and the relationship of motivations and polarization of audiences.

Rubin (1984) identified instrumental viewing as more selective and purposeful; it is associated with greater information seeking and thus greater viewing of news programs. Ritualized viewing, on the other hand, is identified with viewing television for companionship or to pass the time. Findings by Childers and Krugman (1989) indicated more instrumental viewing among subscribers to a new pay service in contrast to traditional viewers of television who were more ritualized in their viewing. Perse (1990) found higher levels of program selection associated with instrumental viewing.

MINORITY AUDIENCES

Even in the age of limited broadcast choices, minority audiences showed distinct patterns of media exposure. For example, when Spanish-language radio was available, it drew more than 40% of the Hispanic audience, according to two different studies (Rosenthal, 1978; Spanish-Language Market Study, 1977). A Spanish-language UHF television station in Los Angeles was selected as the favorite station of 35% of Hispanic respondents (Lopez & Enos, 1973), the choice more positively correlated by those who spoke Spanish at home. A study of a Spanish-language television series by Marshall et al. (1974) indicated that it was preferred by Spanish-speakers.

Going beyond language, Eiselein & Marshall (1971, 1976) found preferences for music and news programming among Hispanics, while a study by Greenberg et al. (1983) concluded that in comparison to whites, Hispanics had greater preferences for situation comedies, soap operas, movies, game shows, and police/detective shows.

Several studies focusing on African Americans have indicated higher priorities for programming containing own-race portrayals (Dates, 1980; Greenberg, 1972; Greenberg & Atkin, 1982; Surlin, 1978). Evidence of this came from Kolbert (1993), who reported that during the first half of the 1992–93 television season, not one of the top 10 rated television programs among African Americans was in the top-10-shows in the overall rating, and among the top 20 shows there were only four matches; this contrasts to 15 matches out of the top 20 shows eight years earlier. The difference, according to Kolbert, was largely due to more programs featuring African American actors that were found mostly on the Fox Network. The trend toward different viewing patterns continued as Nielsen Media Research (2000) reported only two matches between the top 15 shows of African Americans in comparison to the total United States; the two shows common to both lists were NFL Monday Night Football and the pregame show. Much earlier, Carey (1966) documented differences in programming preferences between African Americans and whites. Also, demographic and attitudinal differences among African Americans have accounted for varying programming preferences (Allen & Bielby, 1979; Calhoun, 1979; Shosteck, 1969; Tan, 1978; Tan & Vaughn, 1976).

A few studies focus on minorities in a multichannel environment. In examining television diary information about the viewers of Spanish-language stations, Webster (1986) found a small percentage of Hispanics who spent a disproportionately large amount of time viewing the stations. In a study of African American cable television subscribers, Jones (1990) concluded those who spent more time watching BET (Black Entertainment Television) were younger and had high racial-orientation levels.

Thus, polarization of audiences is documented as occurring not only by demographics, interests, and attitudes, but also within minority groups. Further, polarization may be tied to the motivations of individuals for watching television in the first place.

Research Questions

The foregoing observations lead to the following research questions:

1. To what extent does polarization occur between ethnic groups in a multichannel environment?
2. To what extent do specialized channels aimed at specific ethnic groups lead to polarization within those groups? If there is polarization in these analyses, will it also result in differences in demographics and motivations? Will polarization also account for different television program preferences?
3. To what extent will audiences be polarized who are viewers to specific cable channels?

METHODOLOGY

A telephone survey was administered to adults living in Dallas, Texas, between mid-May and August 1991. In this city of 1.85 million, 57% were white; 20%, African American; 17%, Hispanic; and 6% were Asians and other races (U.S. Census Bureau, 1990). While 60% of the Hispanics in the United States were of Mexican descent, 89% of Dallas Hispanics were of Mexican heritage (Davis, Haub, & Willette, 1988).

Because minorities have been undersampled in studies utilizing a random method of selection, a stratified random method was used in this study with an objective of generating a sample consisting of one-third each whites, African Americans, and Hispanics. Telephone prefixes consisting of the first five digits were selected according to a ratio that would oversample ethnic areas shown on a map provided by the telephone company. Added digit dialing using two random numbers at the end of each phone number was used to reach new and unlisted households (Frey, 1989).[1]

Monitoring revealed that this approach was successful in reaching African Americans and whites, but Hispanics were being undersampled. Therefore, a skip interval method was utilized with selection from the local telephone directory among Hispanic surnames with telephone exchanges in the city.[2] This selection method was used only to reach Hispanics.

The mean duration of telephone interviews was 8.1 minutes. The completion rate was 30% for African Americans and white respondents and 65.9% for Hispanics, the difference in completion rates attributable to different sampling procedures. Those who administered the questionnaire were trained and paid. Questionnaires were available in both Spanish and English, and members of the research team who called Hispanics were bilingual.

MEASURES

Following the introduction, respondents were asked nine items to measure motivations for watching television. Most items were modified from Rubin (1981, 1983, 1984) including "it allows me to unwind," "it entertains me," "It helps me learn about myself and others," "to keep aware of current events," "it's enjoyable," "it relaxes me," "when there is nothing to do," "to learn about new things," and "it gives me something to do." Responses for these items ranged from strongly agree (coded as 5) to strongly disagree (coded as 1).

Respondents were next queried about the frequency of watching certain program types, which included news/newsmagazines, sports, movies, situation comedies, game shows, police/detective, music programs, dramatic shows, soap operas, talk/interview programs, reality programs, and westerns.

Respondents were then asked about the frequency of watching specific cable networks. These included CNN, ESPN, TBS, TNT, MTV, USA, the Weather Channel, and shopping channels; these were selected to represent channels offering specialized information (CNN, the Weather Channel, shopping channels), specialized entertainment (ESPN, MTV), or more broad-based programming (TBS, TNT, USA). To both the program types and the cable networks, responses included always (coded as a 5), frequently, occasionally, rarely, or never (coded as a 1).

Following the query about cable networks, respondents were asked, "What other cable channels do you regularly watch?" Each response was followed by a probe ("Is there another?") until respondents answered negatively. All respondents were within the city limits of Dallas, served exclusively at that time by Dallas TCI Cablevision. Basic subscribers had access to 70 channels.

Demographic variables included age, gender, ethnicity, and household size. Ordinal scales were used to measure education (1 = less than high school, 5 = attended graduate school) and "last year" household income (1 = less than $15,000, 5 = $60,000 or higher).

RESULTS

Altogether, 1,241 respondents were interviewed, including 33.8% whites (n = 412), 28.6% African Americans (n = 348), and 37.6% Hispanics (n = 458). Excluded from further analyses were Asians, individuals who were a part of "other" ethnic groups, and cases where ethnicity was a missing value, totaling 1.9% of the total sample.

Whites had the highest incidence of cable subscription (49.3%), followed by Hispanics (43.5%) and African Americans (36.2%) (X^2 = 13.2, d.f. = 2, p < .001). Only cable subscribers were analyzed for this study. Total cable subscribers interviewed were 529, including 204 whites (38.6%), 126 African Americans (23.8%), and 199 Hispanics (37.6%).

Among these cable subscribers whites were the oldest (mean = 41.3 years), followed by Hispanics (mean = 35.8 years), and then African Americans (mean = 35.3 years) (F = 9.6, p < .0001). Additionally, white cable subscribers had significantly higher levels of education, followed by African Americans, then Hispanics (X^2 = 184.4, d.f. = 4, p < .000001), and whites had the highest income level, again followed by African Americans, then Hispanics (X^2 = 141.4, d.f. = 4, p < .000001). Hispanics ranked highest in size of household number (mean = 3.9), followed by African Americans (mean = 3.4), and whites (mean = 2.5) (F = 48.8, p < .00001). When given the choice, 69.5% of the Hispanics opted to take the questionnaire in Spanish. In comparison to Hispanics who chose the English-language questionnaire, those who chose the Spanish language were older (Spanish mean = 36.1 years; English mean = 32.8 years, t = -2.3, p < .023), came from larger household sizes (Spanish mean = 4.1, English mean = 3.6, t = -3.1, p < .002), and had both lower levels of education (X^2 = 63.1, d.f = 4, p < .000001) and income (X^2 = 29.8, d.f. = 4, p < .00001).

There were significant indications of polarization between ethnic groups in the viewing of selected cable channels. (See Table 4.1.) Out of the eight analyses of variance that controlled for age, education, and income, TBS was the only station where there were not significant differences in viewing by ethnicity. Whites tallied the highest mean on the viewing of CNN. Hispanics were the heaviest viewers of the Weather Channel, and African Americans watched the most of TNT, MTV, and USA. African Americans and Hispanics were nearly identical in their viewing of shopping channels.

To explore polarization within ethnic groups, the open-ended item was used. ("What other cable channels do you regularly watch?") The 28.5% of African Americans who named BET were analyzed in relationship to African Americans who did not name it. As can be seen in Table 4.2, BET viewers were younger with higher levels of education and income, but there were no significant differences in motivations for viewing between the two groups. In the analyses of program types, music was the only type where BET viewers scored a significant difference (BET mean = 3.9, non-BET mean = 3.0, t = 3.3, p < .001). Among the specific cable channels, there were two significant differences with BET viewers watching more of MTV (BET mean = 4.1, non-BET mean = 3.2, t = 3.4, p < .001) but less of TNT (BET mean = 2.5, non-BET mean = 3.0, t = -2.0, p < .047).

To probe polarization among Hispanics, the 42.7% of Hispanics respondents who named one or more of the three Spanish-language networks available (Galavision, Univision, and Telemundo) were contrasted to those who did not. As might be expected, there was a greater likelihood of watching a Spanish-language channel among those who took the questionnaire in Spanish (61.8%) compared to English (16.7%) (X^2 = 38.8, d.f. = 1, p < .000001). While there was not a signifi-

Table 4.1
Mean Scores and ANOVA Results for Cable Channels across Ethnic Segments Controlling for Age, Education, and Income

In a regular week, how often watch . . .	Whites (n = 204)	Afr-Amer. (n = 126)	Hispanic (n = 199)	Total	F Score
CNN	3.47	2.97	3.36	3.31	6.59**
ESPN	2.82	3.10	2.92	2.92	3.08*
Superstation TBS	2.81	2.97	2.70	2.80	1.93
TNT	2.62	2.90	2.47	2.63	4.76**
MTV, music videos	2.33	3.35	2.80	2.74	14.59**
USA Network	2.52	2.98	2.83	2.74	3.67*
Weather Channel	2.40	2.45	2.77	2.55	3.48*
Shopping Channels	1.21	1.66	1.70	1.50	6.34**

(5 = always watch, 4 = frequently watch, 3 = occasionally watch,
2 = rarely watch, 1 = never watch)
*p < .05   **p < .01.

Table 4.2
Demographic Differences of African Americans by BET Viewing

	BET mean	non-BET mean	t =	p <
Age	31.9	37.4	-2.0	.044
Education[a]	3.0	2.5	2.4	.019
Income[b]	3.0	2.5	2.2	.030

a. 2 = high school graduate, 3 = attended college.
b. 2 = $15,000–$30,000, 3 = $30,000–$45,000.

cant difference in age between the viewers and nonviewers of Spanish-language cable offerings, those who did name a network had significantly lower levels of education (named Spanish network mean = 2.0, didn't name Spanish network mean = 2.4, t = -2.4, p < .016) and income (named network mean = 1.9, did not name network mean = 2.2, t = -2.4, p < .02).

As with the BET viewers, no differences were observed among Hispanics in their motivations for viewing ethnic programming aimed at them. Shopping channels was the only selected cable offering where there was a significant difference between the groups. (Named a Spanish network mean = 1.9; didn't name a Spanish network mean = 1.6, t = 2.0, p < .052.) There were five program types where the two Hispanic groups differed, as seen in Table 4.3.

The entire sample of cable subscribers was analyzed to determine polarization by the viewing of the eight cable offerings that were named on the questionnaire. Table 4.1 displays differences in demographics, motivations, the viewing of program types, and viewing of the seven other cable channels named on the question-

Table 4.3
Differences in Program Types[a] among Hispanics by the Watching of
Spanish-Language Channels

	Named Spanish Channel mean	Did Not Name Spanish Channel mean	t =	p <
News	4.3	4.0	2.1	.037
Music	3.4	2.9	2.7	.088
Soaps	3.1	2.4	3.4	.001
Talk	3.7	3.2	3.9	.001
Westerns	2.9	2.5	2.2	.029

a. 5-point scale where 5 = always watch and 1 = never watch.

naire. For these analyses t-tests were used to assess differences between those who said they always or frequently watch a cable offering and those who said they occasionally, rarely or never watch. (Means, t values, and significance levels are available from the authors; they were omitted from Table 4.1 for clarity of presentation.)

As can be seen, there were demographic differences on all cable channels except ESPN, TBS, and TNT. The findings that CNN had an older, more highly educated, upper-income audience could have been predicted, as could MTV with its younger, less educated, lower-income audience. However, lower education levels among the audiences of USA, the Weather Channel, and shopping channels were more of a surprise.

With each of the cable channels, there were differences in motivations, frequency of viewing programming types, and viewing of at least some of the seven remaining cable offerings. Cable channels varied greatly in the number of significant findings. For example, there was only one significant finding in the area of motivations for the heavier viewers of TBS, but there were six motivational differences separating the heavier viewers of TNT from the light or nonviewers. The heavier CNN viewers scored significantly higher on only two program types (news and sports), while the heavier viewers of USA scored higher on 11 programming types. Similar patterns emerged with the viewing of cable offerings.

DISCUSSION

Clearly, the multichannel cable environment observed in this study showed evidence of polarization and thus may serve as an indication of what may happen with the greater choices in the new media environment. Here, there was polarization between ethnic groups. However, it would be an oversimplification to focus solely on those differences because polarization also occurred within ethnic groups and in other ways. Overall, this study supports the Webster and Phalen (1997) notions of greater diversity being a characteristic of the new media environment.

These findings also support the suggestions of Heeter and Greenberg (1985, 1988) that cable should be a more accurate reflection than broadcast television of viewers' content preferences. Selective exposure would seem to go a long way toward explaining audience polarization. With greater diversification in the media, according to Webster and Phalen (1997), "it should be easier for people to find content that more closely conforms to their preferences and avoid content that does not" (p. 111).

What are the societal implications? Comstock (1978) noted that the homogenization effect of (broadcast) television strengthened the then-current social hierarchy and reduced differences in society. It was thought that television programs such as *All in the Family* provided a national forum for topics such as bigotry. If, indeed, broadcast television served to reduce differences, it would seem that polarization in the new media environment would add impetus to an ongoing movement toward greater pluralism, as speculated by Vacker (2000). It is not believed, though, that television as a mass medium will disappear anytime soon (Webster & Phalen, 1997), and it can be speculated with reasonable certainty that some televised events will continue to draw large audiences. This leaves open to speculation the effect of ongoing erosion of the mass audience.

As to specifics from the findings in this study, there was more instrumental viewing among the heavier viewers of both CNN and the Weather Channel, which was to be expected. However, a closer examination reveals segmentation among these viewers seeking informational programming because these channels attracted different audiences. CNN viewers had higher levels of education, while those tuning to the Weather Channel had lower levels of education. Since CNN appealed more to whites and the Weather Channel more to Hispanics and because of the demographic differences between these groups, it may be an indication of information-seeking pertaining to meeting needs specific to one's circumstances in life. For example, unskilled and blue-collar workers are much more apt to work outside and be affected by the weather.

There were two significant motivations for viewers of shopping channels, one of the motivations was instrumental (learning) and the other was ritualistic ("it gives me something to do," a diversionary use of television). Shopping channels appealed more to minorities and individuals with lower levels of education from larger household sizes. The shopping-at-home television experience may be a substitute for a visit to the mall, which would seem to have both diversionary and educational functions.

With Internet use among college students, Papacharissi and Rubin (2000) reported an instrumental orientation as the most salient use, but they also noted the presence of a ritualized element in terms of interpersonal contacts through e-mail. Ferguson and Perse (2000) revealed several ritualized uses of the world wide web among college students but found that an activity like web surfing was more goal-directed toward the acquisition of information.

While there were significant differences in motivations for viewing all of the selected cable networks, there were not differences in motivations among minorities between those who viewed specific programming aimed at those minority groups and those who did not. This was true among African Americans for the viewing of BET and among Hispanics for viewing of Spanish-language programming, despite differences in demographics and programming preferences in each case. One possible reason is the difference in methodology; an aided measure was used for the selected cable channels compared to an unaided measure for the specialized minority programming. Varying results based on this methodological difference are discussed by Ferguson and Perse (1993). Jones (1990) did find different attitudes when examining African American BET viewers in comparison to those who were not. Thus, the question of whether there are different motivations within ethnic groups for the watching of specialized programming warrants further study, perhaps with different measures than used here.

These findings suggest a relationship between polarization and channel repertoire, a relationship about which Heeter and Greenberg (1988) speculated. According to these researchers, repertoire is a phenomenon suggesting that while cable subscribers have a wide array of choices available to them, they have a limited set of channels that they watch regularly. Reagan (1996) speculated that repertoires would grow as technologies made greater choices available.

Shortcomings of this study include the fact that the results are based on a single study; the results show a polarized audience, but due to the nature of the methodology it cannot be said that the results show greater or lesser polarization in comparison to another period of time. A second shortcoming is that the findings come from one market and may not be generalizable. Additionally, there were low response rates to the survey, leaving open the question of self-selection effects.

What this study does provide is evidence that a multichannel environment leads to polarization both between and among ethnic groups. This may be a glimpse of what to expect in the new media environment.

As the expectation of greater choices in the media comes to fruition, the minority audience deserves the scrutiny of researchers. There are many questions that need to be asked, some of which cannot now be anticipated. Based on these results, immediate attention could be placed on both motivations and repertoire.

NOTES

1. According to Survey Sampling, Inc., a professional sampling firm based in Fairfield, Connecticut, approximately 23.1% of all telephones in this market are unlisted.

2. Chang, Shoemaker, Reese, & Danielson (1988) compared random digit dialing and the use of surnames to sample Hispanics and found the two methods produced similar results.

REFERENCES

Allen, R. L. & Bielby, W. T. (1979). Blacks' attitudes and behaviors toward television. *Communication Research*, 6, 437–462.

Baldwin, T. F., Barrett, M. & Bates, B. (1992). Influence of cable on television news audiences. *Journalism Quarterly*, 69, 651–658.

Calhoun, L. E. (1979). *Racial orientation, media habits, and attitudes toward black situation comedy among black viewers*. Unpublished master's thesis. The University of Georgia, Athens.

Carey, J. W. (1966). Variations in negro/white television preferences. *Journal of Broad-casting*, 10, 199–212.

Chang, T. K., Shoemaker, P. J., Reese, S. D., & Danielson, W. A. (1988). Sampling ethnic media use: The case of Hispanics. *Journalism Quarterly*, 65, 189–191.

Childers, T. & Krugman, D. (1989). The pay per view experience: Insights from a field experiment. In R. Vatra & R. Glazer (Eds.) *Cable television advertising* (pp. 156–160). New York: Quorum Books.

Comstock, G. (1978). The impact of television on American institutions. *Journal of Communication*, 28, 12–28.

Dates, J. (1980). Race, racial attitudes, and adolescent perceptions of black television characters. *Journal of Broadcasting*, 24, 549–560.

Davis, C., Haub, C. & Willette, J. L. (1988). U.S. Hispanics changing the face of America. In A. Acosta-Belen & B. R. Sjostram (Eds.), *The Hispanic experience in the United States: Contemporary issues and perspectives* (pp. 3–55). New York: Praeger Publishers.

Eiselein, E. B., & Marshall, W. (February, 1971). "Fiesta"—An experiment in minority audience research and programming. *Educational and Industrial Television*, 3, 11–15.

Eiselein, E. B., & Marshall, W. (1976). Mexican-American television: Applied anthropology and public television. *Human Organization*, 35 (2), 147–156.

Ferguson, D. A., & Perse, E. M. (1993). Media and audience influences on channel repertoire. *Journal of Broadcasting & Electronic Media*, 37, 31–47.

Ferguson, D. A., & Perse, E. M. (2000). The World Wide Web as a functional alternative to television. *Journal of Broadcasting & Electronic Media*, 44, 155–174.

Frey, J. H. (1989). *Survey research by telephone* (2nd ed.). Newbury Park, CA: Sage.

Greenberg, B. (1972). Children's reactions to TV blacks. *Journalism Quarterly*, 49, 5–14.

Greenberg, B., & Atkin, C. (1982). Learning about minorities from television: A research agenda. In G. Berry & C. Mitchell-Kernan (Eds.), *The uses of mass communication* (pp. 71–92). Beverly Hills, CA: Sage.

Greenberg, B., Burgoon, M., Burgoon, J. K., & Korzenny, F. (1983). *Mexican Americans and the mass media*. Norwood, NJ: Ablex.

Greenberg, B. S., Sipes, S., & McDonough, J. (1988). The Playboy profile and other pay channel subscribers. In C. Heeter & B. S. Greenberg (Eds.), *Cableviewing* (pp. 226–236). Norwood, NJ: Ablex.

Heeter, C., & Baldwin, T. G. (1988). Channel type and viewing styles. In C. Heeter & B. S. Greenberg (Eds.) *Cableviewing* (pp. 167–176). Norwood, NJ: Ablex.

Heeter, C. & Greenberg, B. S. (1988). A theoretical overview of the program choice process. In C. Heeter & B. S. Greenberg (Eds.), *Cableviewing* (pp. 33–50). Norwood, NJ: Ablex.

Heeter, C. & Greenberg, B. S. (1985). Cable and program choice. In D. Zillmann & J. Bryant (Eds.) *Selective exposure to communication* (pp. 203–224). Hillsdale, NJ: Lawrence Erlbaum Associates.

Jones, F. G. (1990). The black audience and the BET channel. *Journal of Broadcasting & Electronic Media*, 34, 477–486.

Kolbert, E. (April 5, 1993). TV viewing and selling, by race. *New York Times*, (49, 292), D-7.

Letwin, W. (August 15, 1994). Traffic jam. *National Review*, 46, 43–45.

Lopez, R., & Enos, D. (1973). Spanish-language-only television in Los Angeles County. *Aztlan*, 4, 283–313.

Mann, J. (Aug. 2, 1982). What is TV doing to America? *U.S. News and World Report,* 93 (5), 27–30.

Marshall, W., Eiselein, E. B., Duncan, J., & Bogarin, R. (1974). *Fiesta: Minority television programming.* Tucson: University of Arizona Press.

Nielsen Media Research. (2000). Report on television. New York: Author.

Owen, B. M. (1999). *The Internet challenge to television.* Cambridge: Harvard University Press.

Papacharissi, Z., & Rubin, A. M. (2000). Predictors of Internet use. *Journal of Broadcasting & Electronic Media,* 44, 175–196.

Paugh, R. (1988). Music video viewers. In C. Heeter & B. S. Greenberg (Eds.), *Cableviewing* (pp. 237–245). Norwood, NJ: Ablex.

Perse, E. M. (1990). Audience selectivity and involvement in the newer media environment. *Communication Research,* 17, 675–697.

Reagan, J. (1996). The "repertoire" of information sources. *Journal of Broadcasting & Electronic Media,* 40, 112–121.

Rosenthal, M. (October 23, 1978). Indicators of growth abound in Spanish media community. *Radio/TV Age,* A17-A27.

Rubin, A. M. (1981). An examination of television viewing motivations. *Communication Research,* 8, 141–165.

Rubin, A. M. (1983). Television uses and gratifications: The interactions of viewing patterns and motivations. *Journal of Broadcasting* 27, 37–51.

Rubin, A. M. (1984). Ritualized and instrumental television viewing. *Journal of Communication,* 34, 67–77.

Shosteck, H. (1969). Some influences of television on civil unrest. *Journal of Broadcasting,* 13, 371–385.

Spanish-Language Market Study (November 7, 1977). *Radio/TV Age,* S1-S24, A18-A20.

Surlin S. (1978). "Roots" research: A summary of findings. *Journal of Broadcasting,* 22, 309–320.

Tan, A. (1978). Evaluation of newspapers and television by blacks and Mexican-Americans. *Journalism Quarterly,* 55, 673–681.

Tan, A., & Vaughn, P. (1976). Mass media exposure, public affairs knowledge and black militancy. *Journalism Quarterly,* 53, 271–279.

U.S. Census Bureau. (1990). Washington, DC.

Vacker, B. (2000). Global village or world bazaar? In A. B. Albarran & D. H. Goff (Eds.), *Understanding the web: Social, political, and economic dimensions of the Internet* (pp. 211–237). Ames: Iowa State University Press.

Webster, J. (1986). Audience behavior in the new media environment. *Journal of Communication,* 36 (3), 77–91.

Webster, J. G., & Phalen, P. F. (1997). The mass audience: Rediscovering the dominant model. Mahwah, NJ: Lawrence Erlbaum.

Part II: News

Chapter 5

Use of Minority Sources in News

A. N. Mohamed and Anita Fleming-Rife

INTRODUCTION

Studies of media's handling of race issues invariably note the absence or misrepresentation of minority group perspectives (Martindale, 1986; Campbell, 1995; Johnson, 1987; Shirley, 1992). The oversight is generally a by-product of a "commonsense" approach to newsgathering that is based on identifiable values and practice codes whose legitimacy and fairness are taken for granted.

In view of this, it is significant that some industry groups such as Gannett have instituted measures aimed at influencing the nature of coverage minorities receive (Basheda, 1995). For some time during the 1980s, editors and reporters affiliated with Gannett papers were asked "to quote minority sources in every article they write" in order to achieve what is called a "mainstreaming" effect (Basheda, 1995). The opinions of African American and other minority news sources were to be sought in connection with every subject in the news, not just on "ghettoized" race issues.

This study will explore the possible effects on news that such an approach to news sources will entail. Other chain newspapers will be compared with Gannett papers for variations in how minority news sources are depicted. We expect different editorial policies with regard to use of news sources to produce variations in the racial overtones of news stories.

"MODERN RACISM" AND THE ROLE OF THE MEDIA

Alexis de Tocqueville's American experience was marked by the impression made on him by the American creed proclaiming "justice, freedom, and equality" that were uncommon in Europe and elsewhere during the nineteenth century (de Tocqueville, 1946). Yet he concluded that ingrained racial animosities "would plague the future as they had haunted the past" (quoted in Hacker, 1992, p.215).

This fundamental paradox in the American character has been noted by social scientists who could not reconcile the egalitarian outlook of our collective self with the prejudiced and discriminatory attitudes of individuals (Dovidio and Gaertner, 1986). Although the racial climate in America has improved both socially and legally since the 1960s, individuals still are socialized in an atmosphere of racial animus (Jones, 1986). The openly racist legal and social codes of the past (especially in the South) have been supplanted by politically and socially more tenable attitudes that are nonetheless racist.

While traditional racist sentiments such as segregation and legalized discrimination are no longer a part of mainstream media fare, the literature suggests a preponderance of images and expressions whose collective connotative effect essentially add up to a racist media ideology (Entman, 1990, 1992, 1994; Campbell, 1995; Shah and Thornton, 1994; Rhodes, 1993).

Separate analyses of media content (Ettema, 1990; Entman, 1990) have shown the existence of institutional frameworks of newsgathering practice that feed such tendencies as the proclivities for harboring hostilities toward black political and economic empowerment, for viewing blacks as too demanding, and for dismissing the idea that racial discrimination hampers black social progress (Entman, 1994; Campbell, 1995).

Some social scientists refer to this phenomenon as "modern racism" (McConahay, 1986), others refer to it as "enlightened racism," (Jhally & Lewis, 1992), while still others call it "symbolic racism" (Sears, 1988; Campbell, 1995).

McConahay (1986) has developed a scale for gauging the prevalence of modern racism. His instrument measures three basic characteristics: (1) a general aversion to blacks as a race because of stereotypical images formed through socialization, (2) a resistance to black political and economic demands such as those sought via legislative means, and (3) a denial that racial discrimination exists and that it contributes to an uneven playing field for blacks.

McConahay's survey on modern racism elicited responses to statements such as the following:

- Over the past few years, blacks have gotten more economically than they deserve.
- Over the past few years, the government and news media have shown more respect for blacks than they deserve.
- Blacks are getting too demanding in their push for equal rights.

Positive responses ("agree" and "strongly agree") to these statements were considered indices of modern racism. McConahay (1986) found that even after controlling for legitimate political conservatism, anti-black sentiments were still clearly discernible.

Similar observations were made by Sears (1988) and Hacker (1992). Indeed, the scope of modern racism gets even broader in Hacker's analysis of the status of race relations in America during the 1990s:

At the most visible level, growing numbers of white people are expressing misgivings over how black people are conducting themselves. . . . More and more whites increasingly condemn blacks for casting their race as victims who have no control over their condition. White Americans are franker to admit their support for racial barriers. They describe themselves as bystanders who must watch as their country is held hostage by a demanding minority. In their view, the behavior of blacks is a major explanation for what ails America. (Hacker, 1992, p. 210)

One disturbing aspect of race-related attitudes is the tendency to generalize behavior characteristics in society's minority groups. Social psychologists note that individuals have a natural inclination to favor members of their own groups (the ingroup) than members of other groups (the outgroup) (Linville and Fischer, 1986). Consequently, perceptions of *outgroup homogeneity* become normal and routine just as *ingroup heterogeneity* is taken for granted (Linville and Fischer, 1986). When some minorities misbehave, therefore, others in their group "are homogenized and assimilated to a negative stereotype by the ingroup whereas those in the ingroup (the majority) see themselves as individuated members of a diverse group" (Entman, 1992).

Studies suggest that media help perpetuate these sentiments in several ways. Entman, for example, noted that both local (1992) and national (1994) television news "promoted perceptions that exacerbate whites' racial antagonism" (1994, p. 510) through their coverage of crime and political events involving blacks. His data showed that news of crime by blacks was mostly violent and/or involved drugs. Depictions of white criminals, by comparison, were more varied and included a significant and mitigating "white collar" component (1994). Blacks were more likely to be shown in handcuffs or otherwise being physically restrained by police than were whites; and blacks were more likely to be shown in still mug shots than were whites—thus painting the picture of a more menacing criminal element (Entman, 1994, p. 513). Furthermore, fewer pro-defense sound bites were included in news of black criminals than in news of whites (Entman, 1994, p. 513).

This supports an analysis of newspaper coverage of criminal court trials by Condit and Selzer (1985) who found that media routinely frame their coverage in a way that favors one side, thus cueing readers toward predictable conclusions.

In coverage of political news, Entman (1994) found that black leaders compared unfavorably with their white counterparts. Much more than whites, for example, blacks "complained of racial discrimination and often criticized government policy" for various inadequacies (Entman, 1994, p. 515). Black leaders also tended to speak about a narrow range of issues affecting the black community, whereas white leaders spoke on matters of interest to the general public. Moreover, black leaders and activists in the news spoke in angry tones when registering their complaints about perceived injustices. Former New York City Mayor, David Dinkins (who is black), was concerned about this phenomenon enough to plead with the

media "to seek out and cover those whose views may be less confronta-
tional—even if we're not as loud, even if our words create less controversy"
(Court, 1990, p. 27).

The mayor's concern is understandable, as the cumulative effect of these images
is that they will likely deepen the resentment of blacks by whites (Johnson, 1987;
Entman, 1994).

Although these depictions are not products of a conscious conspiracy, they may,
nevertheless, construct a reality that is at variance with the truth. This was indeed
the conclusion of a study in San Francisco (Stein, 1994) done in conjunction with
four professional associations of minority journalists (National Association of
Black Journalists, National Association of Hispanic Journalists, Native American
Journalists Association, Asian American Journalists Association). The study la-
mented how the "mainstream media's coverage of people of color is riddled with
old stereotypes, offensive terminology, biased reporting and myopic interpretations" (Stein, 1994, p. 12).

The nature of coverage of racial minorities receive could thus be seen as a product of applying one frame of reference to make sense of another. This speaks directly to the frustration expressed by Roland Barthes (1972[1957]) with the
"naturalness" with which newspapers "constantly dress up reality" without acknowledging the role of history in determining that reality. Likewise, Stuart Hall
(1995) explained that the media's construction of the concept of race is determined
by the ideology that informs the social consciousness of a given group at a given
time. Here, ideology refers to the framework "which provides us with the means of
'making sense' of social relations" (Hall, 1995). It is this media ideology that dictates the picture of reality about race relations that emerges, and which in turn
molds audience perceptions.

To place the nature of this coverage in proper perspective, therefore, an examination of some aspects of organizational newsgathering practice is warranted.

EDITORIAL CONTROL AND USE OF NEWS SOURCES

A pivotal relationship in organizational structure is the one between ownership
and content homogeneity and/or editorial autonomy. The overwhelming majority
of U.S. daily newspapers (about 75%) are now owned by chains (Farrar, 1996).
And the trend toward group ownership has long generated interest in the implications of this control for news content (Bagdikian, 1983, Featherstone, 1978,
Wagenberg and Soderlund, 1975).

Organizations like Gannett and Knight-Ridder have gone to some length in trying to allay fears of content homogenization in their papers. Gannett, for example,
often promoted itself as "A World of Different Voices Where Freedom Speaks";
while Knight-Ridder, after buying six more newspapers during the 1980s, tried to
reassure readers: "We don't own their opinions. We don't own their news columns. And quite frankly, we don't want to" (CJR March/April, 1987,17).

But several content studies found evidence of homogenization among papers
owned by the same chain. Glasser, Allen, and Blanks (1989) found that newspa-

pers belonging to the Knight-Ridder group gave more similar news play to a specific story than other papers subscribing to the Knight-Ridder news service. Akhavan-Majid, Rife, and Gopinath (1991) found that editorials in Gannett papers "showed a high level of homogeneity and significant differences between the Gannett and non-Gannett papers." And Gaziano (1989) showed that newspapers belonging to smaller chains tended to be similar in their editorial endorsements of presidential candidates.

But the most conspicuous attempt at influencing coverage is probably Gannett's policy of "mainstreaming" minority images in the news (Basheda, 1995). The concept began in the mid-1980s when Gannett suggested that "someone of African American, Hispanic, Asian, or Native American descent should always be quoted in everyday news coverage, such as stories about tax hikes or new school curricula" (Basheda, 1995). The aim was to avoid pigeonholing minorities by associating them only with certain kinds of stories. That some papers like the *Detroit News* have a special ombudsman to oversee the implementation of the mainstreaming idea attests to Gannett's commitment "to do the right thing."

This is also significant in view of the prominence of political and economic elites as news sources. Sigal (1986) noted that for major U.S. newspapers, "routine channels for news gathering constitute the mechanism for official dominance of national and foreign news." He determined that events under government control such as official press releases, press conferences, official proceedings, and "background" briefings, together accounted for 72% of the news channels for the *New York Times* and the *Washington Post*. About 14 years later, Brown et al. (1987) found that more than half of 5,248 sources cited in 846 front-page stories were official government sources. And almost two decades after the Sigal study, Hansen (1991) found that about 40% of daily reporting relied on official government sources.

This preponderance of official sources is bound to affect not only the kind of information transmitted but also the interpretation of significant situations and events. As Berkowitz and Terkeust (1999) have argued, "what takes place in the public sphere are struggles of meanings to make dominant one of several preferred interpretations of occurrences and issues." Accordingly, Hackett (1985) found that reports on Canadian political discourse mirrored very closely the views of the most dominant political figures. And Weaver and Elliott (1985) found that of 19 prominent local issues, 12 were transmitted by the media exactly as local authorities had framed them.

Thus news sources do shape the *nature* of news; and the media's gatekeeping power derives from "their selection of sources, which largely determines the way stories are framed" (Lasorsa and Reese, 1990).

HYPOTHESES

The foregoing discussion of the images in the media of minority sources of news, as well as Gannett's attempts at "mainstreaming" these sources, leads us to pose the following hypotheses:

H1: Gannett's policy of source diversification will mean less reliance on traditional sources than would be the case with other chain newspapers.

H2: Gannett papers are more likely than other chain newspapers to use minority sources evenly in stories about different subjects.

H3: The thematic content of news will be influenced by the racial background of the sources cited.

METHOD

A content analysis of 15 newspapers from across the United States (five each from Gannett, Knight-Ridder, and Scripps-Howard) was undertaken. They are: *The Clarion-Ledger* (of Jackson, Ms.), *Detroit News, Cincinnati Enquirer,* and *Tucson Citizen* (all owned by Gannett); *Miami Herald, Philadelphia Inquirer, San Jose Mercury News, Fort Worth Star Telegram, Detroit Free Press* (all owned by Knight-Ridder); *Birmingham Post Herald, Cincinnati Post, Rocky Mountain News, Albuquerque Tribune,* and *Ventura County Star* (all owned by Scripps-Howard).

The unit of analysis is the theme. We decided that since source messages come in thematic units, this would be the most appropriate unit of analysis. Therefore all themes within a story in which a source is quoted, directly or indirectly, were coded.

Two classifications of sources were made: (1) Sources were categorized in terms of occupation as elected official, public official, public figure, business leader, national civil rights leader, regional/local civil rights leader, community/religious activist, professional, ordinary citizen, and "other." (2) Sources were also classified according to race as African American, Hispanic/Latino, Asian American, Native American, and Caucasian.

In order to test Entman's theory about qualitative differences in the thematic content of source information based on their race, stories were coded for their inclusion of such themes as anger, criticism of government policies/programs, advocacy of narrow interests, and complaints about government and society. Content was also coded for the presence of opposite themes as advocacy of general interest issues, supportive and/or constructive comments about government, and statements of general solidarity with the American people.

The themes were further coded according to broad topical categories as (1) social, (2) legal, (3) political, and (4) economic.

Five nationally significant stories were selected for analysis. The stories include three that had a strong racial element and two that had no racial overtones at all. The stories, which span a period of six years from the late 1980s to the mid-1990s are: (1) President Ronald Reagan's veto of a civil rights law passed by Congress in March 1988; (2) the Iran-Contra story after the indictment of Colonel Oliver North in March 1988; (3) the Supreme Court's abrogation in January 1989 of a Richmond (Virginia) Affirmative Action ordinance that reserved 35% of city contracts for minority bidders; (4) the debate over, and the passage of, the North American

Free Trade Agreement (NAFTA) in November 1993; and (5) the story of a South Carolina mother who drowned her two young sons and then blamed a fictitious black male carjacker for their abduction in November 1994.

One week's worth of news about each of these stories was coded. Intercoder reliability coefficients (on all variables) between three coders were .84 at the beginning of coding and .86 toward the end of coding.

FINDINGS

The content analysis produced an N of 2,733 themes. Of these, the race of the news source could be clearly identified either through direct references in the stories, photographs, or knowledge of the sources by coders, in 2,159 cases or 78.9% of the time.

Minorities comprised 11.7% of identifiable sources for all the stories. Caucasians comprised 88.3% of the sources. Of the three newspaper chains, Gannett's papers used a slightly higher proportion of black sources (13.5%) than either Knight-Ridder (9.2%) or Scripps-Howard (7.3%) (Chi Square = 63.53, p = .0001). But when the proportion of all minority sources is considered, there is little difference between the three chains, with Gannett using minority sources 16.1% of the time, compared to 13.2% for Knight-Ridder, and 16.5% for Scripps-Howard.

To test our first hypothesis, that Gannett newspapers will depend less on traditional sources of news, a Chi-Square test of the relationship between chain ownership and type of news source was computed (see Table 5.1).

The data show that, overall, Gannett papers relied less on elected and government officials than did either Knight-Ridder and Scripps-Howard newspapers. While a majority of Gannett sources (about 52%) were neither elected or government officials, a majority of sources quoted by both Knight-Ridder and Scripps-Howard papers were government and/or elected officials (about 53% each). With N = 2155, Cramer's V is significant at p = .000.

This shows that Gannett did indeed depart from the news media tradition of relying heavily on "powerful" sources, who are most directly responsible for instituting and executing public policies and programs. It is worth noting that Gannett also has relied more heavily on sources that were identified as civil rights leaders and as local or regional activists. Sixty-two or 7.8% of all sources used by Gannett were civil rights, or other local activists, while Scripps-Howard used only 28 or 3.8% of these sources and Knight-Ridder papers used 51 or only 4.2% of these sources. Cramer's V is significant at the p = .000 level and the hypothesis is therefore supported.

The second hypothesis seeks to compare the three chains on how they use minority sources across different kinds of stories. It was not possible to run statistical comparisons to test this hypothesis because of insufficient frequencies in some data cells.

However, we may state that the data (see Table 5.2) presents inconclusive evidence in this case. The hypothesis states that Gannett papers are more likely than other chain papers to use minority sources in different kinds of stories. The data,

Table 5.1
Newspaper Chain by Kind of News Source

	public/elected officials	civil rights leader	local/regional activist	professional	public figure	business leader	ordinary citizen	other	Total
Gannett N =	380	18	44	123	78	20	115	11	789
raw%	48	2	5	15	10	2	14	1	100
col%	27	42	44	29	39	17	29	20	29
Knight/Ridder	635	16	35	216	49	57	180	16	1204
	52	1	3	18	4	4	15	1	100
	45	37	35	52	24	48	45	29	44
Scripps-Howard	386	9	19	77	74	40	102	27	734
	52	1	2	10	10	5	14	4	100
	27	21	19	4	37	34	25	50	27
TOTAL	1401	43	98	416	201	117	397	54	2727

Cramer's V = .138; p = .00.

Table 5.2
News Source of Five Stories by Race and Newspaper Chain

STORY		Black	Hisp	White	Black	Hisp	White	Black	Hisp	White
Richmond affirm/action	N =	20	-	31	25	2	48	17	-	34
	Raw%	39	-	71	33	2.6	63	33.3	-	66.7
	Col%	22.5	-	7.8	28.4	10.5	5.8	42.5	-	7.4
Reagan veto	N =	4	-	63	5	-	106	2	2	50
	Raw%	6	-	94	4.5	-	95.5	3.7	3.7	92.6
	Col%	4.5	-	11.4	5.7	-	12.8	5	4.5	11
Susan Smith story	N =	49	-	91	53	-	160	9	6	81
	Raw%	35	-	65	25	-	75	9.3	6.2	83.5
	Col%	55	-	16.5	60	-	19	22.5	13.6	17.6
NAFTA	N =	16	13	858	5	16	389	10	34	217
	Raw%	5.6	4.5	89.6	1.2	3.8	91.3	3.8	12.8	82
	Col%	18	100	46.7	5.7	84.2	47	25	77.3	47.2
Iran/Contra	N =	-	-	109	-	1	125	2	2	78
	Raw%	-	-	98.2	-	8	98.4	2.4	2.4	93
	Col%	-	-	19.7	-	53	15	5	4.5	17
Total	N =	89	13	551	88	19	828	40	44	460
	Raw%	13.5	2	83.9	9.2	2	86.8	7.3	8	83.5

however, show that none of the Gannett papers in our study used a minority source (black, Hispanic, Asian, or Native American) in three of the five stories. Only one Native American source was cited in the fourth story, and only two Asian American sources were cited in the fifth story.

Knight-Ridder papers did not cite Hispanic, Asian, and Native American sources in two of the five stories, and no blacks were cited in one of the stories.

Scripps-Howard papers did not cite any Asian American sources in three of the stories. Hispanics were not cited in at least one story, and Native Americans were not cited in four of the five stories.

Overall, Gannett and Knight-Ridder papers used considerably more minority sources than Scripps-Howard papers (102, 107, and 88, respectively).

The third hypothesis is meant to test Entman's theory that there are predictable content themes that are more reliably associated with minority sources than non-minority sources of news. These include advocacy of narrow interests, complaints about their conditions in society, anger about real or perceived social injustices and public policies, and general criticism of the prevailing social order. Entman also argued that minority news sources were cited in circumstances in which they were less likely than other sources to advocate general interest themes or support the prevailing social order.

The data in Table 5.3 show the relationship between race of source and six content themes: anger, complaints, criticism, narrow interest, general interest, and support for the prevailing social order. (Data on Asian and Native American sources were eliminated from the table because of the small numbers of sources from these two groups.)

The largest statistical differences between the news sources of various racial groups is in the presence of complaints and criticism themes in their accounts. African American sources, for example, had complaint themes in their comments 53% of the time compared to 13% for Hispanic sources and only 10% for white sources (Kendall's Tau B = −.314, N = 2133, p = .000).

A majority of black sources also criticized the system (58.5%) compared to 32% of Hispanic sources and only 17% of white sources (Kendall's Tau B = −.279, N = 2132, p = .000).

A majority of black sources spoke about narrow interests (63%) in their accounts to news media as opposed to 25% of Hispanic sources and 26% of white sources. (Kendall's Tau B = −.196, N = 2132, p = .000). A majority of both black and Hispanic sources (71% and 60.5%, respectively) did not speak to general interest themes compared to a majority of white sources (55.5%) who did (Kendall's Tau B = .190, N=2133, p=.000).

Significantly larger majorities of minority sources (84% for blacks; 71% for Hispanics) failed to offer support to the system as opposed to 57% of whites who did not (Kendall's Tau B = .148, N = 2133, p = .000).

Although anger was not registered by a majority of sources of any race, it is noteworthy that black sources registered their anger much more frequently than did other news sources. While 46% of black sources expressed anger or said that

Table 5.3
Race of News Source by Content Themes in Three Newspaper Chains

		Anger		Complaint		Criticism		Narrow interest		General interest		Support	
		yes	no	yes	no	yes	no	yes	no	yes	no	yes	no
Black	N	99	118	115	102	127	90	137	80	45	172	34	183
	Raw%	46	54	53	47	58.5	41.5	63	37	21	79	16	84
Hispanic	N	16	60	10	66	24	52	19	57	30	46	22	54
	Raw%	21	79	13	87	32	68	25	75	39.5	60.5	29	71
White	N	313	1526	182	1658	306	1533	474	1365	1021	819	793	1047
	Raw%	17	83	10	90	17	83	26	74	55.5	44.5	43	57
Kendall's Tau B		-174		-314		-279		-196		.190		.148	
Significance level		.000		.000		.000		.000		.000		.000	
N		2132		2133		2132		2132		2132		2132	

they were angry about something, only 21% of Hispanic sources and 17% of white sources did the same (Kendall's Tau B = $-.174$, N = 2132, p = .000). Our third hypothesis is therefore supported.

CONCLUSIONS

Who the media tap as news sources provides insight into the prevailing social order as Olien and his colleagues (1995) have noted. Potentially, it could also affect whether community consensus is achieved or whether social acrimony is stirred.

Accordingly, conflict theorists suggest that societal groups representing different interests compete constantly for legitimation of their views and for a wider acceptance of their perceptions of social reality. As Berkowitz and Terkeurst (1999, p. 126) put it, the ultimate objective of special interest groups within society "is to protect and strengthen their social position and power through interpretations that facilitate acceptance of their preferred meanings" of events and situations. This is accomplished in large measure through mass media interpretations of those situations and events (Olien, Donohue, & Tichenor, 1995). Consequently, patterns of news source use by media organizations become critical to our understanding of consensus building processes as well as the dynamics of inter-group conflict.

In this study, two conclusions can be drawn from how 15 newspapers belonging to the three largest newspaper chains in the country have used news sources from racial minority groups:

1. Newspapers belonging to all three chains continue to associate minority sources with only certain types of stories—namely, stories with a strong racial/ethnic component. Gannett papers, for example, did not quote any Hispanic sources in any of the stories except in coverage of NAFTA. Both Knight-Ridder and Scripps-Howard papers quoted Hispanic sources in connection with NAFTA significantly more frequently than with any other story (84% and 77% of total number of quotations, respectively). African American sources were used in the greatest proportions by all chains in relation with only race-related stories. Eighty-two percent of the quotations of African American sources by Gannett newspapers came with the three stories on race relations—the Richmond affirmative action story, the Reagan veto of a civil rights bill, and the Susan Smith story out of South Carolina. Knight-Ridder papers associated black sources with "race" stories even more—with 94% of quotations of blacks coming with the three "race" stories.

2. This pattern directly affects how news consumers come to associate racial minorities with certain unpopular dispositions toward some social and political issues as Entman (1994) has previously shown. Our data confirms Entman's hypothesis that minority sources are more likely to speak in angry tones, to complain about their condition in society, to criticize public policies and programs, and to speak against the prevailing social order or social system. Although this is explained in part by the media's association of minorities with stories about certain kinds of issues, the effect is no less detrimental to society as a whole—as it helps feed the climate of racial animus that we live with in the United States.

REFERENCES

Akhavan-Majid, R., Rife, A., & Gopinath, S. (1991). Chain ownership and editorial independence: A case study of Gannett newspapers. *Journalism Quarterly*, 68 (1/2), 59–66.

Bagdikian, B. (1983). Democracy and the media. In Bagdikian, B. (Ed.) *The Media Monopoly* (pp. 176–184). Boston: Beacon Press.

Barthes, R. (1972 [1957]). *Mythologies*. New York: Hill & Wang.

Basheda, V. (1995). When should you quote minority sources? *American Journalism Review*, October, p. 12.

Brown, J., Bybee, C., Wearden, S., & Straughan, D. (1987). Invisible power: Newspaper news sources and the limits of diversity. *.Journalism Quarterly*, 64 (1), 45–54.

Campbell, C. (1995). *Race, myth and the news*. Thousand Oaks, CA: Sage.

Condit, C. & Selzer, J. (1985). The rhetoric of objectivity in the newspaper coverage of a murder trial. *Critical Studies in Mass Communication*, 2(3), 197–216.

Court, A. (1990). Can the press do the right thing? *Columbia Journalism Review*, July/August, p. 27.

de Tocqueville, A. (1946). *Democracy in America*, II. Trans. Henry Reeves. New York: Alfred A. Knopf.

Dovidio, J. & Gaertner, S. (1986). Prejudice, discrimination and racism: Historical trends and contemporary approaches. In J. Dovidio & S. Gaertner (Eds.), *Prejudice, discrimination and racism* (pp. 1–34). Orlando: Academic Press.

Entman, R. (1990). Modern racism and the images of blacks in local television news. *Critical Studies in Mass Communication*, 7, 332–345.

Entman, R. (1992). Blacks in the news: Television, modern racism and cultural change. *Journalism Quarterly*, 69 (2), 341–361.

Entman, R. (1994). Representation and reality in the portrayal of blacks on network television news, *Journalism Quarterly*, 71 (3), 509–520.

Ettema, J. (1990). Press rites and race relations: A study of mass mediated ritual. *Critical Studies in Mass Communication*, 7 (4), 309–331.

Farrar, R. (1996). *Mass communication: An introduction to the field*. Madison: Brown & Benchmark.

Featherstone, J. (1978). Duplication and newspaper content in contrasting ownership situations, *Journalism Quarterly*, 55, 549–554.

Gaziano, C. (1989). Chain newspaper homogeneity and presidential endorsements, 1972–1988. *Journalism Quarterly*, 66 (4), 8.

Glasser, T., Allen, D., & Blanks, S. E. (1989). The influence of chain ownership on news play: A case study. *Journalism Quarterly*, 66 (3), 607–614.

Hacker, A. (1992). *Two nations: Black and white, separate, hostile, and unequal*. New York: Scribner.

Hackett, R. A. (1985). A hierarchy of access: Aspects of source bias in Canadian TV news. *Journalism Quarterly*, 62 (2), 256–265, 277.

Hall, S. (1995). The whites of their eyes: Racist ideologies and the media. In G. Dines & J. M. Humez (Eds.), *Gender, Race and Class in Media* (pp. 18–22). Thousand Oaks, CA: Sage.

Hansen, K. A. (1991). Source diversity and newspaper enterprise journalism. *Journalism Quarterly*, 68 (3), 474–482.

Hynds, E. & Martin, C. (1979). How non-daily editors describe status and function of editorial pages. *Journalism Quarterly*, 56 (2), 318–323.

Jhally, S. & Lewis, J. (1992). *Enlightened racism: The Cosby Show, audiences, and the myth of the American dream*. Boulder, CO: Westview Press.

Johnson, K. A. (1987). Black and white in Boston, *Columbia Journalism Review*, May/June, pp. 50–52.

Jones, J. M. (1986). Racism: A cultural analysis of the problem. In J. F. Dovidio & S. L. Gaertner (Eds.), *Prejudice, discrimination and racism*. pp. 279–314. Orlando: Academic Press.

Lasorsa, D. & Reese, S. (1990). News source use in the crash of 1987: A study of four national media. *Journalism Quarterly*, 67 (1), 60–71.

Linville, P. W. & Fischer, G. W. (1986). Stereotyping and perceived distribution of social characteristics: an application to ingroup-outgroup perception. In J. F. Dovidio and S. L. Gaertner (Eds.), *Prejudice, discrimination and racism* (pp. 165–208). Orlando: Academic Press.

Martindale, C. (1986). *The white press and black America*. Westport, CT: Greenwood Press.

McConahay, J. B. (1986). Modern racism, ambivalence, and the modern racism scale. In J. F. Dovidio & S. L. Gaertner (Eds.), *Prejudice, discrimination, and racism* (pp. 91–125). Orlando: Academic Press.

Olien, C., Donohue, G., & Tichenor, P. (1995). Conflict, consensus, and public opinion. In T. Glasser & H. Sypher (Eds.), *Public opinion and the communication of consent* (pp. 348–369). New York: The Guilford Press.

Rhodes, J. (1993). The visibility of race and media history. *Critical Studies in Mass Communication,* 10 (2), 184–190.

Sears, D. O. (1988). Symbolic racism. In P. A. Katz & D. A. Taylor (Eds.), *Eliminating racism* (pp. 53–84). New York: Plenum.

Shah, H. & Thornton, M. C. (1994). Racial ideology in U.S. mainstream news magazines coverage of black-Latino interaction, 1980–1992. *Critical Studies in Mass Communication*, 11, 141–161.

Shirley, C. B. (1992). L.A. stories: Where have you been? *Columbia Journalism Review*, July/August, 25–26.

Sigal, L. V. (1973). *Reporters and officials: The organization and politics of newsmaking*. Lexington, MA: D. C. Heath.

Sigal, L. V. (1986). Sources make the news. In R. Manoff & M. Schudson (Eds.), *Reading the News* (pp. 9–37). New York: Pantheon Books.

Stein, M. L. (1994). Racial stereotyping and the media. *Editor & Publisher*, (August 6), 12–13.

Thomas, S. (1986). Mass media and the social order. In G. Gumpert & R. Cathcart (Eds.), *Inter/media*. 3rd ed. (pp. 611–627). New York: Oxford University Press.

Wagenberg, R. & Soderlund, W. (1975). The influence of chain ownership on editorial comment in Canada, *Journalism Quarterly*, 52, 93–98.

Weaver, D. & Elliott, S. N. (1985). Who sets the agenda for the media? A study of local agenda-building. *Journalism Quarterly*, 62 (1), 87–94.

Chapter 6

Photo Coverage of Hispanics and Blacks in a Southwestern Daily Newspaper

Sharon Bramlett-Solomon and Priscilla Hernandez

INTRODUCTION

It's said a picture is worth a thousand words. If so, pictures in a newspaper could powerfully influence what people believe about others, especially people they don't know and people of different races. Consider the following cutlines from photos in the local newspaper examined:

Dr. Francis Collins and J. Craig Venter [white males] can't hide their delight with the results of their respective genome research; Convicted rapist Harold Ray [black male] will temporarily remain in the state mental hospital; Janae Bufford [black female], third grader, reads to President Bush [white male] at her school Tuesday in St. Louis; Angela Grant [black female] points to where a water-damaged kitchen cabinet fell off the wall of her apartment, scattering food; Maria Lopez [Hispanic female] is overcome with grief over a lien placed on her finances. At left is her lawyer, Pamela Dion [white female].

Several media studies have focused on the racial content of photos, largely in content analyses of whites and blacks in newspapers or news magazines (Lambert, 1964; Sentman, 1983; Woodburn, 1947; Blackwood, 1983; Lester & Smith, 1990). Researchers have concluded that readers often obtain their first impressions about a story by looking first at the photo on the page (Lester, 1994; Miller, 1975; Woodburn, 1947; Blackwood, 1983; Stempel, 1971). This study examines newspaper photo portrayal of Hispanics and blacks. While several media researchers have conducted systematic examinations of newspaper coverage of blacks and newspaper coverage of Hispanics, studies that have examined news photo coverage comparatively of Hispanics and blacks were not found.

Studies of media coverage and portrayals of people of color are important. The U.S. 2000 census counted 32.8 million Hispanics and 33.5 million blacks. The nation's Hispanic population is rising faster than any other ethnic group and is expected to outnumber blacks by 2004 (U.S. Census Bureau, 2000). Study of localized media diversity is important in states with the demographics of Arizona, where people of color represent 36% of the population (U.S. Census Bureau, 2000; Kamman, 2001a, b). U.S. census population growth figures revealed that Hispanics in Arizona increased 88% in the last decade, one of the largest Hispanic population increases shown across the nation (U.S. Census Bureau, 2000; Kamman, 2001a, b).

Press coverage of Americans of color has grown significantly since the pre-civil rights era when the press rarely focused on people of color unless involved in crimes, and since the 1968 Kerner Commission report criticized the U.S. media for stereotypical and unbalanced news coverage of blacks (Kerner Commission, 1968). However, U.S. press treatment of Americans of color today still draws criticism, most notably with the charge that news media coverage of them tends to be too little, too late, or too stereotyped (Martindale, 1985, 1990; Entman & Rojecki, 2000; Wilson & Gutierrez, 1995). Hispanics and blacks criticize about both news coverage and news portrayals. In particular, Hispanics say that newspapers do not report enough news about them and charge that the news reported is largely negative (VanSlyke Turk, Richstad, Bryson, & Johnson, 1989; Tan, 1978; Greenberg, Burgoon, Burgoon, & Korzenny, 1983).

Studies on news photo coverage of Americans of color in magazines and newspapers largely have focused on black Americans, and tend to show they appear in very low percentages (Shuey, King, & Griffith, 1953; Lambert, 1964; Cox, 1969; Stempel, 1971; Sentman, 1983; Lester & Smith, 1990; Lester, 1994). However, the research reflects increased portrayals of black people over time during the past four decades along with continued stereotypical depictions. In one of the earliest studies of race in magazine pictures, Shuey, King, and Griffith (1953) found that between 1945 and 1950, black Americans rarely were shown in popular white magazines, and when they were portrayed, more likely appeared in editorial content rather than in advertisements. A replication of this study by Cox (1969) also found very scarce images of black people. Lambert's study (1964) of *Look* magazine confirmed earlier studies of minuscule appearances of black people, but found fewer racial references over time.

Greenberg et al. (1983) examined Mexican Americans in news stories and news photos in six Southwestern daily newspapers and found photo coverage more extensive than suggested by prior research. In three of the dailies, Hispanic portrayal in news photos was in proportion to the local Hispanic population, while underrepresentative of the Hispanic population in the other three dailies. Sentman (1983), who looked at *Life Magazine* coverage of blacks from 1932 to 1972, found minuscule portrayal and noted that stereotypes prevailed. Lester and Smith (1990) also examined photo coverage in *Life Magazine* from 1938 to 1988, along with two newsmagazines—*Time* and *Newsweek*. They found increased numbers of photos of blacks over three time periods, with a dramatic rise in everyday life photos over racial stereotypes such as crime, sports, and entertainment. Lester (1994) studied black photo coverage in four daily newspapers from 1937 to 1990 and found increased photo coverage over the three periods, but also found racial stereotypes commonly depicted in the story categories of crime, sports, and entertainment.

Continued research on the visibility, invisibility, and depictions in the press of Americans of color is essential in a society where American Indians, Asians, blacks and Hispanics were largely ignored by the nation's press for almost its first 200 years, and where they still sometimes are unfairly and inaccurately portrayed. The impact of media projection of racial images and issues is apparent in the extensive literature that has developed on press-framing and agenda-setting theories, two theoretical perspectives that, when simplified, focus on the power of the media to prescribe to us what to think or what to think about. Both theories support the idea that media messages influence our views, perceptions, and opinions (McCombs & Shaw, 1972; Tuchman, 1978; Gitlin, 1980). Thus, if we can assume press-framing and agenda-setting power and can assume that newspapers reflect the views and values of the social setting in which they are produced, then by examining news coverage of people of color we can obtain a picture of these values (McCombs & Shaw, 1972; Tuchman, 1978; Gitlin, 1980).

This study examines news photo portrayal of Hispanics and blacks over a three-month period in Arizona's largest newspaper, the *Arizona Republic*. The major questions addressed are: To what extent do Hispanics and blacks appear in news photos in the *Arizona Republic*? How favorable are the portrayals of Hispanics and blacks in news photos in the *Arizona Republic*?

METHOD

This content analysis examines news photo depictions of Hispanics and blacks compared to whites in Arizona's largest daily newspaper, the *Arizona Republic*, which has a weekday circulation of 482,003 and Sunday circulation of 698,886 (National Research Bureau, Inc., 2001). Six weeks of newspaper issues (Monday through Sunday) of the *Arizona Republic* during January, February, and March of 2001 (two weeks in each month) were collected and analyzed. In the 35 issues analyzed, all news photos in the newspaper were examined and coded for people, ethnicity, gender, and favorability of the depictions.

A coding instrument was designed to answer the study questions. Favorable depictions were defined as portrayals that cast subjects in a positive light, such as those showing people successful in life, politically active, gainfully employed, pursuing education, or enjoying lifestyle rewards. Unfavorable depictions were defined as portrayals that cast subjects in a negative light, such as those showing people associated with crime, violence, or other social problems, or that showed them needy or depending on social programs. Photos in this study consisted of those featuring faces of people where race was clearly identifiable. Whites and blacks were identified by skin color or race references, and Hispanics were identified by either surnames or race references. Foreign news photos were eliminated, as well as sports-related photos where helmets or body contact impeded identification.

Intercoder reliability was calculated on 10% of the data using Holsti's formula, which divides coder agreement by the number of items coded. Average coder agreement for all categories was .89 (Holsti, 1969).

FINDINGS

To What Extent Do Hispanics and Blacks Appear in News Photos in the *Arizona Republic*?

Examination of the *Arizona Republic* over the three-month study period resulted in analysis of 2,527 photos depicting 3,297 people of Hispanic, black, and white ethnicity. As shown in Table 6.1, Hispanics and blacks combined constituted 23% (749) of the people in photos. Analysis of people by race in photographs revealed Hispanics were 7% (227), blacks were 16% (522), and whites were 77% (2,548).

These findings are slightly different from studies before the 1980s in which people of color were not often seen in news photos, other than in crime, sports and entertainment depictions. The findings reflect that photos of Hispanics and blacks are very slowly making their way into the newspaper pages examined, though for Hispanics not at a rate to match their population proportions in either Arizona or nationwide. While blacks make up 3% of Arizona's population, their photo portrayal was at 16%. On the other hand, Hispanics make up 25% of Arizona's population, but their photo portrayal was 7%, less than half of the percentage of black photos (Kamman, 2001b).

As shown in Table 6.1, when examined by month, the most people of color appeared during January (27% or 279) followed by March (23% or 249). Somewhat surprising was that February reflected the lowest number of people of color in photos (19% or 221), given that February is Black History Month, a month in which many newspapers often show increased news diversity and visibility of blacks and other Americans of color.

Analysis of Race by Gender

As shown in Table 6.2, it was revealed over the three months examined that males dominated the photos (70% or 2,305) compared to females (30% or 992), and dominated photos across all ethnic groups. Table 6.2 also shows that Hispanic males constituted 4% or 117; Hispanic females 3% or 110; black males 13% or 412; black females 3% or 110; white males 54% or 1,776; and white females 23% or 772.

Data findings of overwhelming male dominance in the current study are consistent with the findings of Miller (1975) and Blackwood (1983). These studies showed men outnumbered women in news photos by at least three to one. No earlier study was found for comparison with the current study that analyzed gender by

Table 6.1
Newspaper Photos by Race: A Three-Month Frequency and Percentage Comparison (N = 3,297)

	January		February		March		Totals	
Whites	736	73%	961	81%	851	77%	2548	77%
Hispanics	116	11%	59	5%	52	5%	227	7%
Blacks	163	16%	162	14%	197	18%	522	16%

race in news photos, thus the baseline findings of this study are important for future research.

How Favorable Are the Portrayals of Hispanics and Blacks in News Photos in the *Arizona Republic*?

Table 6.3 reveals that over the three-month period favorable portrayals in the news photos appeared much less frequently than unfavorable portrayals across all ethnic groups and throughout the study period. Of the 3,297 people featured, 39% or 1,270 were portrayed favorably while 61% or 2,027 were portrayed unfavorably.

When favorability was cross-tabulated by race, the data revealed that Hispanics constituted 3% or 111 of the subjects in favorable depictions and 4% or 116 of the subjects in unfavorable depictions. Blacks constituted 2% or 69 of the subjects in favorable depictions and 14% or 453 of the subjects in unfavorable depictions. Whites constituted 33% or 1,090 of the subjects in favorable depictions and 44% or 1,458 of the unfavorable depictions. Thus, analysis revealed that Hispanics, blacks, and whites in the photos examined all tend to appear in more bad news than good news images. These findings are hardly surprising, given the status and treatment of "conflict" as a news value in American journalism and the prevalence of bad news over good news in daily news reporting.

Study findings were consistent with claims by Hispanics and blacks that their images in the press are more likely to be in an unfavorable light. However, as reflected in Table 6.3, blacks appeared in the most disparaging images with a 12% difference between favorable (2%) and unfavorable depictions (14%).

Also, coverage was not more favorable for blacks or Hispanics during the Black History Month of February, as some would expect, compared to the month preceding and following it. Monthly findings for favorable and unfavorable depictions reflected comparable ratios.

DISCUSSION

Findings in the current study dealt with localized news coverage in a single newspaper and cannot be claimed to be representative of all Southwestern dailies or dailies in states with large Hispanic or black populations. However, the findings

Table 6.2
Newspaper Photos by Race and Gender: A Three-Month Frequency and Percentage Comparison (N = 3,297)

	January				February				March				Totals			
	Male		Female		Male		Female		Male		Female		Male		Female	
Whites	519	51%	217	21%	654	55%	307	26%	603	55%	248	22%	1776	54%	772	23%
Hispanics	57	7%	59	6%	30	3%	29	2%	30	3%	22	2%	117	4%	110	3%
Blacks	134	13%	29	3%	111	9%	51	4%	167	15%	30	3%	412	12%	110	3%

Table 6.3
Favorable and Unfavorable Newspaper Photos by Race: A Three-Month Frequency and Percentage Comparison (N = 3,297)

	January				February				March				Totals			
	Favorable		Unfavor.		Favorable		Unfavor.		Favorable		Unfavor.		Favorable		Unfavor.	
Whites	334	33%	402	40%	419	35%	542	46%	337	30%	514	47%	1090	33%	1458	44%
Hispanics	52	5%	64	6%	29	2%	30	3%	30	3%	22	2%	111	3%	116	4%
Blacks	19	2%	144	14%	31	3%	131	11%	19	2%	178	16%	69	2%	453	14%

in this case study do reveal patterns and trends that are valuable in what they reveal about Hispanic and black photo depictions. Also, since only one study was found on Hispanic visibility in news photos, and since no study was found that compares Hispanic and black news photo portrayal, the findings represent baseline data that would be useful for future examinations in this research area.

Overall, the data showed increased portrayals of people of color compared to research of earlier decades. However, given their growing numbers, the presence of Hispanics in the news media should be greater than their representation found in this study. Hispanic visibility in the photos examined was far below Hispanic local population proportions. The findings suggest that if readers simply go by what they see about Hispanics in the newspaper photos examined, they will not know much about Hispanics and what images they find will be more unfavorable than favorable. On the other hand, the representation of blacks in the newspaper photos examined was much more robust, with twice the number of images found for Hispanics. However, the black images were overwhelmingly negative. Furthermore the findings revealed that news images of both Hispanics and blacks largely presented them as unfavorable stereotypes, as people causing problems or beset by problems.

In summary, overall study findings suggest that while Hispanics and blacks are seen on more news pages than ever before, the content of that coverage needs continued examination. Present study findings show that unfavorable portrayals dominate for both Hispanics and blacks. The findings are consistent with earlier studies that have found greater portrayal of Hispanics and blacks in unfavorable news, such as crime, and greater portrayal of them in sports and entertainment news over other story types, such as politics and business news (Lester, 1994; Sentman, 1983). Socially responsible newspapers are those that reflect the interests and populations of the community in which the newspapers reside. An overwhelming majority of unfavorable photo images of people of color could persist in fueling negative stereotypes of them. Portrayals found in this study may reflect a reliance on stereotypical coverage as opposed to steady progress in eliminating stereotypes.

The findings implicate a need for increased favorable photo portrayals of Hispanics and blacks. Improved photo coverage can be achieved if newsrooms are willing to emphasize news photo diversity. And how is this done? The answer is not simple, but workable strategies exist. As several news observers and scholars have suggested, newspapers can more adequately depict the lives of Hispanics, blacks and other Americans of color by choosing them for everyday life feature pictures and by selecting them as illustrations for trend stories (Byrd, 1997; Lester, 1994).

REFERENCES

Blackwood, R. (1983, Winter). The content of news photos: Roles portrayed by men and women. *Journalism Quarterly,* 60: 711–715.

Byrd, J. (1997). Blacks, whites in news pictures. In S. Biagi & M. Kern-Foxworth (Eds.), *Facing difference: Race, gender and mass media* (pp. 95–97). Thousand Oaks, CA: Pine Forge Press.

Cox, K. K. (1969). Changes in stereotyping of negroes and whites in magazine advertisements. *Public Opinion Quarterly,* 33, 603–606.

Entman, R. M. & Rojecki, A. (2000). *The black image in the white mind: Media and race in America.* Chicago: University of Chicago Press.

Gitlin, T. (1980). *The whole world is watching.* Berkeley: University of California Press.

Greenberg, B., Burgoon, M., Burgoon, J. & Korzenny, F. (1983). *Mexican Americans and the mass media.* Norwood, NJ: Ablex.

Greenberg, B., Heeter, C., Burgoon, J., Burgoon, M. & Korzenny, F. (1983, Winter). Local newspaper coverage of Mexican Americans. *Journalism Quarterly,* 60, 671–676.

Holsti, O. B. (1969). *Content analysis for the social sciences and humanities.* Reading, MA: Addison-Wesley.

Kamman, J. (2001a, March 6). Hispanics soon may be largest U.S. minority group. *Arizona Republic,* p. A11.

Kamman, J. (2001b, March 28). Population of Arizona rose 40% in the '90s. *Arizona Republic,* p. A1.

Kerner Commission. (1968). *Report of the National Advisory Commission on Civil Disorders.* New York: New Bantam.

Lambert, V. (1964, Autumn). Negro exposure in *Look*'s editorial content. *Journalism Quarterly,* 42, 657–659.

Lester, P. M. (1994, Summer). African-American photo coverage in four U.S. newspapers, 1937–1990. *Journalism and Mass Communication Quarterly,* 72, 380–394.

Lester, P., & Smith, R. (1990, Spring). African American photo coverage in *Life, Newsweek* and *Time,* 1937–1988. *Journalism Quarterly,* 67, 136–140.

Martindale, C. (1985, Summer). Coverage of black Americans in five newspapers since 1950. *Journalism Quarterly,* 62, 321–328.

Martindale, C. (1990, Summer). Coverage of Black Americans in four major newspapers, 1950–1989. *Newspaper Research Journal,* 11, 96–112.

McCombs, M. E. & Shaw, D. L. (1972). The agenda-setting function of the mass media. *Public Opinion Quarterly,* 36, 176–187.

Miller, S. (1975, Spring). The content of news photos: Women's and men's roles. *Journalism Quarterly,* 52, 72.

National Research Bureau, Inc. (2001). *Working press of the nation* (Vol. 1, 51st ed.). Newspaper Directory. New Providence, NJ: R. R. Bowker.

Sentman, A. (1983, Autumn). Black and white: Disparity in coverage by *Life Magazine* from 1937 to 1972. *Journalism Quarterly,* 60: 501–508.

Shuey, A. M., King, N. & Griffith, B. (1953). Stereotyping of Negroes and Whites: An analysis of magazine pictures. *Public Opinion Quarterly,* 17: 281–287.

Stempel, G. (1971, Summer). Visibility of blacks in news and news-picture magazines. *Journalism Quarterly,* 48, 338–339.

Tan, A. (1978, Autumn). Evaluation of newspapers and television by blacks and Mexican Americans. *Journalism Quarterly,* 55, 673–681.

Tuchman, G. (1978). *Making news: A study in the construction of reality.* New York: The Free Press.

U.S. Census Bureau. (2000). Year 2000 census. (Online). Available at www.Census.Gov/dmd/www/2khome.htm.

VanSlyke Turk, J., Richstad, J., Bryson, R. & Johnson, S. (1989, Spring). Hispanic Americans in the news in two Southwestern cities. *Journalism Quarterly,* 66, 107–113.

Wilson, C., & Gutierrez, F. (1995). *Race, multiculturalism and the media: From mass to class communication.* 2nd ed. Beverly Hills, CA: Sage Publications.

Woodburn, B. (1947, Autumn). Reader interest in newspaper pictures. *Journalism Quarterly,* 24, 197–201.

Chapter 7

Black, Brown, and Poor: Who You Don't See on Local TV News and Why

Don Heider

INTRODUCTION

When it comes to news, there is one topic where you can see coverage that includes representations of brown and black people. That is in coverage of poverty. Martin Gilens (1999) reports in his review of major newsmagazines and network television newscasts that African Americans have been consistently overrepresented in this coverage since the 1970s. Wilson and Gutierrez have pointed out that in news media there persists "old stereotypes of non-Whites as violent people who are too lazy to work and who indulge in drugs and sexual promiscuity are prominent" (1995). Why is it media only overrepresent brown and black people when it comes to negative news? Why is it we don't see people of color more often in other kinds of news stories? This chapter explores why TV news in one city avoided stories that might deal more directly with issues concerning black people, brown people and poor people. This brings us to questions of class.

It is difficult to think about race and media for long without also considering the question of class. Despite some scholars and politicians' effort to conflate these two concepts, race and class are in no way interchangeable ideas. Each present a separate set of issues in regard to news media.

Like race, class is a concept that we don't discuss all that much in our culture, yet many people assume they have an innate knowledge of what it is. When we meet people, when we see people on the street, drive through neighborhoods, or watch a television program, there are many different ways that we are gathering information and making decisions about social class. In the same way, when we meet people we also make determinations about an individual's racial-ethnic background. Wherein with race we are looking for markers such as skin color, hair texture, the shape and size of certain facial features, and so on, when it comes to class another set of markers comes into play. We are examining clothes, jewelry, accent, speech patterns, and so on. When we drive through neighborhoods we are looking for evidence of wealth, or lack thereof, such as the size of homes, landscaping, and type of automobile. Race may also inform our judgment about one's class status, but rarely is this the lone determinant.

There is another defining difference between race and class. Race and class are both social constructs. That is to say that they are concepts created to distinguish between groups. However, with race, there is no biological or anthropological evidence that supports the idea of distinct racial groups within the larger group of humans (*Harvard Encyclopedia of American Ethnic Groups*, 1980). Despite this, we still live our daily lives as if race is a very real and concrete thing and we make many judgments based upon the idea of race. With regard to class, however, there are fairly concrete measures by which we can distinguish between class groups, such as a family's annual income. Mary and Robert Jackman have put it this way: "Any social system that involves economic inequality will generate social classes" (1983). Not only is there economic inequality in the United States, there is some evidence that it is increasing. Between 1970 and 1990, the average income for families in the bottom fifth of the income scale dropped 5%. Meanwhile income among the top fifth shot up 33% (Stevenson, 2000).

Even though many Americans think of themselves as middle class (doesn't almost everyone?) and we like to think of our society as egalitarian—a society where all people have similar opportunities—many people have a learned sense growing up in the United States that there really are class differences most often decided by material goods. Depending on what city you live in, there are also family names and even accents that may distinguish one group from the next. But overall, we live in a society where money is the largest distinguishing factor between social classes.

Karl Marx argued forcefully that land ownership was crucial in determining class, and in the era he was writing that may have been accurate; but in this era, land ownership may not be as crucial as acquisition of capital.

And what may be just as important in our culture as having money is the appearance of having money. The dominant message on television is a message of consumerism, that is—buy this product and you'll look, feel, or be better.

Given that media plays a role in how we construct ideas about both race and class and because we depend on news programs as a source of reliable information, local news seemed an appropriate place to begin examining some of these questions. I spent 10 years as a photographer, reporter, and producer in local television news and a local newsroom seemed a good place to reenter to begin trying to determine how journalists think about class and race and what message news programs deliver in regard to these ideas.

I went to a top-20 television market in Denver, Colorado, and spent a month in a local newsroom. I sat in on news meetings, went out with reporters on stories, spent each day in the newsroom listening, observing, and talking with news workers. In short, I entered the field as an ethnographer, trying to chart a local culture.

Though unlike many researchers who enter the field, this was a culture I already had much knowledge of, because of my years of experience. This provided me with some insider's status. I could talk the talk, which was helpful for gaining access and information. But since I hadn't worked in news for almost 10 years, I was also able to look at the newsroom and how things occurred with a fresh perspective I had gained from being away for a long period.

I also taped the station's two primary news shows each weekday at 5:00 and 10:00 P.M. and did a content analysis of those newscasts, as a way of checking the observations I made as a newsroom observer. What follows is a detailed discussion of what I found.

NEWS DECISIONS

To understand how local news conceptualizes class and race, we must first think about the way in which news is constructed. Each day local television stations (and other media outlets) are inundated with possible story ideas, especially in the larger markets. Newsrooms receive e-mails, faxes, mail, and phone calls, all with story ideas, details about news conferences and information about events and activities people in the community would like to see covered. Assignment editors or planning editors sift through all this material, plus story ideas turned in by news workers. Also into this mix are events are on local court dockets and upcoming public meetings. These editors put together some type of organized lineup of story ideas, which are generally discussed at a morning editorial meeting. Depending on the newsroom, different people attend this meeting. Most often it is attended by managers (news director, assistant news director, executive producer), assignment editors, and producers. Also often included are reporters, photographers, engineers, and video editors. How do these people decide what the news of the day will be? These professionals use their judgment to decide. This collective judgment is, at times, referred to as a news philosophy. Or, in other words, this is the set of principles that guides these decisions.

As for the station in this study, one reporter described the news philosophy this way: "I don't know if there's so much a news philosophy as there is an effort toward a common goal. And that goal is to get the highest ratings possible to make the most money for the station." Ratings are important to people in newsrooms, especially to news managers. If a station continues to perform poorly in the ratings, these mangers may lose their jobs. But it's rare to hear someone say in a news meeting: "Let's do that story because it will boost our ratings." That's because, other than the drive for ratings, there is another force that is supposed to be at work in the newsroom: the idea that newsrooms in general and journalists in particular are supposed to produce good journalism. Journalism loosely defined is the practice of gathering and disseminating information to serve the public. This is where the tension resides in many news organizations, the rub between what is journalistically sound and what will get viewers to watch.

In day-to-day decision-making, however, neither getting ratings nor producing excellent journalism may be first in the minds of those making news decisions. It is

in most cases more personal. When asked to describe her news philosophy, a producer said: "Well a lot of times it's just what I find interesting. I think I'm a pretty
normal, average person and what concerns me concerns other people."

Despite claims that journalism is objective, it's actually more accurate to say
that ultimately journalism is always subjective. When people talk about objectivity
in journalism, they are usually really referring to the idea that journalism should be
fair, balanced, or even-handed. But journalism is not based upon any kind of scientific method; thus to claim it is objective is without foundation (and for some even
scientific method may not indicate objectivity). Each day a journalist makes doz-
ens of decisions: what story to cover, which people to interview, what questions to
ask, what pictures to shoot, what information to include, and how to edit a piece.

All of these decisions are filtered through each journalist's personal point of
view—through their experience, values, training, education, upbringing—and
through their class orientation and racial-ethnic perception. All of these reflect a
journalist's subjective stance.

NEWS AS CHOICES

Each newsperson each day makes a series of choices that influence what news
viewers see on the evening news. By examining those choices for a month and by
questioning news workers about those choices, certain things became clear. First,
it was clear that this station during this coverage period was largely uninterested in
stories involving either people of color or the poor. Understand first that, although
there is some overlap between these groups, they are distinctly different categc-
ries. When it comes to blacks and Latinos in Denver or almost any other U.S. community, these are remarkably diverse communities. Census data tell us that
African Americans and Latinos can be found in many different class strata. But despite class, this station did not cover issues that were of primary importance to either the black or Latino communities. As well, aside from race, news workers also
did not cover stories of primary importance to poor people.

Consider one particular example. The Environmental Protection Agency (EPA)
sent word via news release that the organization was holding a public meeting to
announce the results of extensive soil testing in a Denver neighborhood. That testing had taken place in Swansea, a neighborhood that was commonly known to be a
poor area, occupied primarily by people of color. There was reason to believe soil
in this area might be contaminated by some of the heavy industry that had historically occupied the neighborhood. There was also a significant historical backdrop
to the story: another Denver neighborhood—Globeville—had been tested and
high levels of contamination had been found. Neighbors in Globeville sued and a
local smelting and refining company eventually paid out $38 million for cleanup.
When the EPA event was discussed at the editorial meeting it became obvious
some of the producers had never heard of Swansea. The executive producer asked:
"Does anyone even speak English down there?" A few people around the table
snickered. The story died after that comment.

In others words, there was no more discussion and it was clear from this manager's question that this story did not fit into his idea of what would be appropriate news for the day. As a result, it went unreported by this station that 3,550 soil samples indicated some properties in the area had levels of arsenic and lead that were so high as to prompt the EPA to promise an extensive cleanup. About 75 neighbors attended the meeting, so there would have been plenty of opportunity to personalize the story and to capture the emotions of neighbors as they discovered the ecological impact of the test results.

Needless to say, no one in that news meeting lived in Swansea. One can only wonder what the reaction would have been had the soil testing taken place in an area where news workers lived. Journalists who decide what is and is not news primarily on what impacts them personally, have a limited view of what might comprise a news story.

On two counts this story failed. It occurred in a poor neighborhood where no news staffers lived, so on a class basis there was no interest. But it also failed because of the racial makeup of the neighborhood. The comment about language was the manager's way of letting people around the table know the story was taking place in a Hispanic neighborhood and therefore not of interest to the station's dominant, white audience. At times, stories are rejected on a class basis. At other times stories are rejected because of race. In this case, both worked to undermine what was a story with arguably substantial news value.

NEWS WHERE YOU LIVE

I gathered the home addresses of all the news workers at the station and compared them to census data for the Denver metro area. Of just under one 100 full-time newsroom employees, only three lived in areas that were predominantly African American or Hispanic and only three lived in areas where at least 40% of the population reported a household income of less than $24,999. Only one of those people lived in an area that was both predominantly people of color and had 40% of the population with an income under $24,999. None of the few living in these areas was a news manager, producer, assignment editor—or in other words in a position that are responsible for most news content decisions.

When asked about coverage of poor people, one producer put it this way: "I think we cover middle class, white issues because I think basically we are not very diverse." Newsrooms are filled with people who are college-educated and middle class. News managers, according to the Radio and Television News Director's Association are largely white, a trend that has remained disturbingly consistent in recent years (Papper, Gerhard & Sharma, 1996). Therefore it should not be terribly surprising that these people make decisions to cover issues that interest them before they choose to cover issues that would affect people not like themselves. One African American news writer said:

It strikes me as we just don't know. Or some of us do know and we just don't say anything or some of us do know and we aren't at the morning meetings to say anything which is a mistake. Somehow we've got to get that knowledge or get our hands on that knowledge if we don't know it and that knowledge comes in various ways. It comes through various contacts whether environmentally or politically or whatever and you can never have enough people who have that knowledge.

Even when news workers know better, when they have experience growing up as a minority or in a lower socioeconomic class, their voices are not always heard in the newsroom. When people of color aren't in the news meeting, their voices cannot be heard. When poor people aren't in news meetings, their voices also cannot be heard. But even when they are in news meetings, their opinions may not always be heard and considered. One producer explained what happens when she pushes for a story idea that a manager doesn't like:

A lot of times you blatantly are told that your ideas are stupid and you're just kind of told what to do versus your opinion. And if a certain manager says this is the way it's going to be and it could be the most ridiculous idea in the whole world, it's still going to get on the air because so-and-so said it. I don't agree with that, I think it should be more like let's all talk about ideas from anyone, it doesn't matter who.

A newsroom with little diversity—racial-ethnic or class diversity—and with no intellectual diversity—when people are not open to ideas that differ from their own norms—leads to an atmosphere where coverage is homogenized. This atmosphere seems to contribute to news programs where viewers see similar stories over and over again and those stories represent a very narrow world: a world that is constructed by the beliefs and values of a few managers and decision-makers.

Black and Latino managers themselves may not feel comfortable pushing story ideas about underrepresented communities, because in order to succeed in news management they have been socialized into a newsroom's organizational culture, where these types of stories are not valued.

NEWS AS PROFIT

On one hand I found that this news operation was not covering people of color or people of lower socioeconomic standing because these viewpoints were not consistently represented in news decision-making. But I also found another reason that was less subtle. "No, I don't think the station does a good job covering poor people or working class people," explained one producer. "They don't have a voice because they don't buy anything so nobody cares. I mean cut and dried they don't buy anything so are we really worried about them? Because they are not the people the advertisers are seeking." An assignment editor put it this way: "I think this newsroom is not in the least bit interested in poor people, because they are not our demographic." By demographic this news worker was referring to a particular profile of a viewer.

In interviews with news workers it became clear they had a particular demographic in mind: women between the ages of 25 and 45. Why? The station's managing editor explained:

It's the demo to bring in dollars. One: for sales and two: to raise the ratings. It's the business side of things. We make personnel changes for that reason, we select stories for that reason.

According to the station's research director, women 25 to 45 is the group that many national advertiser's have identified as crucial in making buying decisions for households.

Of course, there is a problem with targeting coverage toward one particular audience. It means the station is also excluding stories that might interest people who do not fit into the demographic profile. In this case that included people of color and people in lower social classes.

Here we get back to that tension that exists in many newsrooms, which is the conflict between trying to make the news organization a profit center and actually gathering and disseminating the news as part of a larger public responsibility. Many journalism codes of ethics recognize the idea of completeness, wherein journalists are, with each story, supposed to include as much information about the story as possible, given time and space restrictions. Completeness also denotes the idea that many different parts of a community, many different voices, will or should be included in day-to-day coverage. Yet, the idea of targeting one certain audience is completely contrary to this principle.

The station's news director defended his station's practice, arguing that this focus on one particular audience didn't affect the basic coverage of the day. He said that this kind of targeting really only affected some of the less crucial news of the day.

Every day there's a series of stories that are elective. You know: do you want to do this, or do you want to do that? And I think from a business standpoint we have gotten people to think about running those stories through a filter—is this story interesting to people who we would like to watch our news more often?

But not everyone in the newsroom agreed with this assessment, including one assignment editor.

I think a lot of sometimes in catering to target audiences you fail to present a fair and accurate portrayal of news. And let me say I don't think it is primarily a crime of culmination. It is a crime of omission. I think a lot of times there is bias and it's not that the stories aired are biased, it's that stories are aired that should not be aired.

Certainly some other news organizations do target news product to an audience. Think, for instance, of magazines and the differences between the different audiences targeted by say, *National Geographic* and *People* or *Family Circle* and *Sports Illustrated*. However television news is a different matter. The airwaves have been considered by Congress and the courts as owned by the public and stations are given permission or licenses to use those airwaves. Thus came a public service obligation. As well, when one watches local news, including the news of this station in Denver, in the show open the announcer never says: "And now the news for women 25 to 45." Yet in this market, at this station, that was the goal.

Table 7.1
Frequencies of Story Topics

Topic	No. of Stories (N = 672)	Percentage
Crime	147	21.9%
Sports	80	11.9%
Weather	75	11.2%
Economics/Business	69	10.3%
Consumer	59	8.8%
Feature	53	7.9%
Politics/Government	51	7.6%
Disaster	39	5.8%
Health	35	5.2%
The Environment	32	4.8%
Human Rights	13	1.9%
The "Needy"	13	1.9%
Education	6	0.9%

This was reflected in the content analysis of the station's newscasts. As you can see in Table 7.1, during the four weeks of the study, two trained graduate student coders counted 672 news stories in total. Of those only 13 stories or just 1.9% dealt with poor people directly.

This supports what was found in observing the newsroom and interviewing news workers—that news concerning people in lower socioeconomic categories was rarely covered. Coverage of crime led all categories, as is typical in many local news markets. But it is also interesting to note where education coverage ranks, considering in polls of blacks and Latinos education is often listed as a top community concern.

NEWS ON OR OFF TARGET?

There also is the question of whether stations can effectively target audiences. Take, for instance, the example of trying to cater newscasts to women between the ages of 25 and 45. To one show producer, this meant finding and running every story she could on Beanie Babies, the small stuffed animals that had become the rage of collectors. But was there any evidence to support that women in the Denver metro area aged 25–45 were terribly interested in Beanie Babies? Women (and men) had been known to line up outside toy stores for new Beanie Baby debuts, or to mob McDonald's restaurants when mini-Beanies were being given away, but this was purely anecdotal evidence. The bottom line was, the producer was using her own experience and judgment to try and guess what women might like to see in a newscast. Although television consultants might offer news workers general advice, based on research, about what kinds of news generally these women might watch, there is no precise way of determining day-to-day which story might appeal to any given audience.

One reporter at the station said she thought this kind of story selection process often resulted in a type of pandering:

A lot of times I think those stories we come up with are insulting to those women they are trying to target. I'm a professional, I have a disposable income, I'm in the age bracket but a lot of the time I'm doing stories I have no interest in.

The problem lies in trying, with any kind of accuracy, to predict what one person or the next might find interesting each day. The result is a type of narrow thinking where news managers are selecting stories based on stereotypes of the women they are trying to attract. The reporter thought this process often resulted in selection of stories on topics that were:

Very cliche malls, diets, pantyhose, face lifts, very stereotypical, right off the pages of a shallow women's magazine versus sort of real daily concerns about juggling motherhood and professional life, or, you know, investments.

This was further complicated when I interviewed the station's research director, who acknowledged that many news people believed they should be targeting an audience segment. The problem was that she herself couldn't predict with great accuracy who was watching their station:

The way TV works is that you really can't say who your audience is. If you're talking about our news, you still can't say who our audience is. You can't pinpoint it in one general statement.

Television traditionally has been the medium that had a broad-based audience appeal. For advertisers television was the place where a wide audience could be reached. With the advent of cable, that audience has been split into segments. Yet commercial television stations with network affiliations, even given diminished ratings, still by far hold the largest audience. Thus there are serious questions as to whether a station can really target any particular audience and effectively sell that audience's attention to advertisers.

DAILY DISCORD OF NEWS

The issue of targeting one particular audience raises a question of central importance for most news organizations and that is; What is our purpose? As I have documented in earlier research (Heider, 2000) some news workers have to deal with conflict in their newsrooms such as knowing that certain topics are out of bounds—doing consumer stories about large automobile dealers who spend a lot of dollars on advertising. What I found at this station (and what I have found earlier at other stations) was a systematic avoidance of stories that would be of central importance to people of color. There was also ample evidence in this case to see that this station was not interested in covering stories that would be important to people in lower social classes, such as blue collar workers or the poor.

All of this begs the question; Can journalists continue to do basic journalism in this atmosphere? Or will continued commercial interests and profit-making pressure force news workers into so segmenting their practice as to make the news

meaningless to large segments of the audience? Also, how will journalists, trained
with the idea that they are to uphold certain ethical principles, be able to continue
working under conditions that force to them to make daily compromises?

In regard to these issues journalists in this station fell into several different categories. First there was a group that was oblivious to any moral or ethical conflict.
They were either unaware or had rationalized away any dilemma or dilemmas they
encountered in daily news work. They may not know or believe in the idea of trying to be inclusive and complete in news coverage and are not particularly concerned with serving the public (except their own narrow view of the
public—people like themselves) with accurate and complete information.

There was another group of journalists who were aware of the conflict, the defi-
cits, and at times unpleasant realities of news work. But they were able to somehow compartmentalize those conflicts safely away from what they do day-to-day.
Managers in TV newsrooms come and go quite frequently and therefore so do
news philosophies. Perhaps for self-preservation, these people lay low on controversial subjects, they do not look for ethical fights in the newsroom. Each day they
execute their duties as best they can. As long as they are not confronted with a dilemma directly, they continue completing assignments and punching the time
clock.

Of course, by their silence they are complicit in continuing the problems,
whether they acknowledge this role or not.

Finally, there was a group of journalists who were aware of the problems and
worked for change. This small group suggested story ideas outside the norms,
questioned traditional values, and pushed for innovation. These journalists try to
successfully negotiate a space in the newsroom culture where they won't be casti-
gated, stigmatized, or fired; at the same time they try to fight for what they feel are
unwavering principles. Even though this group may push for change, it would take
much more than their effort to constitute widespread change in news coverage. For
that kind of change to take place, management and workers would have to agree to
work together on a wholesale reorientation of how daily news was conceived and
how coverage was executed. All this would have to be done with the blessing and
cooperation of station ownership. This scenario, though, seems unlikely.

BROWN AND BLACK NEWS AUDIENCES

We've heard so many times that the number of people of color is growing in the
United States, that it has almost become cliche. In Denver, it's not difficult to virtually ignore the minority community, because it is indeed a minority community.
But in earlier work, I discovered the trend to ignore communities of color even in
markets where they make up the majority (Heider, 2000).

In entertainment television African American audiences have been segmented
and relegated to one particular network—first Fox and now WB (the Warner
Brothers network). One wonders whether this will also be the case in nonfiction
programming. In some communities, cable-access television has provided an out-
let for some minority programming. In Hawai'i, for instance, many racial-ethnic

groups have shows on cable, programmed specifically for the needs and concerns of say, the Filipino community or the Samoan community. This model raises its own set of concerns. For instance, do we really want a model of news where we only see stories programmed for one community? And if so, how will we ever learn about what other groups are doing? One can only wonder whether the Internet and the new technological changes coming to television will serve to completely segment us off from one another.

In Denver race and class distinguished segments of the market that were systematically ignored, for reasons discussed earlier. Although this study only looked at one city, this does not bode well for the idea of plurality in local news, even as people of color increase in audience percentage. This may even be a harbinger of things to come, where we experience a form of media apartheid resulting in a minority white population owning media resources and controlling messages that are delivered to an audience made up largely of African Americans, Latinos, and Asian Americans. The battle that may be waged in the future may be over ideas and the control of those ideas and over information the media present each day. Whether those ideas will be diverse and wide-ranging or continue to be narrow, homogenized, and dominated by white, upper- and middle-class journalists will be determined in the near future. There is also the question of what role will be played by both market forces—stockholders and the like—and by the influence of new technology. Broad changes in how news is gathered and presented may offer a window of opportunity for change, or it may merely provide a new-fangled platform for the same old power relationships.

REFERENCES

Gilens, M. (1999). *Why Americans hate welfare: Race, media, and the politics of antipoverty policy*. Chicago: University of Chicago Press.

Harvard Encyclopedia of American Ethnic Groups. (1980). S. Thernstrom (Ed.). Cambridge: Harvard University Press.

Heider, D. (2000). *White news: Why local news programs don't cover people of color*. Mahwah, NJ: Erlbaum.

Jackman, M. & Jackman, R. (1983). *Class awareness in the United States*. Berkeley: University of California Press, p. 8.

Papper, B., Gerhard, M. & Sharma, A. (1996). More women and minorities in broadcast news. *Communicator*, 8, 8–15.

Stevenson, R. W. (2000). The nation: In a time of plenty, the poor are still poor. *New York Times*, January 23 (section 4), 3.

Wilson, C. & Gutierrez, F. (1995). *Race, multiculturalism, and the media*. Thousand Oaks, CA: Sage, p. 158.

Chapter 8

The Band Still Plays On: A Content Analysis of HIV/AIDS, African Americans, and Latinos in New England Newspapers

Angela Walker, Diana I. Rios, and James Kiwanuka-Tondo

INTRODUCTION

When you look at the front pages of your newspaper, or even glance through several sections of your newspaper for news about topics that have relevance to you, chances are that you will not find stories about AIDS/HIV. Chances are, the average newspaper reader across the United States will see little coverage of AIDS/HIV and may even conclude that the worry over AIDS/HIV is not reflected in the newspapers, or even other print or electronic media, because a cure for AIDS/HIV has been found. For millions of mass media readers, viewers, and listeners, the decline or absence of news about AIDS/HIV signals its unimportance (Domeyer, et al., 1989; Lee & Davie, 1997; Snyder, 1991) though there is still no cure for AIDS/HIV and it is an epidemic of international concern. Once thought of as a white gay community problem, it is a continued problem today for all. The information that the general public and specifically African Americans and Latinos do not get from news or entertainment media is the huge magnitude of the AIDS/HIV problem in their communities and information about what they can do to curb it.

This research reviews roughly ten years (1988–99) of AIDS/HIV coverage in seven New England newspapers: the *Boston Herald, Boston Globe, Bangor Daily News, Patriot Ledger, Portland Press Herald, Providence Journal Bulletin*, and the *Worcester Telegram and Gazette*. Through content analysis, we examine how much New England newspapers cover AIDS/HIV and how the newspapers treat this topic. Special attention is given to the quantity and quality of AIDS/HIV coverage as it pertains to African Americans and Latinos.

There are several expectations we have regarding New England's coverage. Given that AIDS/HIV is an ugly health problem for national and international publics to continue to face, and that fresher and more exciting topics have emerged over time such as foreign trade and terrorism (Wayne & Yu-Wei, 1993) as well natural disasters such as earthquakes (Moeller, 1999; Rosenblum, 1981), we expect that New England press coverage of AIDS/HIV will illustrate a build and decline over the period under examination. Given that AIDS/HIV was once relegated as only a white gay disease during the initial years of recognition, we expect that AIDS/HIV will be presented as a problem that is only a people of color disease; that is, a problem relegated to African Americans and Latinos. It will not be presented as a national or international problem for all. Also, we expect that brief descriptive statistical data will typify African American and Latino coverage such that substantive issues like health education campaigns, practical methods to reduce the spread, and community action will not be pronounced.

We begin with a review of literature which indicates that most material written about AIDS/HIV, as it is related to mass media content, rests in health communication campaign research. Finally, we discuss the research that deals squarely with newspaper content analysis and AIDS/HIV.

AIDS/HIV COVERAGE BY THE NEWS MEDIA

Although the first cases of the acquired immunodeficiency syndrome (AIDS) were first heard of in the late 1970s and early 1980s in the United States, the national media were completely silent about the disease. According to Shilts (1987), the first cases of a gay person stricken with AIDS surfaced in 1980, but it was not until 1985 when movie star Rock Hudson was diagnosed with the disease that the national media started covering it. Shilts (1987) suggests at that time AIDS was branded a gay disease and the mass media chose to be silent because they did not like covering stories about homosexuals. Others saw AIDS as a problem for male homosexuals, bisexuals, and intravenous drug users (IVDUs) (Clumeck, 1986).

In the international arena, the news media branded AIDS/HIV as a disease ravaging the African continent, backing up the claims with scaring statistics. It was not until the late 1990s and the new millennium that the national news media, such as the *New York Times*, the American Broadcasting Corporation (ABC), and the Cable News Network (CNN), started covering positive stories about Africa. For example, they covered stories about how Africa, especially countries like Uganda, are successfully fighting back against the plague of AIDS/HIV. On a more positive note, the *Baltimore Sun* covered a study by Kiwanuka-Tondo and Snyder (in press) which analyzed the organizational factors that influenced the Uganda AIDS/HIV campaigns.

CONTENT ANALYSES OF NEWS ON AIDS/HIV

Much research has been conducted on the representations of gay communities by the national media (Myrick, 1998). Studies have discussed the stigmatization of the "other," such as homosexual men, and the demonization of people of color such as Hatians and Africans (see review in Sacks, 1996). There are writings on the role of media in disseminating AIDS/HIV information and the construction of public discourses on AIDS/HIV (Reardon & Richardson, 1991; Nelkin, 1991; Hertog & Fan, 1995; Hannaway & Harden, 1995; Brown, Chapman, & Lupton, 1996; Donovan, 1997). Furthermore, there is growing literature on women, AIDS/HIV and media discourses and portrayals (Sacks, 1996; Roth & Hogan, 1998). However, research still needs to be done on the coverage of AIDS/HIV by the regional local media.

News research on AIDS/HIV tends to focus on a few select newspapers and/or elite national presses. For example, Myrick's (1998) research on two major daily newspapers of the southern United States, the *Daily Oklahoman* and the *Birmingham News*, examined the discourse of the power relationships between the homosexual and heterosexual community at their places of work. Myrick concludes that the two newspapers suggest that marginalization and surveillance strategies are the best response to AIDS/HIV and gay identity. Sacks's (1996) excellent research uses discourse analysis, citing potent examples from the *Washington Post*, the *New York Times, Newsweek, US News and World Report*, and other national and international media outlets. This scholar's work concentrated on the discourse of women and AIDS in the media. Sacks argues that the media constantly focus on the themes of self-control, self-discipline, and personal responsibility and therefore neglect the socioeconomic context of poverty, illness, lack of empowerment, and inequalities within which women find themselves.

Using different approaches from discourse analysis, other researchers study media use, media content, knowledge, and public opinion. Stroman and Seltzer (1989) examined mass media use and knowledge of AIDS; Edgar, Hammond and Freimuth (1990) looked at the role of media and interpersonal communication in behavior change. In particular, Hertog and Fan looked at newspaper and magazine coverage of AIDS from 1987 through 1991 on public beliefs using Fan's ideodynamic model of public opinion change. These researchers used newspapers of national stature such as the *New York Times, Washington Post, Los Angeles Times, Chicago Tribune, Time* magazine, *Newsweek, US News and World Report*, and the United Press International newswire. Support was found for the impact of news content on public opinion. Nelkin (1991) discusses "the sources of public perceptions" (p. 283) and focuses on the number of articles published in the *New York Times* and the *San Francisco Chronicle* from 1982 to 1986. Nelkin also presents a historical context for AIDS news coverage and reasons for noncoverage through her discussion on risk reporting and the *Wall Street Journal, Discover*, and other periodicals.

McCombs and Shaw (1972) suggested that the mass media set an agenda of issues for the public to think and talk about. Since McCombs and Shaw's (1972) seminal proposition, numerous studies have been conducted to find out the role of that the media play on the perceptions of the public on the important issues of the day. Mutz and Soss (1977) argue that the news coverage may have important implications on how the public perceives the salience of an issue to their community.

This has serious implications on the coverage of AIDS/HIV issues. The way the national media have and continue to cover the plague of AIDS/HIV may bias the way the public perceives the problem. The more the national news media cover AIDS/HIV as problem for a certain group of people, the more the public is likely to perceive it as one.

Given this information, as well as our own knowledge and exposure to New England newspapers (see the Method section), we formulated the following hypotheses:

H1: New England press coverage of AIDS/HIV will illustrate a build and decline over the period under examination.

H2: AIDS/HIV will be presented as a problem that is relegated to African Americans and Latinos.

H3: Descriptive statistical data will typify African American and Latino coverage.

METHOD

New England papers used in the content analysis were accessed through an abbreviated version of the Lexis-Nexis database available through the University of Connecticut's main library. The newspapers available through this database and used in the analysis were the *Boston Globe, Worcester Telegram and Gazette, Boston Herald, Portland Press Herald, Bangor Daily News, Patriot Ledger*, and *Providence Journal Bulletin*. The *Hartford Courant*, well-known in the region as the country's oldest continuously running newspaper, was sadly unavailable for research using our methods of research. Similarly, newspapers that were not available for this online method of research could not be part of the study. We conducted a general search (see the Results section) in order to discern the quantity of articles within our target time frame. We then conducted more specific searches. Articles selected for the study were those that included the keywords AIDS (HIV), Latinos (as well as Hispanics, Mexican Americans, Puerto Ricans, and Latin Americans) and African Americans (or blacks). The search was conducted across the years 1988 through fall 1999.

A key step in our analysis consisted of grouping the articles into meaningful units; we refer to this general category as "central themes." Because our research is exploratory in nature, the central themes of interest were generated by first reading through the articles and then determining the subcategories. In our initial readings, we found that six subcategories of "central themes" emerged: (1) reporting the rates and trends of the AIDS/HIV epidemic; (2) human interest stories; (3) reporting of an event centered around AIDS/HIV (4) organizations working to manage the AIDS/HIV crisis; (5) health reports; and (6) articles that addressed how the African Americans and Latinos specifically were dealing with the epidemic in our communities.

In addition to central themes, the articles were then analyzed in order to determine which groups of individuals were referred to in the articles. In other words we wanted to find out if writers referenced our communities as a "people of color" bloc, all affected equally by the disease or as specific social groups facing different realities. Again, the subcategories for this general category of "Who is included?" were generated as part of the initial substantial list and then were finalized by skimming through the articles. The subcategories of social groups consisted of (1) Latinos, (2) Latinas, (3) Latino men, (4) African Americans, (5) African American women, (6) African American men, (7) heterosexuals, (8) gay and bisexual men, (9) gay Latino men, (10) gay African American men, and finally (11) lesbians. Additionally, headlines were analyzed for "Who is included?"

A third category was created in order to determine the manner in which the transmission of AIDS/HIV was described by the press. We refer to this category as "vehicles for transmission." As before, we generated seven subcategories based on an initial reading of the articles which implicate: (1) men sleeping with men, (2) IV drug use, (3) cultural barriers, (4) denial, (5) lack of information, (6) unprotected sex, and last, (7) poverty as contributing to the spread of AIDS/HIV.

After the first round of analyses was conducted, we revisited the category of central themes. We reexamined all the articles that were coded as being in the subcategory "rates" to determine, first, if the newspapers were reporting either a decrease or an increase in the number of AIDS deaths and cases and second, if our communities were described as disproportionately affected by the disease. Also reexamined were the articles that were labeled under the subcategory of "organizations." This was done in order to discover first, whether the organizations written about were Latino or African American and second, if these organizations were serving the specific needs of the Latino and African American communities.

In order to further reveal the manner in which African Americans and Latinos are described by the press the subcategory of "cultural issues," falling under the category of AIDS/HIV transmission was analyzed. These articles were coded as implicating (1) machismo, (2) women's reluctance to confront their partners, (3) religion and the church, (4) sex as taboo, (5) bias against condoms, (6) homophobia, and (7) language barriers, as factors and or reasons for the growth of AIDS/HIV cases and deaths specifically within our communities.

RESULTS

In our general search, we needed to gain information about the quantity of articles printed about AIDS/HIV in general. For this search, we specified that the keyword AIDS appear in the headline and HIV in the headline and/or lead paragraph. The results indicated that overall 3,360 articles about AIDS/HIV appeared in New England papers over the last ten years. The *Boston Globe* (1988–99, n = 1528), accounted for 45% percent of our sample. Sixteen percent of the articles were printed in the *Providence Journal Bulletin* (1993–99, n = 545) and *Bangor Daily News* (1993–99, n = 216) accounted 6% of the articles. The *Boston Herald* (1993–99, n = 282) represented 9% of the articles, while 12% of the articles were written by the *Patriot Ledger* (1994–99, n = 391). The *Portland Press Herald* (1994–99, n = 144) accounted for 4% of our sample. Finallly, 8% of the articles were printed in the *Worcester Telegram and Gazette* (1995–99, n = 254). Only 150 articles, account-

Table 8.1
Percentage and Number of Articles Containing AIDS/HIV and Latinos
and/or African Americans in New England Newspapers (n = 150)

Newspaper	Percentage* and Number of Articles	
Boston Globe	53%	(n = 80)
Providence Journal Bulletin	21%	(n = 31)
Boston Herald	11%	(n = 16)
Worcester Telegram and Gazette	7%	(n = 11)
Patriot Ledger	6%	(n = 9)
Portland Press Herald	2%	(n = 3)

*percentages are rounded
The articles were collected from the year 1988 through
Fall 1999 (see Table 8.2): 1988 (n = 1), 1989 (n = 2), 1990 (n = 11), 1991
(n = 10), 1992 (n = 3), 1993 (n = 9), 1994 (n = 14), 1995 (n = 15), 1996
(n = 21), 1997 (n = 27), and 1998 (n = 27). The bulk of the articles were
written during the years 1996, 1997, and 1998. The mean length of the articles
was 736 words (SD = 492).

ing for a meager 5% of all articles printed, contained information referencing, describing, and/or acknowledging AIDS/HIV in our brown and black communities.

The total number of articles we were able to use for analysis was 150 (see Table 8.1 and Figure 8.1). The largest number of articles was obtained from the *Boston Globe* (n = 80) accounting for about 53% of the articles. Twenty-one percent of the articles were from the *Providence Journal Bulletin* (n = 31), 11% of the sample came from the *Boston Herald* (n = 16) and 7% of the articles were gathered from the *Worcester Telegram and Gazette* (n = 11). Six percent of the articles were printed in the *Patriot Ledger* (n = 9), 2% of the articles were found in the *Portland Press Herald* (n = 3). And lastly, the *Bangor Daily News* accounted for just 0% of the sample (n = 0). The *Bangor Daily News* was excluded from further scrutiny. Additionally, we recorded in which sections the 150 articles appeared. The sections were categorized as: News (which included national/foreign, local news, metro/region), city weekly (all magazines that appear in Sunday papers), sports, editorial (op-ed, editorials, commentary), and lifestyle (this included life, religion, science). Most of the articles in our content analysis were located in the news (n = 105) section of the papers. The remaining articles were found in city weekly (n = 14), sports (n = 1), editorials (n = 19) and lifestyle (n = 11) sections (see Table 8.2).

The articles were analyzed for central themes by one coder. Articles concerning *events* (n = 36), represented 24% of the sample, and 23% of the articles reported *rates and trends* (n = 35) and 10% of the articles were *human interest* stories (n = 15). *Organizational* articles (n = 25) accounted for 17% of the sample, 11% of the articles were coded as *health related* (n = 17) and lastly, 14% of the sample focused on *our communities' response* (n = 22).

Regarding the category called *Who is included?*, Latinos (n = 104) were mentioned in 70% of the articles, and African Americans (n = 85) were mentioned in 57% of the articles. More informative though, were the categories of men and women of both communities of color. Each of the social groups were written about

Figure 8.1
**News Coverage of AIDS/HIV and Latinos and/or African Americans
during the Years 1988 through Fall 1999 (n = 150)**

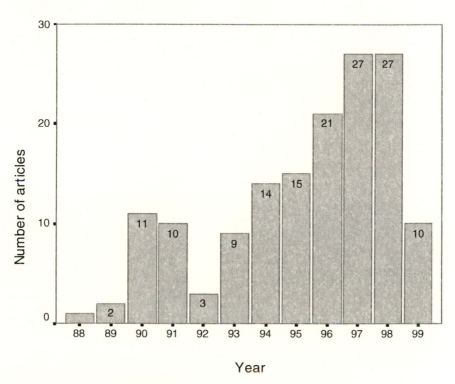

in nearly the same frequencies. Latino men (n = 34) were referred to in 23% of the articles and African American men (n = 38) were referred to in 21% of articles. A similar pattern was observed for the women, in that Latina women (n = 34) were written about in 23% of the articles, while African American women (n = 31) were mentioned in 21% of the articles.

Another social category of interest was that of sexual orientation. Gay men (n = 50) were referred to in 33% percent of the papers; however gay Latino men (n = 7) were mentioned in only 5% of the articles and gay African American men (n = 12) were referred to in just 8% of the articles. Lesbians of any color (n = 6) were rarely mentioned, appearing in just 4% of the articles. The typically unmarked category of heterosexual (n = 35) was also included in the articles about AIDS/HIV and this category appeared in 23% of the articles.

Within the category of *vehicles of transmission*, we found that most often cited sources was IV drug use (n = 74), which appeared in 49% of the articles. Secondly, unprotected sex (n = 61) was listed as a facilitating factor in 41% of the articles. Twenty-four percent of articles mentioned "men sleeping with men" (n = 36), while cultural issues (n = 29) were cited in nineteen percent of the articles. Both

Table 8.2
**Percentage and Number of Articles, per Section, Regarding AIDS/HIV
and Latinos and/or African Americans in New England Newspapers
(n = 150)**

Sections	Percentage* and Number of Articles	
news	70%	(n = 105)
city weekly	9%	(n = 14)
sports	1%	(n = 1)
editorial	13%	(n = 19)
lifestyle	7%	(n = 11)

*percentages are rounded.

denial (n = 15) and lack of information (n =15) each appeared in 10% of our sample of articles.

A more in-depth analysis demonstrated that while our communities are hit hard-
est by this epidemic, this rarely is sufficient for more significant coverage. This is
most clearly illustrated by an analysis of the "rates and trends" subcategory. We
found that an overwhelming 80% of the articles detailing the rates and trends of the
epidemic indicated that the Latino and/or African American communities as being
disproportionately affected by AIDS/HIV. Yet only 26% of the articles discussed
substantively the issue of AIDS/HIV within Latino and/or African American populations (n = 9). Even more dismal is the lack of noteworthiness of the problem in
our communities, as evidenced by our analysis of headlines. Just 17% of articles in
this subcategory contained Latinos (n = 27) in their headlines and merely 9% of the
articles in this subcategory contained African Americans (n = 3) in their headlines.

We also investigated the subcategory of organizations, finding that of the organization articles, 56% pertained to Latino and African American centered organizations (n = 14). Twenty percent of these articles focused on funding issues (n = 5),
while 46% of the articles detailed organizational efforts to provide education about
prevention (n = 14). Of all articles about the organizations, 44% were dedicated to
addressing attempts to meet the specific needs of the Latino and African American
communities (n = 11).

Twenty-nine of the articles indicated that "cultural issues" contributed to the
spread of AIDS/HIV. Of these 25 provided detailed factors. The most often cited
factor was homophobia/denial of homosexuality in the communities (n = 11),
which appeared in 38% of the articles. Machismo (n = 9) and religion/church (n =
9) each were cited as a factor in 31% of the articles. Twenty four percent of articles
suggested that women's fear of confronting their partners (n = 7) functioned as a
contributor and 13% of the articles indicated that language barriers (n = 4) may be
a factor. Lastly, bias against condoms (n = 3) appeared in 10% of the articles implicating "culture" as a significant cause of the growth of AIDS/HIV in Latino and
African American populations.

DISCUSSION

We began the study by posing three hypotheses with regard to press coverage of AIDS/HIV, African Americans, and Latinos. The first hypothesis, that the New England press coverage of AIDS/HIV will illustrate a build and decline over the period under examination was supported by the trends in news coverage during the period of investigation. One must be cautious, however, in noting that almost half of the coverage under scrutiny emanated from the *Boston Globe*. This paper provided the largest amount of news articles on AIDS/HIV and had the largest portion of the smaller pool of articles used for analysis. It was unfortunate that Connecticut's *Hartford Courant* was not available for scrutiny through the academic form of Lexis-Nexis, as it would have provided a fairer comparison across newspapers and would have made a fuller picture of New England newspaper coverage.

Why the news coverage illustrated a slight build and a drop under the years of investigation may certainly have to do with the ocean waves of news worthiness and novelty. Examining the picture in total, we see that even describing the coverage as a build and decline is highly relative, since there was a pittance of coverage to begin with.

During the early 1990s two major developments took place that may also have contributed to the low or inconsistent coverage of AIDS/HIV issues and issues of people of color. We might be seeing what Moeller (1999) has characterized as "compassion fatigue." Moeller (1999) suggests that the American public and journalists have increasingly become tired of images of death, war, famine, and hunger, that the public may be suffering from a short attention span. The issue of AIDS/HIV was so exhaustively covered by the news media in the 1980s that by early 1990s the public and journalists were tired of AIDS/HIV stories. So, the public does not want to hear any more of this type of news and journalists have to cover what the public wants to read and hear.

Indeed, by the latter part of the 1990s, the public had been presented with many forms of information about AIDS/HIV in news and popular culture. It was no longer a great surprise to find out that a popular culture icon or other celebrity was diagnosed HIV positive or was dying of AIDS. The news about AIDS probably became old hat, as editors moved on to newer and more appealing news regarding Clinton administration decisions and scandals, economic outlooks, civility problems and teenagers, U.S. roles in international affairs and many other issues. People in the United States may have thought they were informed enough. The public may even have assumed that a cure had been found for AIDS or that AIDS would never touch them because of their heterosexual lifestyle, social class, ethnicity, and citizenship in a wealthy developed nation.

Since the early 1990s, there has been an increasing feeling among the U.S. public and all developed nations that we have overcome the problem of AIDS/HIV since there are drugs that can prolong a victim's life. The issue of AIDS/HIV has been relegated to developing countries. So, the U.S. public and journalists are increasingly feeling that the problem of AIDS/HIV is an international problem of the "other" and not a national one of "us." In fact, when former President Clinton declared AIDS a threat to national security in the year 2000, many conservatives did not agree with him. Increasingly, therefore, coverage of the AIDS/HIV epidemic is now focused on Africa and somewhat on Russia, India, and China. This shift may also be due to the fact that a number of pharmaceutical companies have started testing anti-AIDS medicines in Africa. For instance, Pfizer is testing AIDS/HIV medicines in Uganda and this has received some coverage by the news media. The cost of AIDS/HIV medicines in developing countries has also attracted some media attention. These developments have helped shift the coverage from the United States to developing countries.

International congresses also helped pushed AIDS/HIV issues back on the international agenda in the late 1990s and early 2000s. Developing regions such as Africa know very well that there is no cure for AIDS/HIV and that problems are becoming magnified. Television news documentaries and specials have been aired in the United States through public broadcasting stations during 2001 drawing U.S. viewers' attention back to the issue of AIDS/HIV. Whether print news coverage jumped up in 2000 and 2001 is a question for future study. What would it take for newspapers in New England to cover AIDS/HIV more heavily? Something groundbreaking involving a major coup, natural disaster and preferably involving a great deal of bleeding (Rosenblum, 1981).

The second expectation of this research was that AIDS/HIV would be presented as a problem that is relegated to African Americans and Latinos. People of color overall, and African Americans and Latinos specifically, did not receive a great deal of coverage in AIDS/HIV stories. Recall that out of 3,360 news articles that contained stories on AIDS/HIV, we were only able to use 150 of these for scrutiny. So, only 5% of all articles printed contained information referencing, describing, and/or acknowledging AIDS/HIV among African Americans and Latinos. In the news articles that did include African Americans and Latinos, however, these groups tended to be presented as part of statistical averages and U.S. infection trends.

As posited in hypothesis three, descriptive statistical data did typify African American and Latino coverage. If one were to rely on these stories, they do indicate to a reader that the AIDS/HIV issue is a problem that African Americans, Latinos, and other people of color need to deal with. People of color do need to deal with the issue. However, AIDS/HIV is a national and international public health problem, not just a U.S. people of color problem. People of color, low-income and otherwise disenfranchised people are disproportionately affected by health problems such as AIDS/HIV. Though statistical trends and averages are useful, more stories discussing how people of color are coping and battling against AIDS/HIV and how the public can get involved in this battle would be more useful and constructive.

CONCLUDING REMARKS

This research examined about 10 years (1988–99) of AIDS/HIV coverage in seven New England newspapers using content analysis. Attention was focused on quantity and quality of AIDS/HIV coverage as it pertained to African Americans and Latinos. We found that AIDS/HIV coverage for people of color was dismal overall. For the news that included African Americans and Latinos, we can see a slight gain and then a drop in 1999. Were these findings surprising to us? The answer is both yes and no. We know that communities of color are in need of fairer news coverage (Heider, 2000). Based on this knowledge, we did not have high expectations for our New England papers, though we had hoped for better. Further research should look at New England press coverage during the years that this study was not able to analyze and include an in-depth qualitative analysis. A future ambitious study would be more comprehensive, using a large number of national newspapers.

REFERENCES

Baltimore Sun. (2000). Op-ed, July 11.

Brown, J., Chapman, S. & Lupton, D. (1996). Infinitesimal risk as public health crises: News media coverage of a doctor-patient HIV contact tracing investigation. *Social Science and Medicine,* 43, (12), 1685–1695.

Centers for Disease Control and Prevention. (Spring, 2000). CDC AIDS data set: Connecticut. University of California, San Francisco: http:hivinsite.ucsf.edu.

Clumeck, N. (1986). Heterosexual transmission: Fear or reality. In Robert F. Hummel, et al. (Eds.), *AIDS: Impact on public policy.* New York: Plenum, pp. 7–13.

Diaz, R. M. (1998). *Latino gay men and HIV: Culture, sexuality, and risk behavior.* New York: Routledge.

Domeyer, C. J., et al. (1989). The effectiveness of an AIDS education campaign on a college campus. *Journal of American College Health,* 38, 131–135.

Donovan, M. C. (1997). The problem with making AIDS comfortable: Federal policy making and the rhetoric of innocence. In M. A. Hallet (Ed.) *Activism and marginalization in the AIDS crisis,* pp. 115–144. Binghamton, NY: Haworth/Harrington Park.

Edgar, T., Hammond, S. L. & Freimuth, V. S. (1990). The role of the mass media and interpersonal communication in promoting AIDS-related behavioral change. *AIDS and Public Policy Journal,* 4, 3–9.

Hannaway, C., Harden, V. A. & Parascandola, J. (1995). *AIDS and the public debate: Historical and contemporary perspectives.* Washington, DC: IOS Press.

Heider, D. (2000). *White news: Why local news programs don't cover people of color.* Mahwah, NJ: Lawrence Erlbaum.

Hertog, J. K. & Fan, D. P. (1995). The impact of press coverage on social beliefs: The case of HIV transmission. *Communication Research,* 22 (5), 545–574.

Kiwanuka-Tondo, J. & Snyder (in press). The influence of organizational characteristics and campaign design elements on communication campaign quality: Evidence from 91 Ugandan AIDS Campaigns. *Journal of Health Communication.*

Lee, Jung-Sook, & Davie, W. R. (1997). Audience recall of AIDS PSAs among U.S. and international college students. *Journalism and Mass Communication Quarterly,* 74 (1), 7–22

McCombs, M. & Shaw, D. (1972). The agenda-setting function of the mass media. *Public Opinion Quarterly,* 36, 176–187.

Moeller, S. D. (1999). *Compassion Fatigue: How the Media Sell Disease, Famine, War and Death*. New York: Routledge.

Mutz, D. C. & Soss, J. (1997). Reading public opinion: The influence of news coverage on perception of public sentiment. *Public Opinion Quarterly*, 61, 431–451.

Myrick, R. (1998). AIDS discourse: A critical reading of mainstream press surveillance of marginal identity, *Journal of Homosexuality*, 35 (1), 75–93.

Nelkin, D. (1981). AIDS and the news media. *The Milbank Quarterly*, 69, (2), 293–306.

Reardon, K. K. & Richardson, J. L. (1991). The important role of mass media in the diffusion of accurate information about AIDS. In M. A. Wolf & A. P. Kielwasser (Eds.), *Gay people, sex and the media*, pp. 63–75. Binghamton, NY: Haworth/Harrington Park.

Rosenblum, M. (1981). *Coups and earthquakes: Reporting the world for America*. New York: Harper Colophon.

Roth, N. L. & Hogan, K. (1998). *Gendered epidemic: Representations of women in the age of AIDS*. New York: Routledge.

Sacks, V. (1996). Women and AIDS: An analysis of media misrepresentations. *Social Science and Medicine*, 42 (1), 59–73.

Shilts, R. (1987). *And the band played on: Politics, people, and the AIDS epidemic*. New York: St. Martin's Press.

Snyder, L. B. (1991). The impact of the surgeon general's understanding of AIDS pamphlet in Connecticut. *Health Communication*, 3 (1), 37–57.

Stroman, C. A. & Seltzer, R. (1989). Mass media use and knowledge of AIDS. *Journalism Quarterly*, 66, 250–261.

Wayne, W. & Yu-Wei, H. (1993). The agenda-setting effects of international news coverage: An examination of differing news frames. *International Journal of Opinion Research*, 5 (3), 250–261.

Chapter 9

Latinos in the Mainstream Media: A Case Study of Coverage in a Major Southwestern Daily

Camille Kraeplin and Federico A. Subervi-Velez

INTRODUCTION

As the fastest growing minority group in the country, Hispanics represent a particularly appealing source of potential readers to newspapers, many of which have
been watching their circulation bases dwindle for the past 20 years or so. Nationwide, the Hispanic population increased from 22.4 million in 1990 to over 30.3
million in 1998, a gain of 35.3 percent or 7.9 million people. Of those 7.9 million
newcomers, 1.5 million of them have settled in Texas. Not surprisingly, a number
of Texas newspapers have led the charge to lure Hispanic readers, be they recent
arrivals or long-time residents, to their pages. One such paper is *The Dallas Morning News* (*TDMN*), a regional powerhouse with a daily circulation of around half a
million.

U.S. Census figures and population estimates suggest that for much of the
1990s, the Hispanic, or Latino, population[1] in the Dallas-Fort Worth metropolitan
area ranked ninth in the nation, and fourth largest within the state of Texas. In the
North Texas area in 1995, the number of Hispanics was estimated at around
657,000 (13 % of total population). Data from the 2000 Census was expected to
put that number at around 920,000 (40% of the population).

With these figures in mind, *TDMN* completed a series of focus groups and a
telephone survey in the mid-1990s to find out what Hispanics in the newspaper's
readership area look for in a paper and what they think of *TDMN*, especially as a
source of Hispanic-related news. At the same time, the newspaper implemented an
extensive content analysis to gauge its own coverage of the Latino community.
The analysis was designed to systematically evaluate both the quantity and quality

of *TDMN*s coverage of Hispanics and Hispanic issues as well as determine how closely that content actually matches Latinos' sense of how they are covered.

When the study was conducted in the mid-1990s, Latinos represented approximately 9% of daily *TDMN* readers and 11% of Sunday readers. By the late 1990s, that figure was about 8% for both Sunday and daily readership. The explanation for this decline lies outside the scope of this study, which did not assess whether editors implemented any changes based on knowledge *TDMN* gathered about Hispanics in the findings reported here. But comparing the results of the poll and focus groups with those of the content analysis, it is not difficult to see why *TDMN* was unable to increase its readership among Hispanics.

LITERATURE REVIEW

Media critics and Latinos have long argued that general market (mainstream) media coverage of Hispanics and the issues important to them is biased (Turk et al.; Tan, 1978; Subervi-Velez et al., 1994). Critics not only deem the amount of attention given to Hispanics insufficient, but they also say the news that is reported often misrepresents Latinos and fosters stereotypes (Ericksen, 1981; Stein, 1994; Fitzgerald, 1994; Gersh, 1993; Navarette & Kamasakir, 1994). A common complaint is that the coverage U.S. media give to Hispanics is too often linked to crime and violence instead of to Hispanics' productive roles in society (Calvo-Roth, 1992). Others maintain that news stories often focus on Hispanics as "problem people" who cause or are beset by problems (Turk et al., 1989).

Some recent media research supports these claims. For instance, a 1995 content analysis of the three major broadcast networks (ABC, CBS and NBC) and CNN found that only 121 stories (or 1 % of the sample) focused on Latinos or issues related to Latinos. And of those items, 85% fell into one of four content categories: crime, immigration, affirmative action, or welfare (Carveth & Alverio, 1996, 1997). Hispanics were rarely pictured on camera as sources. A 1996 follow-up study found little change. Again just 1% of content qualified as Latino, and no Hispanic experts were interviewed for these stories.

Studies examining the content of newspapers present a slightly more positive picture. For instance, a 1983 analysis of six Southwestern dailies found that the proportion of the newshole devoted to Hispanics and Hispanic issues tended to match the proportion of Hispanics in each city's population (Greenberg et al., 1983). This same study determined that crime was not overemphasized in these newspapers. But sports news did outpace other types of Hispanic content. Similarly, the study of two Southwestern dailies during the 1980s by Turk et al. (1989) showed that the proportion of Latino content in those papers corresponded roughly with the Latino presence in their communities. In fact, the researchers reported, Hispanics were represented more equitably than in the past. However, the data from both studies is more than a decade old. And two studies hardly present a definitive picture.

Likewise, little work exists that looks at Hispanics' use of and attitudes toward general market U.S. media. In terms of media use, Subervi-Velez (1984) identified a positive correlation between Latinos' use of general market media and their degree of adaptation into U.S. society. Similarly, Nicolini (1986) found that opinion leaders within the Puerto Rican community in Philadelphia believed Spanish-language media only partially fulfilled the needs of the community. They charged that it left a gap in the coverage of news about the city beyond their neighborhood—a gap that most likely would be filled by general market media.

As noted earlier, a study plan involving three phases was developed to answer three research questions: How much do Hispanics in North Texas use *TDMN* compared with other media? What are Dallas-area Hispanics' attitudes toward *TDMN* and especially its coverage of Latinos? And how much and what kind of coverage does *TDMN* actually devote to Hispanic individuals, groups, and issues? The three methodologies employed (focus groups, survey, and content analysis) provide different but complementary pieces of the puzzle.

FOCUS GROUPS

Focus groups were conducted in July 1995 to explore Latinos' reading habits as well as their attitudes toward *TDMN*. Participants were divided into eight groups based on the criteria of gender, language preference (whether they preferred to read and speak English or Spanish) and readership of *TDMN* (whether they were frequent—3 or more times a week—or infrequent—one or two times a week—readers). Each group included a mix of ages from 18 to 54 and represented all walks of life—from blue-collar workers to professionals, singles to married people with children. They also represented a range of nationalities—although most were U.S.-born citizens of Mexican ancestry, there were several who had been born in Mexico or other Latin American countries.

Participants were asked a range of questions, from what they thought of *TDMN* coverage overall to what they thought of the paper's Hispanic coverage. The opinions of the Latino focus group participants were found to fall into four general topics/themes summarized here.

On Spanish-language versus English-language content:

- Participants were divided over whether *TDMN* should include Spanish-language content.

On international coverage:

- Participants indicated that the Spanish-language broadcast networks Univision and Telemundo were important sources of international news.
- They said that *TDMN* does not cover some international topics of interest to them (for example, many male participants complained about the lack of international soccer coverage).

On their reading habits:

- Participants cited the most common reason among all ethnic groups for not reading: lack of time.
- They said Sunday was a favorite day for reading: "On Sunday we rest, so that's when we have time to read."

On general coverage:

- Participants said that although they think *TDMN* is a good newspaper, they do not think it is a newspaper for Hispanics primarily because *TDMN* has little news about Hispanics and, they believed has few Hispanic employees.
- They said that although the advent of NAFTA in the mid-1990s had increased overall Hispanic coverage in *TDMN*, they were more interested in news of the local Hispanic community.
- They criticized *TDMN*'s coverage of Hispanics as generally "unbalanced," saying that drugs, gangs, and violent crime are overemphasized. As one group member said, *TDMN* "shows more respect for Anglos and blacks and gays than Hispanics—we get gang coverage." Some participants also said the local media have contributed to the public perception that areas where there are large concentrations of Hispanics are unsafe, "so that if you want to take your family to the few events [in these areas] that are publicized, you are afraid."
- Participants generally agreed that the accomplishments of Hispanics receive little attention in *TDMN*. They said they would like to see more positive "Hispanic" content such as profiles of successful business people, teen achievers, or local "heroes" because these types of stories serve as wonderful tools for motivating young people.
- Participants also said that *TDMN*'s sports section showed blatant discrimination by elevating Anglo sports figures over Hispanic athletes who had performed better. The specific examples they noted were coverage of Dallas's White Rock Marathon and coverage of the World Cup playoffs.
- But they didn't place blame only on *TDMN*. In fact, they said that *all* local English-language media give Hispanics only "superficial" coverage and that Hispanics are "invisible" in advertising. "To read the news or watch TV, you'd hardly know there was such a large Hispanic population here," said one. In local TV, the coverage is often limited to stories marking Latino holidays and events, "when they show us dancing at the end of the broadcast."

In summary, Hispanic focus group participants believed that *TDMN* did not serve them well. For one, they said the paper did not cover their community much. When it did, the story usually involved a stereotypical topic such as Hispanic youths in gangs, or was token coverage tied to a Hispanic holiday or celebration.

They also said *TDMN* often gave short shrift to topics they were interested in, such as international soccer. Some participants even charged certain sections of the newspaper with purposely ignoring the achievements of Hispanics in their pages. The telephone survey, the second phase of the study, followed up on many of these ideas.

Table 9.1
Age, Education, and Income Distributions of Hispanics Surveyed in
Dallas-Fort Worth (N = 741)

Age	%	Education	%*	Income	%*
18–24	23	Elementary	16	<$15,000	16
25–34	37	Some high sch	20	$15–29,999	33
35–44	20	High sch grad	29	$30–39,999	13
45–54	10	Some college	18	$40–49,999	7
55+	10	College grad	14	$50+	17

*Percentages for these columns do not add up to 100 because
some participants refused to answer.

SURVEY

In the second phase of the study, a survey was developed to more systematically explore the trends found in focus groups. Between October 31 and December 2,
1995, 741 Hispanic adults in four North Texas counties—Dallas, Collin, Denton and eastern Tarrant counties—were surveyed by bilingual telephone interviewers. To identify Hispanic households, a dual sampling frame was employed, using both a listed Hispanic surname sample and a random digit-dialing sample drawn from high-density Hispanic areas. Overall margin of error for the poll was 3.5. The findings from that section are presented under three categories—demographics, language preferences, and media use and topics of interest to Hispanic readers.

DEMOGRAPHICS

Of the 741 individuals surveyed the vast majority, 84%, were of Mexican descent. Another 4% were Puerto Rican, and 3% said their country of origin was El Salvador. In terms of gender, 55% were male and 45% female, and regarding age, the data clearly mirror 1990 U.S. Census data, which show that Hispanics in the Dallas-Fort Worth area tend to be younger than the general population. For instance, about 60% of the adult Latinos surveyed were between 18 and 34 years old. Only 10% were 55 or older. Education data showed that slightly less than a third had attended or graduated from college, lower than the national average for all ethnic groups. Income may reflect the limited education—about half of the Latinos surveyed had household earnings less than $30,000 per year. Table 9.1 shows the frequency distributions of three of these demographic characteristics.

LANGUAGE PREFERENCE

Many media professionals and researchers today agree that since the Latino community is bilingual, information should be imparted in both languages to better serve and appeal to this population group. As a result, several survey questions addressed this dimension of Latino media use, including language ability and preference. For instance, when asked what language they usually speak at home, 42% of respondents said they use Spanish more than English, compared with 36% who speak English more than Spanish. Another 22% said they use both languages equally.

In terms of reading ability, approximately the same number of respondents feel comfortable reading both Spanish and English; 75% said they found English very or somewhat easy to read, versus 78% who said Spanish was very or somewhat easy to read. Not surprisingly, given these findings, respondents used both English-language and Spanish-language media, with the largest percentages relying on Spanish-language broadcast outlets for their news.

When respondents identified as readers of *TDMN* were asked what, if any, portion of the paper should be in Spanish, well over half (66%) said there should be some content in Spanish. A quarter believed there should be no content in Spanish, and 1% believed all the content should be in Spanish. Readers who preferred speaking Spanish at home were more likely to say there should be some content in Spanish.

MEDIA USE AND TOPICS OF INTEREST TO HISPANIC READERS

Two other issues that the survey explored were how often readers pick up *TDMN* as well as what type of content they find most interesting. In general, they said they read *TDMN* more often than other newspapers, including Spanish-language papers. But both Spanish-language radio (used by 68%) and Spanish-language television (used by 77%) were much more popular. In terms of topics, respondents' interests tended to lean toward the local, the focus on community mentioned by focus group participants.

Hispanics in Dallas-Fort Worth do appear to read *TDMN* less than the general public. For instance, 32% of Hispanics said they read *TDMN* on an average weekday compared with half of the general public in *TDMN* circulation market. Similarly, on most Saturdays, one-fourth of Hispanics read versus half of the general market. Even on Sunday when focus group participants said they were most likely to read, reading was lower among Hispanics than among the general population. Some 37% of Hispanic survey respondents said they read *TDMN* most Sundays compared with 66% of the general public.

The topics that Hispanic *TDMN* readers (respondents who had read *TDMN* within the past week) said they are most interested in reflect a strong interest in local coverage. For instance, 84% of readers said they are somewhat or very interested in education and local school administration (see Table 9.2). This rings true since nearly nine in 10 respondents have school-age children. Readers also expressed an interest in local crime news, including gang activity (80%) and drug use (71%). (Interestingly, recall that focus group participants criticized *TDMN* for focusing too much on Hispanic involvement with gangs and drugs.) Readers were also interested in traditional "Hispanic" issues such as immigration (70%) and news of Mexico and other Latin American countries (approximately 70% in both cases).

Table 9.2
Topics of Interest to Hispanic Readers of *The Dallas Morning News*
(N = 393)

	% very interested	% somewhat/very interested
Topics		
Education/schools	58	84
Gang activity	50	80
Illegal drugs	40	71
Housing/neighborhoods	39	73
Immigration	38	70
News from Mexico	34	70
News from other Latin American countries	27	66
International soccer	18	40
Boxing	26	54
Other sports	47	74

Finally, despite the fact that focus group participants criticized *TDMN* for failing to cover international soccer, only four out of 10 readers were interested in this topic.

Survey results also suggest that Hispanic readers pay attention to newspaper stories that have an "Hispanic link." For instance, nearly nine in 10 said they would read a story in *TDMN* if it dealt with issues that involve Hispanics. Around eight in 10 would read a story if they noticed it referred to Hispanic culture or customs, focused on Hispanic individuals, or was about a Hispanic organization. Nearly seven in 10 would read a story that contained a Spanish surname or referred to a Spanish-speaking country.

CONTENT ANALYSIS

In the third phase of the study, content analysis was used to determine how Hispanics are portrayed in *TDMN*. All issues of *TDMN* from July 1995 were analyzed for Hispanic-related content, including coverage both of Hispanics in the United States and of Spanish-speaking countries. This parameter was selected based on previous studies that suggest this time frame should provide an acceptable number of stories and photographs.[2] July was chosen primarily because that was the month when the focus groups were held. Availability was also a consideration. We wanted to use hard copies of the paper for coding, and many older papers were no longer stocked in back issues.

As a result of choosing the July date, sampling coincided with the professional baseball season, a sport with many Hispanic players. In addition, the annual conference of the National Council of La Raza, one of the nation's largest Latino advocacy organizations, took place in Dallas the second week of July. These factors should be kept in mind when interpreting the content analysis results. Four University of Texas students were hired as coders.[3] To measure the reliability of both the coders and the coding instrument, an intercoder-reliability score was calculated using the results of a pretest. This score reflects the number of coding decisions on which coders agreed. Using the Holsti method, researchers calculated a reliability score of 83%.

On average, "Hispanic coverage" was found to represent just over 6% of *TDMN* coverage during the month of July. Coders identified a total of 138 photographs and 499 "news items"—an umbrella term for stories, columns, news briefs, etc.—that qualified as Hispanic coverage. Weekly zoned sections were excluded from the study. All other sections of the newspaper, including occasional special sections and other sections were analyzed.

Five criteria were used to identify "Hispanic coverage." Again, existing studies that look at newspaper coverage of Hispanics were used to develop this list (Greenberg et al., 1983; Turk et al., 1989). A news item was labeled as Hispanic content if the text or headline (1) contained Hispanic surnames; (2) referred to a Spanish-speaking country; (3) dealt with issues that involve Hispanics, or that have been identified by Hispanic organizations or leaders as Hispanic issues; (4) referred to Hispanic culture or customs; and/or (5) referred to Hispanics as members of a minority group.

When a Hispanic person, issue or topic, or a Spanish-speaking country did appear in the text of a news item, that person, issue or topic was a primary focus of that story about 74 percent of the time. In other words, the stories in our sample did not qualify as "Hispanic" content because of a single reference to Mexico buried in the story. Most of the news items in the sample—69%—were standard news stories or articles. Columns and news briefs each comprised just over one-tenth of the sample. The rest of the news items, about 7% of the sample, were coded as "other." They included reviews, such as music reviews, editorials, letters to the editor, obituaries, and bulletins or announcements, such as wedding announcements.

News items were most likely to be included in the sample because they contained Spanish surnames. These names appeared in about 82% of the sample stories and 12% of the headlines. Approximately 44% of the sample stories and one-fourth of headlines referred to a Spanish-speaking country. And about 44% of stories and 30% of headlines dealt with a Hispanic issue. References to Hispanic culture or customs appeared in about one-tenth of the stories, as did references to Latinos as members of a minority group. However, these references were almost completely absent from headlines.

IDENTIFYING TOPICS AND COUNTRIES

As noted earlier, nearly half of the news items in the sample referred to a Spanish-speaking country. Coders were asked to identify which Spanish-speaking country or countries were mentioned in stories. They were also asked to determine the primary topic—from sports to accidents to economics—of the story they were coding.

Table 9.3
Frequency and Percentage Distribution of the Main Topics in News Items

Main topic	Frequency	%
Sports	134	27
Judicial/crime*	77	15
Economics/trade/business	60	12
Foreign affairs/defense	51	10
Government/politics	32	6
Arts/culture/entertainment	27	5
Human interest	24	5
Social issues	22	4
Accidents/disasters	19	4
Education	14	3
Immigration	12	2
Other**	27	7
Total	499	100

*4%—19 stories—of total Hispanic coverage was drug-related;
less than 1%—2 stories—was gang-related.

**The "other" category includes the environment, transportation/travel,
housing, science/health/medicine, religion, and consumer/lifestyle.

Not surprisingly, of the 218 news items (44% of the 499 sampled items) that referred to a Spanish-speaking country or countries, 56% mentioned Mexico. No other country even came close. Next was Spain, which appeared in 10% of news items, and Colombia, which appeared in 7%. Cuba was mentioned in about 5%, and both Guatemala and Puerto Rico in about 3%.

As Table 9.3 shows, when news items were categorized by subject or topic, sports showed up at the top of the list. Of the sample items, 27% were classified as sports. That was followed by crime and judicial coverage, which comprised about 15% of Hispanic coverage. However, the "stereotypical" topic of gangs made up only a small portion of this 15%.

Economics/trade/business and foreign affairs/defense were also fairly common topics. Government/politics, arts/culture/entertainment, human interest, accidents/disasters, social issues, and education were the topics of a smaller number of stories.

Stories about immigration accounted for only about 2% of Hispanic coverage.

In our focus groups we found that many participants believed that much of the coverage of Hispanics in *TDMN* focused on crime, especially gang-related crime, and "token" stories about holiday celebrations and the like. Table 9.3 shows that while 15% of the Hispanic content in our sample did focus on crime, less than 1% dealt with gang activity. And although some human-interest stories that may have covered Hispanic celebrations did appear in the sample, this category accounted for only about 5% of the total.

These findings raise the question of whether other factors influenced readers' perceptions of the type of coverage Hispanics receive in *TDMN*. An answer, we thought, might be sought by assessing the role of Latinos in the stories, and the placement of the news items pertaining to this population.

Editors typically place the stories they consider most important on the front page of each section of the newspaper. The most salient general interest stories of the day will generally appear on the first page of the section A, while the most important business stories usually appear on the first page of the business section. Likewise for the most important sports, metropolitan, and lifestyle or entertainment stories, depending on the structure of the particular newspaper. Most readers understand this method of signaling importance. In addition, since many people do not read the entire newspaper, stories that appear on the first page of any section are more likely to leave a lasting impression.

To explore the question of whether certain Hispanic-related content topics were more likely to appear on the front page of a section of the newspaper and thus perhaps carry greater symbolic weight, a cross-tabulation was performed. The variables involved included story placement (inside page or page 1) and content topic. Overall, we found that 21% of Hispanic content appeared on a section cover, while 79% ran on an inside page. The analysis also detected statistically significant relationships between placement and topic; as one might expect, a story's topic appears to influence whether it gets page-1 treatment.

Only about 2% of the articles with or about Latinos were front-page stories about crime or judicial issues. In fact, the front-page coverage of Hispanics in stories about crime/judicial matters was nearly equal to the percentage of Latinos in page-1 stories about four other topic categories—government,/politics/foreign affairs/social issues and economics/trade/business. The most common topic category on page 1 was sports. Of course, sports stories dominated the sample of news included in this study. But sports stories were also more likely than stories about other topics to appear on page 1. For instance, nearly a third of all sports stories in the sample appeared on the front page of a section, followed by human interest and business stories, each with about a quarter on page 1. In contrast, 16% of crime stories that involved Hispanics appeared on a section front.

However, most crime stories ran on the front page of Section A or Metropolitan (75%). Likewise, most human interest stories (nearly 60%) ran in one of these two sections. Since *TDMN* research shows that the A and Metropolitan sections are the most widely read, the stories that dominate the front pages of these sections arguably may also dominate Hispanic readers' impressions of this newspaper's coverage of Latinos and Latino issues, even if they are fewer in number. For instance, the crime and human interest stories may have been seen by more Hispanic readers than the Latino-related sports and business stories, which usually appeared on the front page of those specialized sections, sections that appeal to a narrower readership. Nearly nine in 10 business-themed stories in the sample appeared in the Business section, and eight in 10 sports-themed stories ran in Sports Day.

Table 9.4
Percentage and Distribution of Hispanics in News Items and Photos by Social Role

Social Role	News (N = 861)	Photos (N = 156)
Athlete	30	24
Politician/govt official	19	12
Professional	12	9
Business/executive	7	5
Entertainer/artist	6	10
Criminal	5	5
Laborer/blue-collar worker	3	4
Law enforcement/judicial	3	3
Student/youth	2	12
Other	6	6
Can't determine	7	10
Total	100	100

SOCIAL ROLE OF HISPANICS IN NEWS ITEMS AND PHOTOS

Another goal of the content analysis was to assess how Hispanic individuals were portrayed. Thus, several facets of that form of portrayal were analyzed, including the individual's social role, defined as the individual's profession or identifying function in society. Coders were able to record information for up to four people in each news item, in order of appearance in the particular story. This resulted in data pertaining to 861 individuals. Given the prominence of sports as a topic of Hispanic coverage, not surprisingly, nearly a third of the individuals in *TDMN*'s stories were athletes (see Table 9.4). The other major category of Latino individuals covered by *TDMN* was politicians or government officials. And about one in 10 Hispanics were identified as professionals.

The data indicate that only about 5% of stories portrayed Hispanic individuals as criminals. The other role that could be considered stereotypical portrayal of Hispanics would be that of a laborer or unskilled worker, for example, the restaurant, hotel or construction worker. Again, the analysis shows that only 3% of Hispanics appeared in this role. However, the proportion of Hispanics portrayed in the more positive roles of entertainer/artist and businessperson/executive also hovered in the single digits.

And the numbers of law enforcement/judicial personnel and young people/students who appeared in the sample were especially low. Insufficient information was provided to determine the social role of about 7% of the Hispanics in the sampled stories.

To analyze the portrayal of Latinos in photographs, up to two individuals could be coded for each of those graphics. (If a photo contained more than two people, they were defined and coded as being part of a group and analyzed accordingly.) A total of 156 Hispanic individuals were coded in the sample photos. Nearly a fourth

of the Hispanics pictured were identified as athletes. Politicians/government officials and young people also appeared fairly frequently, with members of each
group showing up in 12% of the studied photos. This was lower than the number of
politicians/government officials featured in news items, but much higher than the
number of Latino youth mentioned in stories. Entertainers or artists appeared in
10% of the photos—a number that would probably be larger today given the popularity of Latino artists such as Ricky Martin and Jennifer Lopez. Latinos were
rarely pictured as law officers/judges or as businesspeople/executives. Nor did
Hispanic laborers or criminals appear in many photos.

Again, for various reasons, portrayals that appear on the front page of a section
most likely make more of an impression on readers than those that appear on inside
pages. Therefore, a cross-tabulation analysis was conducted to assess which portrayals turned up most often on section covers. As was noted earlier in this chapter,
up to four individuals could be coded for each news item. However, the vast majority of stories referred to only one Hispanic individual. Therefore, the cross-tabulation was performed using the variable social role 1, to indicate the first individual
coded in each news item. The analysis found that 23% of stories featuring a Hispanic appeared on a section cover, and 77% ran on an inside page. The analysis
also showed that there are statistically significant relationships between the social
role of a Latino featured in a news item and where that item appears.

As suggested by the data, very few Hispanics appeared in the stereotypical,
marginalized social roles of criminal or laborer on a front page of a section in
TDMN during the sample period—only about 2% of all portrayals. In percentage
terms, they were more likely than most other Latino individuals to make it to the
front page—but total numbers for both categories were small. Of course, Latino
athletes and government officials were much more plentiful throughout the paper,
and both categories of individuals were more apt to end up on page 1 than say a Latino entrepreneur or even a Latino entertainer.

ROLE OF HISPANICS IN NEWS ITEMS AND PHOTOS

Another way to gauge *TDMN*'s coverage of Hispanics was by assessing what
role they played in the stories in which they appeared. For this, coders were asked
to choose one of seven category options that best described the role an individual
played in the sampled news stories and photos. Table 9.5 indicates that 57% of the
Hispanics were coded as subject/participant in the news, which means they played
a central role in the story. Another 11% were classified as bystanders, meaning
they played a more peripheral role. Some 10% could be described as a perpetrator
or wrongdoer, 9% as an expert or official and 7% as a victim. Only 6% of the Latino individuals who appeared in the sample stories could be described as heroes or
role models.

Compared with news stories, 10% of the individuals who appeared in photos
were portrayed as heroes or role models. The number of victims or wrongdoers appearing in studied photos was also very low. Understandably, the "bystander" cat-

Table 9.5
**Percentage and Distribution of Hispanics in News Items and Photos by
Role Played in the News/Photo**

News/Photo Role	News (N = 861)	Photos (N = 156)
Subject/participant	57	70
Bystander	11	3
Perpetrator/wrongdoer	10	5
Expert/official	9	8
Victim	7	4
Role model/hero	6	10
Total	100	100

egory was small, since photos generally feature only people who are central to the issue or event illustrated.

This analysis was taken one step further by computing a cross-tab to compare the role in the photo for individual 1 with the placement of that photo (front page of section or inside page). The results showed that role models/heroes were pictured significantly more often than either perpetrators or victims on the front pages of *TDMN*.

HOW HISPANIC INDIVIDUALS AND GROUPS WERE PORTRAYED IN NEWS ITEMS AND PHOTOS

Coders were also asked to determine whether Hispanic individuals were portrayed in news stories in an essentially negative, positive, or neutral manner. A portrayal was coded as "favorable" if the story (1) reflected positively on the person, (2) highlighted his or her talents or accomplishments, (3) associated him/her with positive characteristics or actions; or (4) honored his or her culture. A portrayal was "unfavorable" if it (1) reflected negatively on the person; (2) associated him/her with unethical, illegal, or immoral behavior; (3) suggested he/she was the source of problems; or (4) associated him or her with a negative experience or failure. A portrayal was neutral or balanced if the news item was neither positive nor negative toward the individual, or if it provided nearly equal amounts of positive and negative information. Using the same criteria, coders assessed the way Hispanic groups that appeared in the sampled news items and photos were portrayed. A "group" was defined as anything from an informal gathering of friends to employees of Hispanic-owned business to a formal organization with primarily Hispanic members. Up to two "groups" could be coded for each story. A total of 114 group news items and 17 group photos were analyzed for this treatment.

As Table 9.6 shows, slightly more than half of the Latino individuals and groups in the sample news items and more than two-thirds of the individuals and groups in the photos were coded as receiving favorable treatment by *TDMN*. However, a notable number of Hispanic individuals (19%) and groups (30% were featured in a

Table 9.6
**Percentage Distribution of Tone of Presentation of Hispanic Individuals
and Groups in News Items and Photos**

Tone	Individuals		Groups	
	News (N = 861)	Photos (N = 156)	News (N = 114)	Photos (N = 17)
Favorable	53	69	51	71
Neutral/balanced	28	21	19	17
Negative	19	10	30	12

negative way. Evidently, *TDMN*'s unfavorable coverage of Latinos is found in stories more often than photos, and focuses more on groups than individuals.

This analysis was taken one step further by cross-tabulating the treatment of individuals with the topics of the stories. Data shows there is a correspondence between these variables. For example, human interest stories—pieces about local people with interesting stories—were most likely to present Latinos in a positive way. However, the number of these stories as a percentage of total sample content was low, 5%. Latinos in sports stories, arts and entertainment stories, and stories about social issues (education, race, immigration, and welfare all might be included) were also highly likely to be favorably portrayed. This is especially significant in the case of sports stories because there were so many of them that ran during the sample period—due to sheer numbers, people were more likely to see these stories. Latinos were also presented favorably more than half of the time in stories about government and politics and in business stories. Not surprisingly, they were most likely to be presented in a negative light in stories about crime and the justice system.

Another variable that clearly influenced whether a Latino individual presented in our sample stories and photos was favorably portrayed was the individual's social role. A cross-tabulation showed a statistically significant relationship between these two variables, both in news items and in photos. As expected from earlier findings, Latino athletes were clearly presented in a highly positive way in *TDMN* stories—75% of these portrayals were favorable. They were featured even more favorably in photos. Likewise, Latino entertainers were celebrated in stories, and more so in photos. In contrast, Hispanic government officials, including politicians, and law enforcement personnel were favorably portrayed only about half of the time in both stories and photos. About a third of them appeared as neutral official sources. It came as no surprise to find that Latino criminals were uniformly portrayed in a negative way in stories, but in photos they were nearly as likely to receive more neutral treatment. Professionals, businesspeople, and young people received highly positive treatment in both stories and photos. Blue-collar workers and laborers, however, received favorable treatment less than half the time. In photos, they were just as likely to be portrayed in a negative way.

DISCUSSION AND CONCLUSIONS

When *USA Today* instituted its policy of featuring at least one photo of an ethnic minority or woman on its cover in the 1990s, many hailed it as a well-intentioned and useful means of boosting the visibility of these groups in this popular newspaper. Others criticized the move as "tokenism" and noted that many of the photographs featured athletes or entertainers rather than more legitimate newsmakers or "real" people. And although the policy may have heightened the awareness of journalists making editorial decisions at *USA Today*, it could certainly be argued that it most likely had no real effect on what appeared in the rest of the paper.

The results of this study suggest that in the mid-1990s, at a time when journalists were becoming increasingly aware of the need to diversify both the newsroom and the news content, the *TDMN* may have suffered from what critics of the *USA Today* policy described above would call "tokenism." Latino athletes were celebrated in photos on the front page of *TDMN*'s popular Sports Day section. A few Hispanic businesspeople and professionals were profiled or otherwise featured in news stories. Smiling Hispanic children occasionally appeared in color photos on the cover of Metropolitan. And every now and then a Latino official was quoted as an expert source. But although these efforts to include Hispanics were laudable, they certainly did not meet the mark one would expect from the newspaper of record in a community with a burgeoning Latino population like that of Dallas-Fort Worth.

Applying the general rule that the amount of coverage a newspaper gives to any group should approximate the percentage of the local population that group comprises, *TDMN*'s coverage of Hispanics was low. Only 5% of coverage during July 1995 was found to be "Hispanic," while Hispanics made up about 13% of the population in the area at that time. However, as noted earlier, the portrayal of those Hispanics who did appear in news stories or photos was predominantly favorable. One common criticism of general market media treatment of Hispanics is that much of the reporting is unbalanced or negative. In focus groups, for example, Hispanic readers of *TDMN* said that gangs, drugs, and violent crime are emphasized and that the accomplishments and successes of Hispanics receive little attention. These content analysis findings suggest that this is not the case. In fact, just over half of the Hispanic individuals and groups in the sample were favorably treated in news stories and headlines. In photos, that percentage was even higher: more than two-thirds of Hispanic individuals and groups that appeared in sample photos were favorably portrayed. And when Hispanics were not favorably treated in photos or stories, they generally were portrayed in a neutral or balanced way.

Keeping in mind the fact that most editors would agree that crime is news, no matter who it involves, this study also suggests that crime is not overemphasized in Hispanic coverage in *TDMN*. News items that dealt primarily with the judicial system or crime comprised about 15% of the sample. But this does not mean Hispanics were portrayed as criminals in all of these stories. In fact, Hispanic individuals were portrayed as criminals in only 5% of sample stories and photos. In some cases, a crime story may have been identified as Hispanic coverage if a Hispanic was the victim of a crime, or if a Hispanic police officer or other official appeared as a news source. In addition, only very small portions of crime-related coverage dealt with illegal drugs or gang activity.

It's difficult to explain this disconnect between what Hispanic readers perceived and what actually appeared in *TDMN*. Clearly further research needs to be done to explain this discrepancy. Story placement may have something to do with it. This analysis shows that sports, business, and human-interest stories were more likely to appear on the front page of a section of *TDMN* than crime news. But of the nearly two in 10 stories about Latinos and crime that ran on a front page, most were on the cover of Section A or Metropolitan, the two most widely read sections of the newspaper. In other words, Hispanic readers may have the perception that *TDMN* portrays Latinos as criminals and Latino neighborhoods as wracked with crime because these stories appear on the cover of the Metropolitan section they look at every day to keep up with local news.

Internal characteristics of the story or message—such as the level of negativity and/or conflict—may also be involved. In other words, those stories that are more conflictual may be perceived as more salient, regardless of where they appear. Another possible explanation is that some past negative portrayals of Latinos left lasting impressions that are difficult to overcome. We must also acknowledge the possibility that our sampling method may have overlooked some egregious negative portrayal that feeds the critical perceptions that are held by the Dallas-Fort Worth Latino community. We also could not compare size of photos with their treatment. It is possible that a large number of the 30% of the group photos that were evaluated as being negative were significantly larger than many or most of the positive group photos. This would indeed contribute to the community's perception (as indicated by members of the focus groups) that *TDMN* has a tendency to treat Latinos in a negative way. Of course, this does not negate the possibility that the negative treatment is a reflection of the problems faced by Latinos in the Dallas-Fort Worth area.

However, even if *TDMN*'s portrayal of Hispanic life is not overtly negative, it is problematic for several reasons alluded to earlier. First and foremost, nearly a quarter of the Hispanic content during the sample period consisted of sports stories; nearly a third of the newsmakers featured in stories and a quarter in photos were athletes. Granted, the study period coincided with the height of the baseball season. But even with that caveat, the limited range of what little Latino content did appear in *TDMN* during this time is unacceptable due to what Marilyn Gist suggests is a very fundamental reason:

It may limit what young Latinos envision for their future by restricting the roles in which they see themselves. Where are the physicians, the architects, the teachers? Others may argue that such a limited portrayal may perpetuate myopic stereotypes of Latinos among other ethnic groups simply by offering few alternative visions of Latino life. Both effects are pernicious and further steps must be taken to ensure that the general market media offer a broader picture of Hispanics and the Hispanic community.

The two best ways to begin this process have been identified many times in the past. First, the general market media must make a commitment to recruit more Hispanics and other minorities as reporters, editors, and station managers. This will not ensure an integrated news product, but it is a necessary first step. Second, mass media courses in high schools and universities must educate media consumers to recognize the importance of an integrated news product. Savvy media consumers, one can only hope, may then demand news and entertainment programming that more accurately reflects the social realities of the twenty-first century.

NOTES

1. The terms Hispanic and Latino are used interchangeably throughout this chapter.

2. The Turk et al. (1989) study looked at 27 issues of each of two newspapers; the Greenberg et al. (1983) study examined two weeks' worth of issues of each of six newspapers.

3. All four speak Spanish and know something about Hispanic culture. Two are Hispanic, one is married to a Hispanic, and one has lived and studied in Latin America.

REFERENCES

Calvo-Roth, F. (1992). The good and the bad: Press coverage of Hispanic Americans. *Hispanic, 5,* 80.

Carveth, R. & Alverio, D. (1996). *Network brownout: The portrayal of Latinos in network television news.* Washington, DC: National Association of Hispanic Journalists/National Council of La Raza.

Carveth, R. & Alverio, D. (1997). *Network brownout: The portrayal of Latinos in network television news.* Washington, DC: National Association of Hispanic Journalists/National Council of La Raza.

Carveth, R. & Alverio, D. (1998). *Network brownout: The portrayal of Latinos in network television news.* Washington, DC: National Association of Hispanic Journalists/National Council of La Raza.

Carveth, R. & Alverio, D. (1999). *Network brownout: The portrayal of Latinos in network television news.* Washington, DC: National Association of Hispanic Journalists/National Council of La Raza.

Carveth, R. & Alverio, D. (2000). *Network brownout: The portrayal of Latinos in network television news.* Washington, DC: National Association of Hispanic Journalists/National Council of La Raza.

Ericksen, C. A. (1981). Hispanic Americans and the press. *Journal of Intergroup Relations,* 9, 3–16.

Fitzgerald, M. (1994). State of Hispanic America: National Council of La Raza says negative stereotyping by both Hollywood and news organizations is holding down Latino progress in civil rights, education, housing and the economy. *Editor & Publisher,* 127, 11.

Gersh, D. (1993). Portrayals of Latinos in and by the media. *Editor & Publisher,* 126, 12.

Gist, M. (1990). Minorities in media imagery: A social cognitive perspective on journalistic bias. *Newspaper Research Journal,* Summer 1990, 52–63.

Greenberg, B. S., Burgoon, M., Burgoon, J. K. & Korzenny, F. (1986). *Mexican Americans and the mass media.* Norwood: NJ: Ablex.

Greenberg, B. S., Heeter, C., Burgoon, J. K., Burgoon, M. & Korzenny, F. (1983). Local newspaper coverage of Mexican Americans. *Journalism Quarterly,* 60, 671–676.

Navarette, L., & Kamasaki, C. (1994). *Out of the picture: Hispanics in the media. The state of Hispanic America 1994.* Washington, DC: National Council of La Raza.

Nicolini, P. (1986). Philadelphia Puerto Rican community leaders' perceptions of Spanish-language media. *Mass Communication Review,* 13, 11–17.

Stein, M. L. (1994) Racial stereotyping and the media. *Editor & Publisher,* 127, 12.

Subervi-Velez, F. A. (1984). Hispanics, the mass media and politics: Assimilation vs. pluralism. Doctoral dissertation, University of Wisconsin, Madison.

Subervi-Velez, F. A. (1986). The mass media and ethnic assimilation and pluralism: A review and research proposal with special focus on Hispanics. *Communication Research,* 13, 71–96.

Subervi-Velez, F. A., Berg, C. R., Constantakis-Valdez, P., Noriega, C., Rios, D. & Wilkinson, K. (1994). Mass communication and Hispanics. In F. Padilla (Ed.), *Handbook of Hispanic cultures in the United States: Sociology* (pp. 304–357). Houston: Arte Publico Press.

Tan, A. (1978). Evaluations of newspapers and television by blacks and Mexican Americans. *Journalism Quarterly,* 55, 637–681.

Turk, J. V., Richstad, J., Bryson, R.L., Jr., & Johnson, S. M. (1989). Hispanic Americans in the news in two Southwestern cities. *Journalism Quarterly,* 66, 107–113.

Vivian, J. (1997). *The Media of Mass Communication.* Needham Heights, MA: Allyn & Bacon.

Chapter 10

News Media, Immigration, and the Priming of Racial Perceptions

*David Domke, Kelley McCoy,
and Marcos Torres**

INTRODUCTION

One issue in which racial and ethnic tensions have been apparent in recent years is immigration.[1] Public discourse in the United States about immigration has been characterized by two features—a tendency to "reduce all questions to simple cost-benefit analyses" (New & Petronicolos, 1996, p. 1) and a distinct racial subtext (Macias, 1996; Suarez-Orozco, 1996). For example, Borjas (1996, p. 77) suggests that the discussion about immigration "is not over whether the entire country is made better off by immigration—it is over how the economic pie is sliced up" (see also Passel & Fix, 1994). This debate is reflected in public opinion polls, which show that U.S. adults are deeply divided over the material impact of immigration (Gallup Organization, 1999; NBC News/Wall Street Journal, 1998). Some argue that race, while rarely explicit, is also at the heart of this debate.[2] Johnson (1997) suggests that economic concerns coupled with a "new nativism" directed against Mexican immigrants helped drive the passage in California of anti-illegal immigration.

Proposition 187 in 1994 (see also Tolbert & Hero, 1996). Further, national polls show that concern about Hispanic immigrants, primarily from Mexico, has risen. The percent of adults reporting an unfavorable impression of immigrants from Mexico nearly tripled between 1993 and 1997, rising from 7% to 20%, while there is no similar trend for immigrants from other nations (Knight-Ridder, 1997; Time/Cable News Network, 1993).

*This chapter is condensed from Domke, D., McCoy, K., & Torres, M. (1999). News media, racial perceptions, and political cognition. *Communication Research, 26*, 570–607. Copyright © 1999 by Sage Publications, Inc. Reprinted by permission of Sage Publications, Inc.

While there has been some analysis of news content about immigration (Hufker & Cavender, 1990; Miller, 1994; Simon & Alexander, 1993), insufficient attention has been given to how media coverage of immigration affects the public. This gap in scholarship is reflective of a broader pattern in media and race research, which often has focused solely or primarily on media content with little examination of how citizens evaluate and utilize such information. The result is that much research must *assume* that media coverage of issues that intersect with race plays a role in citizens' thoughts and subsequent policy decisions and social interactions. This is not an unreasonable assumption and, indeed, some survey evidence is suggestive that news media help to establish the contexts in which whites come to understand race relations and form their opinions on various policies (see Gandy & Baron, 1998; Pan & Kosicki, 1996). This perspective is buttressed by a small but growing body of experimental research, which indicates that "public opinion on race . . . depends in a systematic and intelligible way on how the issues are framed" by elites and interest groups (Kinder & Sanders, 1996, p. 165; also Peffley, Shields, & Williams, 1996; Sniderman & Piazza, 1993; Valentino, 1999). Nonetheless, virtually unexplored are the *cognitive processes* involved when citizens encounter news coverage of political issues that intersect in some manner with race relations. It seems particularly important to examine these processes in light of the complex nature of contemporary discourse about politics and race, in which explicit references to racial groups are rare yet citizens' racial perceptions are nonetheless thought to significantly contribute to their political judgments (Gilens, 1996; Jamieson, 1992).

With this in mind, this study examines the linkages among news media, racial perceptions, and citizens' political cognitions. Specifically, we conducted an experiment in which we altered the news frame of immigration—as either material or ethical in nature—within controlled political information environments to examine how individuals process, interpret, and use issue information in forming political judgments. The sample consisted of undergraduate students at a major Midwestern university, a particularly relevant population for two reasons: (1) many university students hold jobs and many others are cognizant of their future roles in the nation's economy; and (2) the ideas and perceptions of university students provide insight into the climate of race relations among individuals entering their adult years.

THEORETICAL ARGUMENT

Considerable research (e.g., Ball-Rokeach et al., 1990; Iyengar & Kinder, 1987; Price, Tewksbury, & Powers, 1997) suggests that media presentation of political issues, by selecting and emphasizing certain values and "considerations" (Zaller, 1992) while excluding others, influences which cognitions are activated as citizens evaluate a political environment. However, these relationships have received little consideration in the arena of race relations. We posit that news coverage of issues influences not only people's thinking about the issues but also the role and import of racial cognitions in their political evaluations and behavior. Specifically, we theorize that news coverage of issues, first, activates existing racial or ethnic stereotypes held by individuals and then, second, influences whether these perceptions are applied in politically meaningful ways, such as in the formation of issue positions or evaluations about whether certain political, economic, or legal outcomes are positive for U.S. society. It is not that media texts determine citizens' political cognitions or behavior; rather, we argue, media coverage interacts with individual predispositions to guide information processing and subsequent judgments.

On the basis of conceptual distinctions developed by Shah, Domke, and Wackman (1996), we contend that individuals may form distinct interpretations of issues based on the activation of particular cognitions. Individuals who form an *ethical interpretation* of an issue understand it in terms of human rights, civil rights, religious morals, or personal principles. Individuals who form a *material interpretation* of an issue understand it in terms of economics, expedience, practicality, or personal self-interest. Many issues that intersect in a significant way with race relations—such as welfare, immigration, and crime—have significant material components and, as a result, are often discussed in terms of economic resources, government services, and pragmatic policy goals. Indeed, social and political elites in the 1990s have predominantly framed immigration in material terms by emphasizing the costs and benefits of particular policies (Borjas, 1996; Citrin et al., 1997).[3] It is not surprising, then, that economic considerations are central to public opinion on this issue, in particular in citizens' evaluations of whether to maintain or reduce current immigration levels.

With this in mind, we theorize that news coverage about U.S. immigration that emphasizes jobs and resources will foster a material interpretation of the issue, since evidence suggests that such a framing of immigration is consonant with (1) much of contemporary public debate and (2) many of the considerations that people already hold. It is almost certainly the case, we recognize, that individuals may also have ethical or moral considerations about immigration and other issues intersecting with race relations. However, because of the substantial emphasis on economic opportunities and resources in both public discourse and opinion, we posit that material-based schema about immigration are likely for most citizens to be both cognitively "available"—that is, present in long-term memory—and "accessible"—that is, relatively salient and thus easily retrieved from memory (see Fiske & Taylor, 1991; Higgins & Bargh, 1987; Higgins & King, 1981). These factors increase the likelihood that a material media frame will foster a material interpretation, particularly among individuals for whom jobs and economic resources are salient. Because of the contemporary political conversation it may be the case that material considerations also will be drawn upon by citizens when news coverage frames immigration in *ethical* terms, but this seems less likely than when the frame is material in emphasis. Accordingly, we now state Hypothesis 1:

H1: Individuals receiving a race-related issue (e.g., immigration) with a material news frame will be more likely to form a material interpretation of the issue than individuals receiving the same issue with an ethical news frame.

We also are interested in how news coverage may influence the cognitive associations formed by individuals as they evaluate a political environment. Some research suggests that a person's mental framework consists of a network of integrated and intersecting concepts and constructs, with the linkages between constructs strengthened each time they are activated in tandem (Anderson, 1985; Collins & Loftus, 1975; Judd & Krosnick, 1989). As a result, Berkowitz and Rogers (1986, pp. 58–59) argue, "When a thought element is activated or brought into focal awareness, the activation radiates out from this particular node along the associative pathways to other nodes," thereby increasing the probability that related constructs will come to mind and influence subsequent evaluations (Goidel, Shields, & Peffley, 1997; Krosnick & Brannon, 1993; Krosnick & Kinder, 1990; Johnston, et al., 1992; Mendelsohn, 1996; Pan & Kosicki, 1997). It may be, then, that news media are in a position to "trigger" priming effects that begin with individuals' thoughts about issues and then, through spreading activation, "carryover" to activate *associated* cognitive elements (Domke, Shah, & Wackman, 1998; Iyengar & Kinder, 1987). In this process it seems likely that news frames, by emphasizing certain considerations and relationships and not others, may help to strengthen (or weaken) the linkages between one mental construct and related ones. Such processes may have substantial implications for politics and race.

In particular, we posit that news frames may influence the relative strength of linkages between people's positions on issues and their perceptions of racial and ethnic groups. Research indicates that certain stereotypes of racial minorities are virtually inevitable and widely held among U.S. adults (Devine, 1989; Marin, 1984; Power, Murphy, & Coover, 1996). Such stereotypes, due to their culturally embedded and enduring nature, are likely to be woven in varying degrees throughout an individual's ideas and judgments about the political landscape. In particular, racial perceptions seem likely to be closely associated with political topics that directly affect race and ethnic relations, such as the issue of immigration. News frames, then, that draw upon *common* patterns of discourse about race-related topics, such as an emphasis on jobs and economic resources in debate about U.S. immigration levels, may activate not only thoughts about the issue *but also associated cognitions about relevant racial and ethnic groups*—in particular Hispanics in the case of immigration. Such a process of spreading activation is likely to occur, we contend, because the mental linkages among race-related policy issues and racial perceptions have developed over time for many citizens and, therefore, are activated with relative ease—even when racial and ethnic groups are *not* explicitly referenced in the discussion—when news coverage emphasizes the dominant framing of the debate.

In contrast, our expectation is that such priming of racial cognitions would be much less likely to occur if news media frame race-related policy coverage in a less common or "alternative" manner, such as by emphasizing human rights or personal responsibility (rather than material concerns) in debate about immigration levels. In such a case, it seems plausible that the news frame, by focusing on ideas and relationships not commonly emphasized, might weaken—or at least temporarily hinder or impede—the linkages between thoughts about the issue and relevant stereotypes because recognition of such relationships would require additional mental effort on the part of citizens, who prefer to expend limited cognitive effort in their information processing and judgments (see Fiske & Taylor, 1991). In essence, then, our view is that the ways in which news media frame political issues may significantly influence the cognitive associations that citizens form between the issue and their racial perceptions. Accordingly, we now state Hypothesis 2:

H2: The relationship between individuals' positions on current immigration levels and their racial perceptions (e.g., of Hispanics) will be much stronger among individuals receiving a material news frame of immigration than among individuals receiving an ethical news frame of immigration.

Further, emphasis on jobs and economic resources in political debate about race-related issues, particularly when this is the dominant framing, may foster close linkages among individuals' racial stereotypes, issue positions, and broader "sociotropic" appraisals—what Kinder and Kiewiet (1981, p. 131) call "rough evaluations of national economic conditions." For example, it seems likely that a material news frame of immigration would strengthen the associations between both (1) an individual's racial perceptions and (2) an individual's position on whether to maintain current immigration levels, with (3) one's evaluation of *whether the U.S. economy, in general,* benefits from immigration. Indeed, research suggests that media coverage plays a crucial role in spurring and shaping sociotropic appraisals among voters in presidential campaigns (Hetherington, 1996; Shah et al., 1999). An ethical frame of immigration, in contrast, by emphasizing considerations essentially unrelated to jobs and economic resources, would seem likely to *weaken*, or at least hinder, linkages among individuals' immigration positions and racial perceptions with their evaluations of whether immigration contributes in a positive manner to the national economy. Accordingly, we now state our final hypothesis:

H3: The relationships between (1) individuals' racial perceptions (e.g., of Hispanics) and (2) positions on immigration with (3) their evaluations of whether the U.S. economy, in general, benefits from immigration will be much stronger among individuals receiving a material news frame of immigration than among individuals receiving an ethical news frame of immigration.

METHODOLOGY

The sample consisted of 172 undergraduate students at a large university in a major metropolitan center in the Midwest (for all study materials, see Domke, McCoy, & Torres, 1999).

Research Design

The core of this research strategy is the controlled presentation of political information environments. Each environment contained newspaper articles that contained the contrasting views of three candidates on four issues in a congressional primary campaign. All subjects received the same articles on three issues—education, crime, and tax cuts. Two experimental conditions were created by differently framing a fourth issue, immigration. In one condition, immigration was framed in material terms; in the second condition, immigration was framed in ethical terms. In carrying out the manipulation, candidate positions and policy implications were the same in both conditions. Thus, this design draws upon the definition of framing as "the presentation of an identical set of consequences of a policy proposal in different ways" (Lau, Smith, & Fiske, 1991, p. 645).

As argued by Entman (1993), framing requires selecting and emphasizing in a text some aspects of a perceived reality so as to promote a particular definition or interpretation of that item. Further, Ball-Rokeach et al. (1990) assert that media frames often implicitly and explicitly link particular values to social issues. Therefore, to textually frame immigration in terms of material values, its material dimensions were stressed: the issue was presented in terms of economics, expedience, tangible resources, and practicality; quotations expressed candidate positions in this manner. To textually frame immigration in terms of ethical values, its ethical dimensions were stressed: the issue was presented in terms of human rights, principles and morality, and personal responsibility; quotations expressed candidate positions in this manner. Notably, no references were made to any racial groups in either version of immigration. The other issues—education, crime, and tax cuts—were framed in material terms and hereafter are referred to as the "controlled" issues.

Several steps were taken to ensure that (1) any observed differences *between* subjects in the two research conditions were due to the framing of immigration, and (2) any observed cognitive effects *within* subjects were initiated by processing of issue—not image—information. Across the political environments, all information was held constant except for varying the frame of immigration. Within environments, subjects were provided with only four items of (identical or nearly identical) personal information about the candidates: gender, age, educational background, and occupational background. Candidates and issues were then rotated in each packet of articles to avoid order effects. Each subject read the articles, then filled out the questionnaire described next. Most subjects took 35 to 45 minutes to complete the materials.

Measurement

The questionnaire began by asking subjects to make a candidate choice and then probed their thoughts and evaluations of several components of the political environment.

Subjects' positions on the issues were measured by their level of agreement with statements corresponding to the policy positions of issues. For each issue, candidates disagreed about whether a policy proposal should be pursued, so subjects were asked their level of support for the same policy; for crime, subjects were asked their positions on two differing proposals suggested by candidates because no candidates oppose taking steps to reduce crime. For all issues, responses were placed on a five-point continuum, ranging from "strongly disagree" to "strongly agree." To facilitate interpretation in analysis, subjects' responses were coded in a directionally consistent manner, from 1 = conservative to 5 = liberal on each issue.

Individual interpretations of the issues were measured by open-ended questions that engaged subjects in a thought-listing procedure to tap how the issues related to their personal values, concerns about society, and personal life situations. Three subjects did not answer the question about crime, and one did not answer the question about tax cuts. In all other cases, each issue was coded for whether it received a material interpretation, an ethical interpretation, or both. Issues were coded as receiving a *material interpretation* if the individual discussed the issue in terms of economics, expedience, practicality, or personal self-interest. Issues were coded as receiving an *ethical interpretation* if the individual discussed the issue within the framework of human rights, civil rights, religious morals, or personal principles. To be clear, individuals could receive a coding of material, ethical, or both, regardless of their position on an issue; the interpretation of the issue focuses on what considerations are in active thought about an issue. Four coders working in pairs agreed on 585 of 688 individual-issue codings, producing an inter-coder reliability coefficient of .85, which was 78% greater than by chance. The remaining 103 individual-issue codings were discussed and then classified.

Next, subjects were asked to indicate their impression of how common certain characteristics are among members of particular racial and ethnic groups. The seven attributes were violent/hostile, quiet, nurturing/caring, rich, lazy, intelligent, and weak; responses were placed on a seven-point scale, ranging from 1 = very uncommon to 7 = very common. This measurement approach was drawn from research identifying these attribute dimensions as part of commonly held stereotypes of racial and ethnic minorities (Devine, 1989; Power, Murphy, & Coover et al., 1996). In this study, our focus is on evaluations of Hispanics because public discourse and opinion about immigration shows clear linkages to perceptions of immigrants from Mexico, Latin America, and/or Hispanics.[4] However, to ascertain whether the participants in this study linked Hispanics with immigration, subjects (later in the questionnaire) were asked to estimate what percent of legal immigrants arriving to the United States in the past year originated from Mexico and what percent originated from "all Asian countries." The mean responses were 27.4% from Mexico and 25.1% from Asia. In reality in 1997, 18.4% of legal immigrants arrived from Mexico and 33.3% arrived from Asian nations (Immigration and Naturalization Service, 1999). It appears, then, that these subjects did indeed perceive a close linkage between people from Mexico, that is, Hispanics, and legal immigration while, at the same time, they substantially underestimated the linkage between people from Asia and immigration.

Subjects' "sociotropic" impressions of whether or not the U.S. economy, in general, benefits from immigration were measured by responses to three statements:

(1) "immigrants to this country tend to take jobs away from people already here"; (2) "immigrants to this country tend to contribute to lower wages for many workers"; and (3) "immigrants to this country tend to provide needed labor for new jobs." These questions were drawn from previous research on immigration and national economic perceptions (Citrin, Reingold, & Green, 1990; Citrin et al., 1997). For each statement, subjects placed their responses on a five-point continuum ranging from 1 = strongly disagree to 5 = strongly agree. Items were coded so that a low score meant a respondent thought immigrants contributed negatively to the U.S. economy, and a high score meant that a subject thought immigrants contributed positively to the U.S. economy. Responses to these items were then used to build an additive "U.S. economy" index, which had mean inter-item correlations of .45 and a Cronbach's alpha of .71.

Finally, demographic information also was collected, as part of a preexperimental questionnaire completed one month before subjects were presented with experimental materials. Subjects indicated their race (87% white), age (91% between ages of 18 and 22), income of the household in which they grew up (ascending fairly evenly beginning at $20,000), and, on a seven-point scale from 1 = very liberal to 7 = very conservative, political ideology (53 percent on liberal side of scale, 28 percent at mid-point, and 19% on conservative side).

RESULTS

Hypothesis 1 was tested at the experimental level. Hypotheses 2 and 3 were tested within experimental conditions, an approach that allowed us to get "within the cognitive system of the individual" (Lavine et al., 1996, p. 298).

Hypothesis 1

In general, Hypothesis 1 posits that news frames will influence how individuals think about issues, including race-related topics such as immigration. Specifically, the prediction is that individuals presented with a material textual frame of immigration will be more likely to form a material interpretation of the issue than individuals presented with an ethical textual frame. To test this hypothesis, crosstabulations were run between the experimental conditions and subjects' interpretations of immigration (see Table 10.1).

The hypothesis received strong support. As the results in Table 10.1 show, almost 72% of subjects who received immigration with a material frame interpreted the issue in solely material terms, compared to the roughly 52% of subjects who received the ethical frame of immigration. Indeed, subjects who received the ethical frame of immigration were much more likely to include a mixture of ethical and material considerations in their thinking about the issue, while the percentage of subjects interpreting immigration in solely ethical terms was low and virtually identical (roughly 10%) regardless of experimental condition. These results, then, simultaneously suggest that (1) the dominant conception of immigration is based on material concerns, as suggested by previous evidence, and (2) the framing of a

Table 10.1
Textual Frame of Immigration by Interpretation of the Issue

Issue Interpretation	TEXTUAL FRAME	
	Ethical	Material
Ethical	9.2% (n = 8)	10.6% (n = 9)
Ethical & Material	39.1% (n = 34)	17.6% (n = 15)
Material	51.7% (n = 45)	71.8% (n = 61)
Totals	100% (n = 87)	100% (n = 85)

$X^2 = 9.8$, d.f. = 2, p <.01.

news story can indeed alter the considerations that come to mind about an issue. In particular, it appears that the ethical news frame *added* ethically based considerations to subjects' already existing material concerns about immigration, rather than *replacing* the prior cognitions.

Hypothesis 2

Hypothesis 2 examines whether a connection exists between subjects' positions on U.S. immigration levels and their perceptions of Hispanics on several attributes. We focus on appraisals of Hispanics because, as suggested by public discourse and opinion as well as subjects' estimates of the area of origin of recent U.S. immigrants, it seems likely that perceptions of Hispanics would be cognitively linked with individuals' schema, particularly material-based schema, about immigration. Our hypothesis predicts that this cognitive association will be stronger for individuals who receive the material frame of immigration than for individuals who receive the ethical frame.

To test this hypothesis, we examined the correlation between subjects' immigration positions and Hispanic evaluations *separately* for subjects within the differing experimental conditions. Among subjects receiving the material frame of immigration, we expected an identifiable pattern of linkages, which would suggest a close association between subjects' immigration positions and racial perceptions and that these mental constructs were consistently activated in tandem. In contrast, among subjects receiving the ethical frame of immigration, there should not be a distinguishable pattern of linkages, which would suggest that immigration positions and racial perceptions were essentially unassociated in subjects' information

Table 10.2
Partial Correlations between Position on Immigration and Hispanic
Evaluations Controlling for All Other Hispanic Evaluations

POSITION ON IMMIGRATION[a]

Hispanic Evaluations[b]	Ethical Frame	Material Frame
Violent	.17	-.38**
Quiet	.04	-.01
Nurturing	.02	.26*
Rich	-.05	.03
Lazy	-.06	.22*
Intelligent	.11	-.17
Weak	-.05	-.06
	(n = 83)	(n = 85)

Notes: Correlations control for subjects' evaluations of
Hispanics on other attributes a) Immigration position: 1 = reduce
current levels, 5 = maintain current levels b) Hispanic evaluations:
1 = attribute very uncommon, 7 = attribute very common.
**p < .001, *p < .05.

processing. Partial correlations were run, controlling for subjects' perceptions of
Hispanics on the other attributes (see Table 10.2).

Several points are noteworthy about these results. First, there were *no* significant correlations between immigration position and subjects' evaluations of Hispanics on the seven attributes when immigration was framed in an ethical manner. While these results do not necessarily indicate that the ethical news frame *weakened* the linkages among these cognitions, it clearly did not facilitate *strong* associations among them.

In contrast, for subjects receiving a material frame of the issue, three significant correlations are present. First, there is a strong negative correlation ($r = -.38$) between a perception of Hispanics as violent and immigration position, indicating that subjects who perceive Hispanics as violent want to reduce immigration levels. Second, there is a positive correlation ($r = .26$) between a perception of Hispanics as nurturing and a desire to maintain current immigration levels. These two correlations intuitively make sense. Third and a bit more surprising, however, is the modest positive correlation ($r = .22$) between a perception of Hispanics as lazy (and to a lesser degree, a view of Hispanics as not intelligent) and a desire to maintain current immigration levels. It may be that subjects want to maintain immigration levels *despite* a perception of Hispanics as lazy or unintelligent. Or perhaps, in part *because* of a perception of Hispanics as not highly ambitious and unintelligent—and thus not likely to provide significant competition in the work force—these subjects support immigration levels. Hypothesis 3 analysis may provide further insight into these data.

Hypothesis 3

The third hypothesis examined whether priming individuals to think in material or ethical terms influenced the cognitive linkages between (1) evaluations of Hispanics and (2) positions on appropriate immigration levels, *with* (3) subjects' "sociotropic" assessments about immigration. Specifically, our prediction is that the associations between both issue positions and perceptions of Hispanics with evaluations of whether immigrants contribute positively to the U.S. economy will be much stronger among subjects receiving the material frame of immigration than among subjects receiving the ethical frame.

Consistent with the approach used to test Hypothesis 2, we again conducted analysis separately for subjects within the differing experimental conditions. To test this hypothesis, we ran step-wise linear regressions with the "U.S. economy" index (range: 3 to 15) as the dependent variable and 16 predictor variables entered in three distinct blocks. Demographics were entered in the first block as a baseline.[5] Block two consisted of perceptions of Hispanics on the seven attributes. The third block consisted of positions on each of the issues. Within blocks, variables were entered simultaneously (see Table 10.3). Regression analysis was performed for two reasons: (1) to assess the simultaneous influence of subjects' racial perceptions and issue positions, which might offer insights beyond the correlational analysis in Table 10.2; and (2) to examine whether the news frames influenced the amount of variance explained in subjects' evaluations of whether immigrants contribute positively to the U.S. economy.

Several points are noteworthy about the results in Table 10.3. First, equations in both conditions explained a sizable amount of variance in subjects' assessments about the role of immigration in national economic conditions.

Nonetheless, the final equation in the material news frame condition explained nearly *three times* more variance, 59%, in subjects' appraisals of the role of immigration in the U.S. economy than the equation in the ethical news frame, 22%. These results indicate that demographic factors, perceptions of Hispanics, and the issue positions exerted considerably more influence upon subjects' appraisals of whether immigration benefits the U.S. economy when the issue was framed in terms of jobs and tangible resources.

Second, the demographic blocks, entered first, accounted for virtually the same variance (15% and 18%) in the two conditions. Notably, though, once all three variable blocks were entered into the equations, no demographic factor was a consistent predictor across experimental conditions of subjects' sociotropic evaluations about immigration. These results, then, are suggestive that information processing and subsequent judgments about race and politics are guided by the *interaction* between media coverage and individual predispositions.

Third, the results indicate that as predicted, the news frames significantly influenced the role of subjects' Hispanic perceptions in their sociotropic assessments.

Table 10.3
U.S. Economy Index Regressed on Relevant Variables

TEXTUAL FRAME OF IMMIGRATION

	Ethical Frame			Material Frame		
	Eq 1	Eq 2	Eq 3	Eq 1	Eq 2	Eq 3
Demographics						
Ideology	-.22*	-.23*	-.11	-.31*	-.36*	-.31*
Race	-.31*	-.34*	-.38*	-.24*	-.20*	-.13
Household income	.08	-.11	-.08	.11	.14	.03
Age	.21*	.19+	.19+	.23*	.27*	.14
Hispanic Evaluations[a]						
Violent		.03	.02		-.50**	-.20+
Quiet		.08	.05		-.11	-.07
Nurturing		.22+	.23+		.22+	.10
Rich		-.16	-.13		.17+	.09
Lazy		.07	.10		.30*	.11
Intelligent		-.05	-.02		-.42*	-.25*
Weak		-.03	-.02		-.14	-.15+
Issue Position[b]						
Immigration			.32*			.53**
Education			.05			-.11
Crime (programs)			-.04			-.19+
Crime (police)			.06			.02
Taxes			-.04			-.04
Incremental R^2	.18	.01	.03	.15	.21	.23
Adjusted R^2	.18	.19	.22	.15	.36	.59
	(n = 78)	(n = 78)	(n = 78)	(n = 74)	(n = 74)	(n = 74)

Notes: U.S. economy index: Low = immigrants contribute negatively, high = immigrants contribute positively. a. Hispanic evaluations: 1 = very uncommon, 7 = very common
b. Issue positions: 1 = conservative position, 5 = liberal position.
**$p < .001$, *$p < .05$, +$p < .10$.

Before the issue positions were added to the regression equations, the attributes block accounted for 21% of variance in the material frame condition, compared to only 1% of the variance in the ethical frame condition. Further, among subjects receiving the material frame of immigration, perceptions of Hispanics on the attributes of intelligent (beta of -.25) and to a lesser degree violent (-.20) and weak (-.15) made meaningful contributions even after the issue positions were added to the equations. In combination with Table 10.2 findings (which indicate that there also are linkages between these subjects' Hispanic perceptions and issue positions), the data suggest the following associative patterns among these subjects:

those who want to reduce immigration levels and see it as a negative for the U.S. economy may hold these views, in part, because they see Hispanics as violent, while subjects who want to maintain immigration levels and see it as a positive for the U.S. economy may hold these views, in part, because they see Hispanics as being nurturing and not overly ambitious or intelligent yet providing needed low-skill (and, likely, relatively low-wage) labor for the U.S. market—the latter two of which are likely to *not* be the future that university students imagine for themselves. In contrast, among subjects who received the ethical frame of immigration, a perception of Hispanics as nurturing (a final beta of .23) was the only attribute evaluation that contributed to subjects' views of whether the U.S. economy benefits from immigration. These results, then, further highlight the complexity of these relationships and the need for further research.

Finally, when all the variable blocks were entered in the equations, the role and import of immigration position differed considerably between the research conditions, as indicated by both the issue position beta weights and the incremental variance explained by the final variable block. Among subjects receiving the material news frame, immigration position clearly exerted the greatest influence on subjects' sociotropic assessments: immigration position had a beta of .53 and the final variable block of issue positions explained 23% of variance in the U.S. economy index. Among subjects receiving the ethical frame of immigration, while immigration position had a beta of .32 the final variable block explained only 3% of variance in subjects' sociotropic assessments. The evidence, then, strongly suggests that news coverage influenced the strength of the cognitive associations among subjects' racial perceptions, positions on immigration levels, and their sociotropic evaluations about the role of immigrants in the national economy.

DISCUSSION

These findings offer insights into the relations among news media, individuals' racial perceptions, and political cognitions. The results suggest that (1) news coverage influences the considerations that individuals draw upon in thinking about political issues, as suggested by previous work (Ball-Rokeach et al., 1990; Iyengar & Kinder, 1987; Price, Tewksbury, & Powers 1997; Shah, Domke, & Wackman, 1996; Zaller, 1992); and (2) news coverage of issues *also* influences which racial cognitions are activated and how strongly those cognitions are linked to political judgments. For example, data in Table 10.2 show a significant relationship between perceptions of Hispanics on several attributes and positions on U.S. immigration levels among people presented with a material frame of immigration, while such relations were *not* found among individuals presented with an ethical frame of immigration. In a similar pattern, data in Table 10.3 show a link—indeed, a strong link—between racial perceptions and sociotropic evaluations of the role of immigration in the U.S. economy only among people presented with a material frame of immigration. Further, the results in Table 10.3 indicate that among individuals receiving the material frame, perceptions of Hispanics substantially contributed to sociotropic evaluations about immigration even when issue positions were taken into consideration.

The findings provide strong support for our theory that news coverage of issues that intersect substantially with race relations, by *priming* subjects to focus on some considerations and relationships and not others, influences the linkages between individuals' racial cognitions and their political evaluations. Specifically, it appears that news frames about race-related issues—in this case, immigration—not only activate thoughts about the issue, but also engage associated schema about relevant racial and ethnic minority groups—in this case, Hispanics. Such a process of spreading activation is likely to occur, we suggest, because the cognitive linkages among race-related policy issues and racial perceptions already exist for many citizens and, therefore, are activated with relative ease when such issues are emphasized in news coverage. Further, the associations among issue positions, racial perceptions, and sociotropic assessments may be particularly strong when news coverage focuses on ideas and relationships—in particular, material considerations—that are commonly emphasized by social and political elites and are a dominant feature of the political discourse. These findings, then, support the perspective that news media are in position to "trigger" priming effects that begin with individuals' thoughts about issues and then activate associated cognitive elements (Domke, Shah & Wackmman, 1998; Iyengar & Kinder, 1987; Krosnick & Kinder, 1990; Pan & Kosicki, 1997).

This research suggests that even when specific racial images, which have been the focus of considerable research, are *not* present in the news, coverage of politics nonetheless still intersects in important ways with race relations. In particular, how elites and media frame issues may significantly influence whether individuals apply existing racial stereotypes in a politically meaningful manner, such as in the formation of issue positions or evaluations about whether certain political, economic, or legal outcomes are positive for U.S. society. For example, although no references were made to any racial or ethnic groups, the news frames in this study influenced whether individuals drew upon common, stereotypical perceptions of Hispanics in their judgments about immigration. While this study is not without limitations, some of which are noted later, such insight into how individuals process, interpret, and use race-related information and images in their political decision making is, for the most part, missing from scholarship interested in the linkages between mass media and race. As this study and some recent survey analyses (Gandy & Baron, 1998; Pan & Kosicki, 1996) suggest, much further research is needed on the often subtle—and, we suspect for many individuals, unconscious and undesired—cognitive routes through which news coverage and citizens' racial perceptions *interact* to influence political judgments and social relations more broadly.

For example, understanding the linkages among news media, racial perceptions, and political cognitions may shed light on how individuals process information in forming judgments about a number of policy domains. Consider welfare, which has significant material dimensions *and* racial overtones. Polls indicate that citizens support adding job training and day care to welfare reform, but only as long as such efforts do not cost taxpayers more money (Princeton/Kaiser/Harvard, 1996). At the same time, Gilens (1996) found that anti-black attitudes were the single most important factor shaping whites' views of welfare funding (see also Sniderman & Piazza, 1993). Our findings, however, suggest that a crucial mediating factor in these relationships may be the manner in which the debate about welfare is framed by elites and news media. In particular, the linkage between citizens' racial perceptions and issue position may be strengthened by an emphasis in discourse upon material concerns, because of the central role of these features in the political conversation. In contrast, these linkages may be weakened—or at least temporarily hindered or impeded—by an emphasis in discourse upon alternative or less-commonly heard considerations, such as ethical or moral values, collective rather than particularized goals (see Gamson, 1992), and consensus over conflict (see Patterson, 1993). In addition to welfare, these relationships should be explored with other issues that intersect in significant ways with race relations, such as affirmative action and crime, both of which have been the focus of considerable debate and legislation in recent years.

Further, it is noteworthy that, in this study, negative perceptions of Hispanics were associated with individuals' positions on both sides of immigration, which seems suggestive of the culturally embedded nature of racial and ethnic stereotypes *regardless of issue preferences and political ideology*. Among people who received the material frame, individuals who perceived Hispanics as violent wanted to reduce immigration, which is an association that might be expected. More surprising is that individuals who supported current immigration levels and believed that immigration contributed positively to the U.S. economy *also* perceived Hispanics as relatively unintelligent, lazy, and weak. It may be that support for immigration is tied, in part, to a perception of Hispanics as less-intelligent, less-ambitious, and non-threatening individuals who provide needed low-skill labor. While such a viewpoint seems plausible among this subject population of undergraduate students, who are not likely to see themselves as pursuing the types of jobs they may envision for Hispanic immigrants, support for this interpretation is also available outside the laboratory. For example, in a recent survey 71% of randomly sampled U.S. adults said that immigrants "mostly take low-paying jobs Americans don't want" (Gallup Organization, 1999). At a minimum, therefore, it seems important for future research on news media and race to distinguish citizens' political ideology or positions on race-related policy issues *from* their racial perceptions, since we suspect that the latter is the stronger predictor of how individuals of differing racial and ethnic groups interact on a daily basis.

While this study offers insights into media effects in race relations, we recognize that it has some weaknesses. In particular, we theorize that priming effects spurred by media coverage depend on the associations and inter-connections within an individual's mental system; with this perspective, we found that news coverage substantially influences the strength of the linkages among individuals' racial perceptions, positions on immigration, and sociotropic assessments. We are unable, however, to offer concrete evidence of the relations among mental constructs, partly due to the difficulty in getting inside the cognitive "black box." Fu-

138   News

ture research on news media, race, and politics should explore media effects by
using measurement strategies that explore in greater depth (1) whether an individual's amount of *contact* with differing racial and ethnic groups serves as a mediating factor in the link between racial cognitions and political judgments, as Allport
(1954) and others have suggested (Sigelman & Welch, 1993; Tan, Fujioka, &
Lucht, 1997), and (2) the potential explanatory power of variables such as degree
of political sophistication, need for cognition, amount of political knowledge,
level of integrative complexity, and extent of public affairs media use. Research
that examines these factors—with, for example, politically active populations living in urban areas—would be an important step toward understanding the contributions to contemporary politics of news media and racial cognitions.

NOTES

1. About 1 million people immigrate to the United States each year, the vast majority of
these through legal avenues (American Immigration Lawyers Association, 1998; Fix &
Passel, 1994; National Research Council, 1997).

2. In this article, we follow Bobo (1997) in using, for the sake of simplicity, the term
"race" rather than "ethnicity" or the cumbersome phrase "race and ethnicity." Our perspective is that both "race" and "ethnicity" constitute social constructions that are "historical,
cultural, and, above all else, interpretative products of the human capacity for creating
'meaning' " (Bobo, 1997, p. 2).

3. To gain additional insight into the relative presence in news coverage of material and
ethical arguments about immigration, we searched news stories in the NEXIS database using terms indicative of the differing frames. The search string for *material* was "United
States or America and immigration and econom! or job or work or labor or employ! or wage
or material or resource," while the search string for *ethical* was "United States or America
and immigration and human right or civil right or freedom or moral or ethical or liberty or
fair! or equal! or responsibility." We searched content from 1994 to 1999 in the following
news outlets: *New York Times, Los Angeles Times, San Francisco Chronicle, Miami Herald, Houston Chronicle*, and *Washington Post*. A total of 1,415 stories were identified by
the material search string, 780 stories were identified by the ethical search string, and 145
stories were identified by both search strings. While obviously lacking the detail of a content analysis, these results suggest, as do previous research and essays that we draw upon in
our theoretical argument, that material concerns have been more central to the immigration
debate than ethical concerns. Further, these results suggest that, at least in news coverage,
relatively little overlap exists between material and ethical viewpoints, which is consistent
with the design of our experiment in which the two frames were distinct. To be clear, we
recognize that other frames of immigration either exist or could exist, as we discuss in the
discussion section.

4. Subjects' mean scores on the Hispanic attributes were largely unaffected by the experimental manipulation. For violent/hostile, means were 4.0 (material frame) and 3.9 (ethical
frame); for quiet, 4.0 and 4.0; for nurturing/caring, 4.7 and 4.5; for rich, 2.8 and 2.6; for lazy,
3.6 and 3.8; for intelligent, 4.2 and 3.9, a difference significant at p < .05; for weak, 3.3 and
3.5. This general pattern in the data provided further confidence that perceptions of Hispanics were cognitively available to a similar degree for the subjects in this study. The *role* and
impact of these perceptions in a political environment is the focus of Hypotheses 2 and 3.

5. The demographic variables were coded as follows for the regression equations. Age is just that. Race is 0 = nonwhite, 1 = white. Household income (from home raised in) ascends in $20,000 increments from 1 = less than $20,000 to 6 = more than $100,001. Political ideology ranges from 1 = very liberal to 7 = very conservative.

REFERENCES

Allport, G. W. (1954). *The nature of prejudice*. Cambridge: Addison Wesley.

American Immigration Lawyers Association. (1998). About immigration. http://www.a-ila.org/aboutimmigration.html, 1–6.

Anderson, J. R. (1985). *Cognitive psychology and its implications*. New York: Freeman.

Ball-Rokeach, S. J., Power, G. J., Guthrie, K. K., & Waring, H. R. (1990). Value-framing abortion in the United States: An application of media system dependency theory. *International Journal of Public Opinion Research, 2*, 249–273.

Berkowitz, L., & Rogers, K. H. (1986). A priming effect analysis of media influences. In J. Bryant & D. Zillman (Eds.), *Perspectives on media effects* (pp. 57–81). Hillsdale, NJ: Erlbaum.

Bobo, L. (1997). Race, public opinion, and the social sphere. *Public Opinion Quarterly, 61*, 1–15.

Borjas, G. J. (1996, November). The new economics of immigration. *Atlantic Monthly, 278*, 72–80.

Citrin, J., Green, D. P., Muste, C., & Wong, C. (1997). Public opinion toward immigration reform: The role of economic motivations. *Journal of Politics, 59*, 858–881.

Citrin, J., Reingold, B., & Green, D. P. (1990). American identity and the politics of ethnic change. *Journal of Politics, 52*, 1124–1154.

Collins, A. M., & Loftus, E. F. (1975). A spreading activation theory of semantic processing. *Psychological Review, 82*, 407–428.

Devine, P. G. (1989). Stereotypes and prejudice: Their automatic and controlled components. *Journal of Personality and Social Psychology, 56*, 5–18.

Domke, D., McCoy, K., & Torres, M. (1999). News media, racial perceptions, and political cognition. *Communication Research, 26*, 570–607.

Domke, D., Shah, D. V., & Wackman, D. (1998). Media priming effects: Accessibility, association, and activation. *International Journal of Public Opinion Research, 1*, 51–74.

Entman, R. M. (1993). Framing: Toward clarification of a fractured paradigm. *Journal of Communication, 43* (4), 51–58.

Fiske, S., & Taylor, S. (1991). *Social cognition*. New York: McGraw-Hill.

Fix, M., & Passel, J. S. (1994). *Immigration and immigrants: Setting the record straight* (pp. 1–84). Washington, DC: The Urban Institute.

Gallup Organization (1999). Poll with questions about immigration. Conducted February 26–28. Obtained through Roper Center at the University of Connecticut.

Gamson, W. (1992). *Talking politics*. New York: Cambridge University Press.

Gandy, O. H., & Baron, J. (1998). Inequality: It's all in the way you look at it. *Communication Research, 25*, 505–527.

Gilens, M. (1996). "Race coding" and white opposition to welfare. *American Political Science Review, 90*, 593–604.

Goidel, R. K., Shields, T. G., & Peffley, M. (1997). Priming theory and RAS models: Toward an integrated perspective of media influence. *American Politics Quarterly, 25,* 287–318.

Hetherington, M. J. (1996). The media's role in forming voters' national economic evaluations in 1992. *American Journal of Political Science, 40,* 372–395.

Higgins, E. T., & Bargh, J. A. (1987). Social cognition and social perception. *Annual Review of Psychology, 38,* 369–425.

Higgins, E. T., & King, G. (1981). Accessibility of social constructs: Information-processing consequences of individual and contextual variability. In N. Cantor & J. Kihlstrom (Eds.), *Personality, cognition, and social interaction* (pp. 69–121). Hillsdale, NJ: Erlbaum.

Hufker, B., & Cavender, G. (1990). From freedom flotilla to America's burden: The social construction of the Mariel immigrants. *Sociological Quarterly, 31,* 321–335.

Hurwitz, J., & Peffley, M. (1997). Public perceptions of race and crime: The role of racial stereotypes. *American Journal of Political Science, 41,* 375–401.

Immigration and Naturalization Service, U.S. Department of Justice (1999). *Legal immigration, fiscal year 1997.* Washington, DC: U.S. Government Printing Office.

Iyengar, S., & Kinder, D. R. (1987). *News that matters.* Chicago: University of Chicago Press.

Jamieson, K. H. (1992). *Dirty politics.* New York: Oxford University Press.

Johnson, K. R. (1997). The new nativism: Something old, something new, something borrowed, something blue. In J. F. Perea (Ed.), *Immigrants out: The new nativism and the anti immigrant impulse in the United States* (pp. 165–189). New York: New York University Press.

Johnston, R., Blais, A., Brady, H. E., & Crête, J. (1992). *Letting the people decide: Dynamics of a Canadian election.* Stanford: Stanford University Press.

Judd, C. M., & Krosnick, J. A. (1989). The structural bases of consistency among political attitudes: Effects of political expertise and attitude importance. In A. R. Pratkanis, S. J. Breckler, & A. G. Greenwald (Eds.), *Attitude structure and function* (pp. 99–128). Hillsdale, NJ: Erlbaum.

Kinder, D. R., & Kiewiet, D. R. (1981). Sociotropic politics: The American case. *British Journal of Political Science, 11,* 129–161.

Kinder, D. R., & Sanders, L. M. (1996). *Divided by color: Racial politics and democratic ideals.* Chicago: University of Chicago Press.

Knight-Ridder. (1997). Poll with questions about immigration. Conducted May 2–26. Obtained through Roper Center at the University of Connecticut.

Krosnick, J. A., & Brannon, L. (1993). The media and the foundations of presidential support: George Bush and the Persian Gulf conflict. *Journal of Social Issues, 49,* 167–182.

Krosnick, J. A., & Kinder, D. R. (1990). Altering the foundations of support for the president through priming. *American Political Science Review, 84,* 497–512.

Lau, R., Smith, R. A., & Fiske, S. T. (1991). Political beliefs, policy interpretations, and political persuasion. *Journal of Politics, 53,* 644–675.

Lavine, H., Sullivan, J. L., Borgida, E., & Thomsen, C. J. (1996). The relationship of national and personal issue salience to attitude accessibility on foreign and domestic policy issues. *Political Psychology, 17,* 293–316.

Macias, J. (1996). Resurgence of ethnic nationalism in California and Germany: The impact on recent progress in education. *Anthropology and Education Quarterly, 27* (2), 232–252.

Marin, G. (1984). Stereotyping Hispanics: The differential effect of research method, label, and degree of contact. *International Journal of Intercultural Relations, 8*, 17–27.

Mendelsohn, M. (1996). The media and interpersonal communications: The priming of issues, leaders, and party identification. *Journal of Politics, 58*, 112–125.

Miller, J. (1994). Immigration, the press, and the new racism. *Media Studies Journal, 8* (3), 19–28.

National Research Council. (1997). *Overall U.S. economy gains from immigration, but it's costly to some states and localities*. Released in May by the Commission on Behavioral and Social Sciences and Education, and the Committee on Population.

NBC News/Wall Street Journal (1998). Poll with questions about immigration. Conducted December 3–6. Obtained through Roper Center at the University of Connecticut.

New, W. S., & Petronicolos, L. (1996). Rereading the record: The rhetoric of anti-immigrant legislation and education. Paper presented at the annual meeting of the American Educational Research Association, Chicago. (http://www.uwosh.edu/faculty_staff/petronic/pages/paper-2.htm, 1–10).

Pan, Z., & Kosicki, G. M. (1996). Assessing news media influences on the formation of whites' racial policy preferences. *Communication Research, 23*, 147–178.

Pan, Z., & Kosicki, G. M. (1997). Priming and media impact on the evaluation of the president's performance. *Communication Research, 24*, 3–30.

Passel, J. S., & Fix, M. (1994). Myths about immigrants. *Foreign Policy, 95*, 151–160.

Patterson, T. (1993). *Out of order*. New York: Vintage Books.

Peffley, M., Shields, T., & Williams, B. (1996). The intersection of race and crime in television news stories: An experimental study. *Political Communication, 13*, 309–327.

Power, J. G., Murphy S. T., & Coover, G. (1996). Priming prejudice: How stereotypes and counter-stereotypes influence attribution of responsibility and credibility among ingroups and outgroups. *Human Communication Research, 23*, 36–58.

Price, V., Tewksbury, D., & Powers, E. (1997). Switching trains of thought: The impact of news frames on readers' cognitive responses. *Communication Research, 24*, 481–506.

Princeton Survey/Kaiser Family Foundation/Harvard. (1996). Poll with questions about welfare and taxpayer dollars. Conducted in November. Obtained through Public Agenda Online, http://www.publicagenda.org.

Shah, D. V., Domke, D., & Wackman, D. (1996). "To thine own self be true": Values, framing, and voter decision-making strategies. *Communication Research, 23*, 509–560.

Shah, D. V., Watts, M. D., Domke, D., Fibison, M., & Fan, D. P. (1999). News coverage, economic cues, and the public's presidential preferences: 1984–1996. *Journal of Politics, 61*, 914–943.

Sigelman, L., & Welch, S. (1993). The contact hypothesis revisited: Black-white interaction and positive racial attitudes. *Social Forces, 71*, 781–795.

Simon, R. J., & Alexander, S. H. (1993). *The ambivalent welcome: Print media, public opinion, and immigration*. Westport, CT: Praeger.

Sniderman, P. M., & Piazza, T. (1993). *The scar of race*. Cambridge, MA: Harvard University Press.

Srull, T., & Wyer, R. (1989). Person memory and judgment. *Psychological Review, 96*, 58–83.

Suarez-Orozco, M. M. (1996). California dreaming: Proposition 187 and the cultural psy-
    chology of racial and ethnic exclusion. *Anthropology and Education Quarterly, 27*
    (2), 151–167.
Tan, A., Fujioka, Y., & Lucht, N. (1997). Native American stereotypes, TV portrayals, and
    personal contact. *Journalism & Mass Communication Quarterly, 74*, 265–284.
Time/Cable News Network (1993). Poll with questions about immigration. Conducted Sep-
    tember 8–9. Obtained through Roper Center at the University of Connecticut.
Tolbert, C. J., & Hero, R. E. (1996). Race/ethnicity and direct democracy: An analysis of
    California's illegal immigration initiative. *Journal of Politics, 58*, 806–818.
Valentino, N. A. (1999). Crime news and the priming of racial attitudes during evaluations
    of the president. *Public Opinion Quarterly, 63*, 293–320.
Zaller, J. (1992). *The nature and origins of mass opinion.* Cambridge: Cambridge Univer-
    sity Press.

Part III: Advertising

Chapter 11

Hispanics, Advertising, and Alcohol: Cultivation Theory and Panethnic Beer Commercials on the Univision Television Network

Frank G. Perez

INTRODUCTION

Recent demographic changes have prompted the growth in popularity of Spanish-language television in the United States. The increase of multinational corporations that advertise on Spanish-language television to specifically target Hispanics[1] exemplifies this shift. This study examines the construction of Hispanic identity in beer commercials on Univision, the Spanish-language television network with the largest market share of Hispanic viewers in the United States. (Univision, 1998a). Specifically, it analyzes beer commercials for Bud Light and for Miller Genuine Draft (MGD) to determine their possible ramifications for Spanish-language advertising.

This chapter addresses two important media issues related to the Hispanic population. First, the images in these commercials potentially illuminate how Univision viewers are influenced to perceive Hispanics. Scholars argue that television influences how people view themselves and others (Gerbner et al. 1994; Lull, 1995; Real, 1989). Second, the present study examines a topic outside the realm of current scholarship. Most Hispanic mass media research focuses on film (e.g., Keller, 1994; Noriega, 1992, 2000). My interest here is to promote better understanding of how Hispanic identity is constructed in Spanish-language beer commercials from the perspective of *cultivation theory,* which argues that frequent viewer exposure to mass mediated messages alters individual perceptions of reality (Shanahan & Morgan, 1999). Cultivation analysis provides a theoretical perspective and methodology that examines the potential effects of frequently repeated images or stereotypes in media, particularly television.

Beer commercials on Univision typically use stereotypic constructions of Hispanic identity for product promotion. This strategy minimizes cost and establishes
a precedent for future marketing. In addition to saving money for advertisers, this
strategy is important because it is used in the television commercials produced for
Univision. As the most popular Spanish-language television network in the United
States, Univision serves as a trendsetter in its industry. Smaller, less influential
media outlets typically copy the leaders in their field (Dearing & Rogers, 1996).
Beer companies also sponsor many Univision-produced programs (e.g.,
"Republica Deportiva," "Sabado Gigante").

The Political Economy of Univision

Like all commercial television networks, Univision requires solid economic resources, a number of affiliated television stations, broadcast outlets, programming
that attracts a large market share, and continual marketing and promotion in order
to remain profitable (Bagdikian, 1999). When judged by these criteria, Univision
is the most successful national Spanish-language television network in the United
States.

The Univision network currently consists of 47 stations in the US, 20 of which
are owned and operated by Univision (the other 27 stations are Univision affili-
ates). The network is available on over 800 cable systems across the United States.
(Univision, 1998b). It is owned by three principal entities—Jerry Perenchino, a
media entrepreneur (50%); the Cisneros brothers, owners of Venevision, a Vene-
zuelan broadcasting company (25%); and Televisa, a Mexican broadcasting and
media conglomerate (25%) (Rodriguez, 1996). These connections with foreign
media entities allow Univision to purchase and broadcast Mexican, as well as Ven-
ezuelan, programming. The network also has television production studios in Miami, Florida.

As the primary source for Spanish-language television programming in the
United States, Univision provides a "foreign" market through which multination-
als can reach bilingual (English/Spanish) and Spanish-dominant consumers.
These consumers constitute a growing market segment that spent an estimated
$380 billion on consumer goods in 1998; this amount is expected to reach $938 bil-
lion by 2010 (DRI/McGraw-Hill, 1995, cited in Univision, 1998b). Thus
Univision provides multinationals access to a highly coveted market
(Chan-Olmsted & Albarran, 1998).

This study analyzes four beer commercials that aired on Univison during October and November 1998, two commercials each for Bud Light and for MGD. It
seeks to examine the marketing strategy used and how beer commercials on
Univision construct Hispanic identity. Univision's marketing strategy is to present
the network's audience as a homogenous category, both to its viewers and its advertisers. Rodriguez (1996) terms this a panethnic marketing strategy, whereby all
Hispanic ethnicities are presented as a single group, "regardless of differences in
national origin, race, class, U.S. or immigration history" (p. 60). I argue that
Univision constructs the Hispanic market as a homogeneous unit in order to create

an image of its audience that is most appealing to advertisers at a loss of specific ethnic identity (e.g., nationality). This tendency is illustrated in the commercials aired on the network.

THEORETICAL PERSPECTIVE

Cultivation theory examines the relationship between frequently televised images and individuals' perceptions of reality. As exemplified by Gerbner and Gross' (1976) landmark study, television violence is the most popular subject for this research approach. Cultivation theory suggests that heavy television viewers shape their perceptions of reality in relation to what they see on television, especially in relation to law enforcement, crime, trust and danger (Shanahan & Morgan, 1999). Heavy viewers saw the world as being more violent than indicated by statistical measures of crime in their area. According to Shanahan and Morgan (1999) individuals who spend more time viewing television tend to perceive the world more as it is portrayed in broadcasts than it is in reality.

Cultivation theory also serves other areas of study because it posits that frequent and long-term exposure to any mediated message—not only television—can affect individuals. In recent years, cultivation studies examined a variety of topics including the perception of East German youth toward the Federal Republic of Germany (Klimet, 1994), public perception of biotechnology (Priest, 1995), public awareness of global environment issues (Mikami, et al. 1995), and reality-based television programming (Valkenburg & Patiwael, 1998). Cultivation theory presents a perspective that acknowledges the cultural impact of television on individuals, while admitting that other factors also impact individuals' perceptions and behavior.

Cultivation analysis "teases" out the ways in which media may influence viewer perceptions because television is said to homogenize viewers toward a narrow set of widely accepted principles. This tendency is termed *mainstreaming* and "means that heavy viewers may absorb or override differences in perspectives and behavior that ordinarily stem from other factors and influences" (Gerbner et al., 1994, p. 28). Television's ability to influence viewers' perceptions of reality most impacts heavy viewers (Shanahan & Morgan, 1999).[2] Typically, children and the elderly are heavy television viewers (Gerbner and Gross, 1976). This relationship is relevant to Hispanics because collectively they are a youthful population in the United States (Horner, 1996).

Hispanic identity in the selected beer commercials can best be understood via an examination of gender, race, and social class. These criteria partly compromise the identity for mass mediated characters (Denzin, 1991; Dines & Humez, 1995). Enteman (1996) argues that viewers can have cognitive interactions where mediated characters are thought to represent "real" people or ethnic groups. Viewers may cultivate a perception of a social group based upon their frequent interaction with mediated characters. To understand how these commercials potentially cultivate viewer perceptions of Hispanics, the following research questions are posed:

RQ1: How is gender constructed in these commercials?

    1a. What clothing and physical attributes predominate in the images of men?

    1b. What clothing and physical attributes predominate in the images of women?

RQ2: How is social class status portrayed?

RQ3: How are relationships with whites portrayed?

RQ4: Do the beer commercial portrayals indicate a panethnic marketing strategy?

To answer these research questions, the four selected commercials were analyzed with attention paid to a variety of elements, including gender, race and class representations and their relationship to Hispanic and white identity.

METHODOLOGY

This analysis seeks to identify the potential perceptions that the selected beer commercials cultivate in Univision viewers. The commercials were chosen for four reasons. First, alcohol ads are disproportionately aimed at people of color (Kilbourne, 1999). Second, Univision created a sports audience to draw in beer commercials (Sinclair, 1990). Third, each commercial appeared to have distinct aesthetic and ideological components, making it possible to identify as part of a larger campaign. Finally, each campaign presents a distinct marketing approach through which to appeal to Hispanic consumers. Bud Light presents Hispanic characters in apparently middle-class settings interacting with two white protagonists. The MGD campaign consists of black-and-white commercials where Hispanics are typically shown "drinking" MGD[3] at exclusively Hispanic social events. This campaign uses the *bato loco* (gang member) stereotype, which is often linked to Hispanic youth gangs.

The selected commercials were recorded in October and November 1998, from a Univision affiliate in a midsized Southwestern city.[4] Univision prime-time broadcasts, other than *telenovelas* (soap operas), were recorded for the selected period. *Telenovela* commercials were omitted because beer companies rarely sponsor them. Five beer commercials were recorded in total. However, one ad was part of a separate campaign for Miller Lite and was omitted from the current study.

I titled the four selected commercials and call the reader's attention to this situation to avoid confusion should these titles not match those used by the beer companies or their advertising firms. The first Bud Light commercial analyzed is titled, "Fiesta" and involves two white protagonists who climb 45 flights of stairs to attend a party in a twin-tower high rise. Upon their arrival they learn that they have climbed the stairs in the wrong tower. They proceed to climb the stairs in the other tower in order to drink Bud Light, which is being served at the party. The second Bud Light commercial is titled "Camping," and features the same two white protagonists "rescuing" a boat filled with Bud Light. The boat apparently belongs to two Hispanic women. The first MGD commercial is titled, "Car Show" and features a lowrider Impala "hopping" in the center of what appears to be a lowrider show. The final MGD commercial is titled, "Woman with Cars." It features a tight shot of a woman in sandals, a short skirt and light-colored top with long dark hair walking between two rows of lowriders and away from the camera. As the woman progresses through the rows of cars they begin to "hop." The further she progresses through the cars the more animated they become.

Gender focuses on the physical appearance of females and males. This distinction is important because commercials occasionally feature transvestites or transsexuals as women (Kilbourne, 1999). This distinction is neither sought nor analyzed in the current study. However, gender in relation to ethnic representation is an important element in mediated identity. For example, the most common stereotypes of Hispanic females include the sensual peasant, the spitfire, and the vamp (Keller, 1994; Woll, 1977). Similarly, Hispanic males are typically stereotyped as bandits, greasers, and Latin lovers (Keller, 1994; Woll, 1977). Hispanics, regardless of gender, have increasingly been associated with the *bato loco* (gang member) stereotype since the 1960s (Fregoso, 1993). However, the previous stereotypes also remain in use.

Another important element in the creation of mediated identity is race or ethnic labeling. A character's ethnic or racial identity is typically related to geographic locale, physical appearance, speech, surname, and wardrobe (Cortes, 1992). The preceding elements are tied to representations of race from an aesthetic perspective because the use of color schemes is linked to cultural identity (Buricaga, 1995). Characters are categorized as Hispanic if they possess the following media-ascribed traits: dark hair, dark or olive skin color, fluency in Spanish, physical characteristics, and wardrobe (Cortes, 1992; Rodriguez, 1997). Characters that speak in fractured English are traditionally understood in mainstream media to represent people of color (Lichter & Amundson, 1997). The current study inverts this perspective and identifies characters that speak a fractured Spanish as white. Characters fluent in Spanish are identified as Hispanic.

Wardrobe is used to determine racial category in two ways. First, a character's wardrobe can identify a person as a member of a subculture (Clarke, 1976; Hebdige, 1979). For example, a character dressed as a *bato loco* is understood to be Hispanic. Second, when characters are of different ethnicities but of the same social class, clothing and decor color are used to identify their racial identity. This use of color builds on Burciaga's (1995) observation that soft colors reflect the aesthetic tastes of middle-class whites and that bright colors reflect the aesthetics of Hispanics. Characters in soft colors are identified as white, while characters in bright colors are identified as Hispanic.

Social class is determined via the analysis of a character's dress, material possessions, manner of speech, and physical environment because these elements differentiate social classes and subcultures (Clarke, 1976). For example, a character driving a sports car conveys more status than one driving an economy car. Other material possessions and presentations of self function similarly. Social class was further determined by the relationship of Hispanic characters to whites.

Typical media representations of Hispanics of low socioeconomic status portray them within an ethnically homogeneous context (e.g., *Bound by Honor*, 1993), where few or no whites are central to the story line or within an ethnically heterogeneous context with whites in positions of power (e.g., *The Border*, 1982). Panethnic elements will be identified in relation to these interactions or lack thereof. The current data analysis was completed via a *generic analysis* (Foss, 1996), which is a research method that "seeks to discover commonalties in rhetorical patterns across recurring situations" (p. 225). Here the commercials were analyzed in terms of framing, language, and aesthetic codes to identify the recurring situations in each commercial.

FINDINGS

Gender Construction: As described previously, analysis of gender construction focused on the clothing and physical attributes of men and women. The image of men in the Bud Light commercial is described in relation to both whites and Hispanics. The first white protagonist is a tall, blond male with blue eyes. The second white protagonist is slightly shorter with light brown eyes and light-colored skin. Both white males are presented as friendly, casually dressed "guys next door." This construction of white male identity is one of many positive representations readily found in mainstream media (e.g., Woody Boyd played by Woody Harrelson on *Cheers*). In terms of clothing, the white males typically wear blue jeans with a casual top in subtle colors. They also speak a fractured Spanish stating, "*Yo quiero un [sic] Bud Light*" (I want a Bud Light.)

The Hispanic male image in the Bud Light commercials fits the media stereotypes as well. Although they serve primarily as "backdrops" (i.e., people not actively involved with the protagonists) these Hispanic males have dark hair, brown eyes, and darker skin than the white males. The Hispanic males in this beer campaign are presented as middle-class with a distinctly Hispanic style, reflected in the use of brightly colored clothing. For example, in one commercial a Hispanic male wears a bright lime-colored shirt and a pair of casual white pants. His outfit conforms to mainstream fashion conventions with the exception of color. Hispanic male identity is constructed through the actors' clothing, their physical attributes, and the white protagonists' attempts to speak Spanish. Many Univision viewers may interpret these commercials as humorous and nonoffensive. However, some may take exception to the stereotypic portrayals of both ethnic groups.

The MGD commercials create Hispanic identity through clothing and other elements of the lowrider subculture. There is an apparent absence of any non-Hispanic ethnic group in the MGD commercials. The male MGD models are dressed in baggy pants and tank-top style undershirts and wear short slicked back hair. The MGD campaign relegates Hispanic males to a negatively stereotyped population. Many apparently Hispanic actors in the MGD campaign are shown with a beer in hand and are linked to the "macho" stereotype of the *bato loco*.

Females in both campaigns are distinctly Hispanic sexual objects. However, the sexual framing of Hispanic females in the Bud Light commercials presents them as aesthetically desirable, without making them appear sexually threatening. Unlike the sensual peasant, spitfire, or vamp (Rodriguez, 1997; Woll, 1977), these Hispanic females are dressed in a contemporary, middle-class manner and are not apparently promiscuous. They neither seduce the white males nor lead to their downfall. The Bud Light models appear confident but do not use their sexuality to seduce males. For example, one Hispanic female in the "Fiesta" commercial is shown in a pink party dress with a six pack of Bud Light. Her role appears to be that of someone attending a party. At the end of the commercial the same young woman is shown commenting to another female that she loves men of few words. Her comment references the white males, who by this time have climbed 135 flights of stairs in their quest for a Bud Light. She is presented as a responsible drinker, apparently sober, and is not sexually threatening to the protagonists. She admires them from afar.

The Bud Light commercials potentially cultivate a favorable perception of Hispanics. First, Hispanics are depicted in middle class settings while maintaining their cultural identity. Second, the Hispanic characters interact well with the white characters. Finally, not every Hispanic character is shown with a beer, suggesting that Hispanics may drink responsibly.

The MGD commercials feature Hispanic females dressed in a manner that suggests a "hip hop" style that mimics the *bato loco* male stereotype. Most Hispanic females in the "Car Show" commercial appear as backdrops. Their wardrobe implies that Hispanics are involved in the gang member lifestyle regardless of gender. This erroneous perception is often imposed upon lowrider enthusiasts, although the subculture typically excludes drug dealers and gang members (Gradante, 1982). The most obvious female in the "Car Show" commercial, however, wears a bikini and the viewer only sees her from behind. At one point, her posterior occupies half of the screen as she jumps in rhythm with a "hopping" lowrider. The "Car Show" commercial reinforces the idea that Hispanic females are sexual objects, a common trait imposed upon them in the media (Cortes, 1992; Woll, 1977).

The "Woman with Cars" commercial alludes to sexual intercourse by having the model walk through two "aroused" rows of cars. Her role implies that Hispanic females serve the sexual desires of lowrider owners. This commercial reinforces the negative stereotypes Hispanic females constantly battle (Rodriguez, 1997). The MGD commercials either minimize the woman's role, as when their presence is limited to being in the background, or reinforce the supposed link between Hispanic females and sexual promiscuity.

Social Class

The importance of examining social class portrayals is that such portrayals can either reinforce the perception of Hispanics as unable to attain middle-class status or they can support the idea that Hispanics interact well with other ethnic groups, in this case whites. The Hispanic characters in the two Bud Light commercials are apparently middle-class, as reflected in their lifestyles. For example, the party in "Fiesta" occurs in a high-rise apartment building, not in a barrio setting. This depiction allows the white characters to interact with an educated, professional segment of the Hispanic population. This commercial campaign alludes to Hispanic upward mobility and suggests that mediated middle-class Hispanics do not associate with their culture in the same manner as working-class Hispanics. The latter are often presented in the media via signifiers, such as flags from their homeland or other symbols of ethnic origin. The Hispanics in the Bud Light campaign are non-threatening to the mainstream because they mimic mainstream norms.

The Hispanics in the Bud Light commercials speak fluent Spanish with no discernable accent, cultivating the idea that Hispanics are a panethnic group. Hispanics use variations of the Spanish language that are tied to specific ethnic populations. The standardized Spanish used here erases these distinctions. This use of language also cultivates the idea that Hispanic national distinctions are secondary to their shared language.

Social status is equally obvious in the MGD commercials. Hispanic identity here is created through clothing and other elements of the lowrider subculture. There is an apparent absence of any non-Hispanic ethnic group in these commercials. This strategy cultivates a negative view of Hispanics with a subculture that is often vilified in mainstream media. The MGD campaign propagates the perception of Hispanics as a social problem, a recurrent theme in mainstream United States media (Fregoso, 1993). Further, they alienate Hispanics from other ethnic groups, implying that Hispanics are ethnocentric.

Both commercial campaigns create Hispanic identity through stereotypes that emphasize the differences between the mainstream and non-mainstream populations. However, the Bud Light campaign does so in a more positive manner. The white protagonists want to drink beer with Hispanics. In contrast, the MGD campaign relegates Hispanics to a negatively stereotyped and marginalized population.

Ethnic Relations

The third research question examined in the current study regards ethnic relations, specifically portrayals of relationships with whites. A peaceful coexistence between whites and Hispanics is increasingly important given the current political climate in the United States (e.g., attacks on affirmative action programs) and the increasing large Hispanic population.

The Bud Light commercials present a positive view of inter-ethnic relations. Here, the white protagonists find Hispanic females attractive. This observation is based on their willingness to help the Hispanic females reclaim their beer in "Camping." When a male needs help, the white protagonists hide because they now have Bud Light and Hispanic female companionship. Further, the Hispanic female in "Fiesta" takes an interest in the white protagonists by jokingly stating to a friend, "*Me encantan los hombres de pocas palabras*" (I love men of few words) as she looks at him and his friend. These interpersonal exchanges potentially cultivate the idea that attraction, or friendship, across ethnic lines is acceptable to both whites and Hispanics. However, Hispanic couples are also presented as backdrops also. This implies that attraction does not have to be linked to ethnicity. The absence of Hispanic characters that do not fit the physical stereotype is troubling; there are no black, blonde, or redheaded Hispanics, for example.

The Bud Light campaign potentially cultivates a more positive view of Hispanics for viewers, regardless of race. Non-Hispanic viewers may cultivate the perception that Hispanics are potentially middle class and accepting of other ethnic groups. Hispanic viewers may cultivate the views that middle-class status does not equate with a loss of culture and that non-Hispanics are potential friends.

No white characters are apparent in the MGD commercials. This omission is negative; it implies that Hispanics do not interact with other ethnic groups. While there are many negative institutional machinations that discriminate against Hispanics, racial isolation is not a solution. Further, these commercials consistently use the lowrider subculture to present a negative and overly masculine representation of Hispanic social interaction. One can read these commercials as implying that Hispanic males are only concerned with drinking beer, driving lowrider automobiles, and pursuing sexually available women. These campaigns are potentially damaging to Hispanic self-understanding and to inter-ethnic interaction between Hispanics and others. The MGD campaign propagates the view that Hispanics are a social problem, a recurrent theme in mainstream media (Fregoso, 1993; Rodriguez, 1997). Both commercial campaigns present Hispanic identity through the use of stereotypes that emphasize the otherness of minority populations. However, the Bud Light campaign is more positive.

Panethnic Marketing

The final research question investigates whether commercial portrayals seem to indicate a panethnic marketing strategy. Analysis of this marketing strategy is important because of the need for culturally sensitive advertising in Spanish-language media. The Bud Light commercial contains elements of panethnic marketing, namely the identifiably Hispanic characters with unidentifiable cultural backgrounds and the positive interaction between whites and Hispanics. Panethnic marketing eradicates the differences between various Hispanic groups and focuses upon their commonalities—in this case, aesthetic tastes and common language. What makes this campaign panethnic is the omission of any cultural distinction among the various Hispanic characters; not one is identified along national or regional lines. The positive interactions between whites and Hispanics are panethnic, encouraging inter-ethnic communication between the two groups.

The MGD commercials contain no apparently panethnic elements. This situation may stem from the geographic area in which the commercials were broadcast and the target audience of that area. The Southwest Hispanic population is predominantly Mexican American and constitutes a number of lowrider enthusiasts (Stone, 1990). One can speculate that this marketing strategy stems from a specific aim to target the largest Hispanic group in the Southwest.

DISCUSSION AND CONCLUSION

Both Anheuser-Busch and Miller Brewing Company adopted different approaches to the portrayal of Hispanics in beer commercials. The most positive elements in the Bud Light commercials are the interactions between whites and Hispanics. The differences between Hispanics and whites are reduced to matters of aesthetic or taste differences that still allow for favorable intercultural exchanges. The aesthetic appeal of these commercials may cultivate a positive response because these Hispanic representations counter the gang member image often ascribed to the Hispanic population.

The beer commercials studied contain one overlapping element: The use of sex appeal to sell beer. Hispanic females in the Bud Light campaign receive more character development and do not sexually seduce men, although the men in these campaigns find them attractive. The MGD campaign reduces Hispanic females to "body parts" for viewer consumption. These women are only developed at an aesthetic level. Hispanic female representation in these beer commercials may lead viewers to see Hispanic women as sex objects but not as fully developed humans. These commercials potentially cultivate sexist perceptions of Hispanic women.

The commercial campaigns analyzed illustrate how difficult it is for advertisers to penetrate the Hispanic market in a culturally accurate way. Hispanics are a heterogeneous population with myriad levels of language proficiency, social norms, and socioeconomic status. The problem with panethnic marketing is that it obliterates, or at least distorts, these dynamics. Panethnic marketing presents Hispanics as homogeneous. This homogenization cannot hold beyond attempts to address its various segments at a superficial level.

The Bud Light campaign succeeded in presenting generic Hispanics in a positive light. Here the panethnic tendency to homogenize Hispanics also cultivates the perception that Hispanics drink responsibly and are part of the professional class. The strategy may minimize tensions between various ethnic groups within the Hispanic community. It also, however, homogenizes the unique characteristics of this community's ethnic subgroups. Thus its mainstreaming effect may be to encourage Hispanics to identify with the larger Spanish-speaking community, at the expense of their specific ethnic identity.

The MGD commercials are apparently aimed at individuals who identify with, or are members of, the lowrider subculture. Lowriders are typically popular across several age groups but are frequently identified as part of Hispanic youth culture in media. In reality, however, adults often build lowriders because most teenagers cannot afford such expensive vehicles (Rojas, 1999; Trillin & Koren, 1980). Thus the MGD commercials advance common misconceptions of Hispanics in order to promote their product. Regardless of their intent, these commercials cultivate the view that only Hispanics like lowriders. Further, the manner in which these commercials are framed promotes the idea that Hispanic lowrider enthusiasts are gang members. The mainstreaming effect of these commercials may be to encourage Hispanic youths to identify with the *bato loco* subculture. More positive role modes would better serve the Hispanic community.

Advertisers need to apply cultural sensitivity to their portrayals of Hispanics at the same level as they apply "good production values" (Jhally, 1990) to commercials. Anheuser-Busch illustrates a sense of cultural sensitivity in its current Bud Light campaign but is exclusionary of Hispanics outside the current physical stereotype and outside the middle-class realm. However, Miller Brewing Company needs to reevaluate its willingness to stereotype an entire culture in so negative and limited a manner.

Univision's dominance in the Spanish-language television arena is drawing scholarly attention (Rodriguez, 1996; Sinclair, 1990 & 1996). Future research needs to trace the use of panethnic advertising to positively or negatively portray Hispanics. The analysis of other panethnic commercials on Univision could also provide insights into which products or advertising campaigns possibly cultivate positive Hispanic images. Finally, scholars may consider other panethnic elements on the Univision network or in other ethnic-oriented media.

The analysis of Spanish-language media is important because it shapes perceptions of self and other (Gerbner et al., 1994; Kellner, 1995; Real, 1989). Cultivation theory suggests that we see others as they are portrayed in media and not as they may be in actual life. Spanish-language media have the potential to cultivate positive impressions of Hispanics. The Bud Light commercials function at this level, showing that Hispanics can be responsible middle-class beer drinkers. Future advertising campaigns that adopt this perspective can potentially cultivate a better societal view of Hispanics. A better and more accurate social understanding of Hispanics is necessary for this growing population to gain access to upward mobility. As the fastest growing ethnic group in the nation, Hispanics must be allowed to succeed; if not, they will continue to be relegated to the lowest echelons of American society.

NOTES

1. The term "Hispanic" is used here in reference to all people of Latin American cultural heritage. Despite its problematic nature, the term is used because its generic attributes reflect Univision's tendencies to combine all Latinos into one ethnic category.

2. The exact definition of a heavy television viewer varies in each specific study. When television viewing is divided into categorical terms, determinations of light, medium, and heavy viewership are typically made using a three-way split of the self-reported television viewing (Shanahan & Morgan, 1999).

3. Television commercials imply that a person is drinking by either showing the actors putting a beer to their mouths or simply holding cans of beer. Either of these two strategies was used to determine who in the commercial is consuming alcohol.

4. Efforts to acquire the complete commercial campaigns were unsuccessful because both companies declined to provide the commercials on videotape, citing "legal reasons." Representatives from each company suggested that the commercials be videotaped from a local broadcast.

REFERENCES

Bagdikian, B. (1999). *The media monopoly.* 6th ed. Boston: Beacon Press.

Burciaga, J. A. (1995). *Spilling the beans: Loteria Chicana.* Santa Barbara, CA: Joshua Odell Editions.

Chan-Olmsted, S. M., & Albarran, A. B. (1998). A framework for the study of global media economics. In A. B. Alabarran. & S. M. Chan-Olmsted (Eds.), *Global media economics: Commercialization, concentration and integration of world media markets* (pp. 3–16). Ames: Iowa State University Press.

Clarke, J. (1976). Style. In S. Hall & T. Jefferson (Eds.), *Resistance through rituals* (pp. 175–191). Boston: Unwin Hyman.

Cortes, C. E. (1992). Who is Maria? What is Juan? Dilemmas of analyzing the Chicano image in U.S. films. In C. Noriega (Ed.), *Chicanos and film: Representation and resistance* (pp. 74–93). Minneapolis: University of Minnesota Press.

Dearing, J. W., & Rogers, E. M. (1996). *Agenda-setting.* Thousand Oaks, CA: Sage.

Denzin, N. K. (1991). *Images of postmodern society: Social theory and contemporary cinema.* Thousand Oaks, CA: Sage.

Dines, G., & Humez, J. M. (1995). *Gender, race and class in media: A text reader.* Thousand Oaks, CA: Sage.

Enteman, W. F. (1996). Stereotyping, prejudice, and discrimination. In P. M. Lester (Ed.), *Images that injure: Pictorial stereotypes in the media* (pp. 9–14). Westport, CT: Praeger.

Foss, S. K. (1996). *Rhetorical criticism: Exploration and practice.* 2nd ed. Prospect Heights, IL: Waveland Press.

Fregoso, R. L. (1993). *The bronze screen: Chicana and Chicano film culture.* Minneapolis: University of Minnesota Press.

Gerbner, G., & Gross, L. (1976). Living with television: The violence profile. *Journal of Communication, 26,* 173–199.

Gerbner, G., Gross, L., Morgan, M., & Signorielli, N. (1994). Growing up with television: The cultivation perspective. In J. Bryant & D. Zillmann (Eds.), *Media effects: Advances in theory and research* (pp. 17–41). Hillsdale, NJ: Lawrence Erlbaum.

Gradante, W. (1982). Low and slow, mean and clean. *Natural History, 91,* 28–39.

Hebdige, D. (1979). *Subculture: The meaning of style.* New York: Routledge.

Horner, L. L. (Ed). (1996). *Hispanic Americans: A statistical sourcebook.* Palo Alto, CA: Information Publications.

Jhally, S. (1990). *The codes of advertising: Fetishism and the political economy of meaning in the consumer culture.* New York: Routledge.

Keller, G. D. (Ed.). (1994). *Hispanics and United States film: An overview and handbook.* Tempe, AZ: Bilingual Press/Editorial Bilingue.

Kellner, D. (1995). *Media culture: Cultural studies, identity and politics between the modern and the postmodern.* New York: Routledge.

Kilbourne, J. (1999). *Deadly persuasion: Why women and girls must fight the addictive power of advertising.* New York: Free Press.

Klimet, E. T. (1994). TV viewing in East Germany and the image of the Federal Republic of Germany: A contribution toward the cultivation hypothesis. *Rundfunk und Fernsehen, 42,* 483–509.

Lichter, S. R., & Amundson, D. R. (1997). Distorted reality: Hispanic characters in TV entertainment. In C. E. Rodriguez (Ed.), *Latin looks: Images of Latinas and Latinos in the U.S. media* (pp. 57–79). Boulder, CO: Westview Press.

Lull, J. (1995). *Media, communication, culture: A global approach.* New York: Columbia University Press.

Mikami, S., Takeshita, T., Nakad, M., & Kawabet, M. (1995). The media coverage and public awareness of environmental issues in Japan. *Gazette, 54,* 209–226.

Noriega, C. A. (2000). *Shot in America: Television, the state, and the rise of Chicano cinema.* Minneapolis: University of Minnesota Press.

Noriega, C. A. (Ed.). (1992). *Chicanos and film: Representation and resistance.* Minneapolis: University of Minnesota Press.

Priest, S. H. (1995). Information equity, public understanding of science, and the biotechnology debate. *Journal of Communication,* 45, 39–54.

Real, M. R. (1989). *Super media.* Newbury Park, CA: Sage.

Rodriguez, A. (1996). Objectivity and ethnicity in the production of the Noticiero Univision. *Critical Studies in Mass Communication,* 11, 141–161.

Rodriguez, C. E. (Ed.). (1997). *Latin looks: Images of Latinas and Latinos in the U.S. media.* Boulder, CO: Westview Press.

Rojas, J. (1999). The Latino use of urban space in East Los Angeles. In G. Lecler, R. Villa, & M. J. Dear (Eds.), *Urban Latino cultures: La vida latina en L.A.* (pp. 131–138). Thousand Oaks, CA: Sage.

Shanahan, J., & Morgan, M. (1999). *Television and its viewers: Cultivation theory and research.* New York: Cambridge University Press.

Sinclair, J. (1990). Spanish-language television in the United States: Televisa surrenders its domain. *Journal of Latin American Popular Culture,* 9, 39–63.

Stone, M. C. (1990). Bajito y suavecito [low and slow]: Low riding and the "class" of class. *Studies in Latin American Popular Culture,* 9, 85–126.

Trillin, C., & Koren, E. (10 July 1980). Our far-flung correspondents: low and slow, mean and clean. *New Yorker,* 70–74.

Univision. (1998a). *Univision: 1992–1997.* (Brochure). Dallas: Univision Sales Offices.

Univision (1998b). *Univision: The Hispanic market in brief, 1998.* (Brochure). Dallas: Univision Sales Office.

Valkenburg, P. M., & Patiwael, M. (1998). Does watching Court TV "cultivate" people's perceptions of crime? *Gazette,* 60, 227–238.

Woll, A. L. (1977). *The Latin image in American film.* Los Angeles: UCLA Center of Latin American Publications.

Chapter 12

Beauty in Brown: Skin Color in Latina Magazines

*Melissa A. Johnson, Prabu David,
and Dawn Huey-Ohlsson*

INTRODUCTION

Mass communication literature shows that, except for brief periods in the twentieth century, Americans with brown or black skin have been the subject of negative stereotypes or exclusion from general market media. One supposed refuge from these negative stereotypes has been ethnic media.

Portrayals of brownness and blackness in media have been studied because of scholars' concerns for their impact on non-group members and societal institutions and processes—effects from prejudice to political or workplace exclusion. For instance, lightness and whiteness are associated with political and socioeconomic power in the United States (Entman & Book, 2000; Robinson & Ward, 1995). Chabram-Dernersesian points out that Chicano intellectuals have also studied the construction of whiteness, although there is debate in Chicano/a studies scholarship about studying white or brown identities (1997). Physical portrayals in media also are important because of the way individuals use media in the construction of self-identity.

This chapter examines one genre of ethnic media—magazines targeted to Latinas in the United States. The purpose is to examine editorial photographs of women in 13 Latina magazines to investigate how these ethnic media portray one aspect of diversity among Latinas—skin color. In doing so, we discuss the theoretical functions of ethnic media and question whether ethnic media are portraying brownness in a manner that differs from mainstream or other ethnic media. In addition, we look at the portrayals' possible effects on Latina identity.

The terms Latino and Hispanic are used interchangeably in this chapter to refer to a U.S. resident who self-identifies with the indigenous or Spanish-speaking cultures of Mexico, Puerto Rico, Cuba, Central America, or South America. Hispanics are also of European Spanish origin, and Portuguese-speaking Brazilians may self-identify as Latin American (although normally not as Hispanic). The feminine form of Latino, Latina, refers to Latin American women. Someone can place an ethnicity on somebody else, or that person can self-identify as she sees fit. For instance, someone might self-identify as Mexican American or Puerto Rican, but institutional forces (e.g., government agencies, universities) might categorize that person as Hispanic. Another term used throughout the article is ethnic media. Ethnic media is defined as mass media targeted to particular ethnic or racial groups.

Latino media distributed in the United States has paralleled the exponential growth of U.S. Latinos, who currently comprise about 11% of the U.S. population. Most of the research on U.S. Latino media has described the content, audience uses and gratifications, and effects of usage of Spanish-language broadcasting and newspapers. Little attention has been paid to Latino magazines. Latino magazines in the United States originated as a Spanish-language genre, currently dominated by the behemoth publisher Editorial Televisa. But in the late 1990s, a number of English-language and bilingual magazines started publication in the United States. Once publishers and advertisers recognized that the Hispanic market is under served and that the market has considerable purchasing power, Latino magazines have aggressively targeted the Hispanic population. Latina magazines were chosen as the genre in which to pursue our research questions because of two reasons: (1) women's use of magazines has been found to have a stronger correlation with constructed self-image (Harrison & Cantor, 1997) than other media such as television; and (2) the vivid images in these magazines provided the ideal framework to rigorously pursue our research questions on skin color.

REVIEW OF THE LITERATURE

Ethnic Media Research: From Assimilation to Pluralism to Millennium Identity

Several phases of social science research have investigated the role of mass media in an immigrant's adjustment to mainstream United States' culture. The first research phase took place in a major United States. immigration era, the 1920s, and was primarily assimilative in its approach (e.g., Park, 1922). During this phase of research, assimilation, which meant giving up one culture and taking on another (Gordon, 1964; Gudykunst & Kim, 1997) was the influential theoretical model among academics. Social scientists studying ethnicity in the early twentieth century viewed assimilation as the ideal, which implied rejecting one's culture in order to become "American."

Later, communication scholars dropped the term assimilation in favor of the concept of acculturation (Berry, 1980). This concept became dominant in the second wave of social science and communication research in the 1960s, most likely tied to civil rights movements rather than immigration trends. Research emphasized that participation in mainstream communication channels was necessary for acculturation to the host culture (Gordon, 1964; Shibutani & Kwan, 1965) but the expectation was that one would retain aspects of one's own culture. The focus during the 1960s was on minorities' instrumental use of dominant information channels (general market media) to gain a footing in the mainstream culture. During this phase, ethnic media, especially broadcast media, were classified as vehicles for entertainment or relaxation, and buffers from the assimilation forces of the dominant culture.

Current definitions of acculturation refer to gradual adaptation to the new culture by replacing some norms and values of the old culture with those of the new (Chen & Starosta, 1998; Kim, 1988). Although some intercultural communication scholars focus on minority adaptation to the majority culture, other definitions suggest a reciprocal process (Kim, 1988). The majority culture, too, adapts to the norms or customs of the new culture and the acculturating group can retain some of its customs or values.

Beginning in the late 1970s and continuing through the 1990s a robust third period of media scholarship focused not only on immigrants and minorities, but began to include Hispanics, who had been relatively absent from the first two phases. Subervi-Velez's touchstone piece (1986) profiled Hispanics and found substantial support for the pluralistic function of media. At the individual level, pluralism is defined as an internal view of one's group membership, but not a required cultural identity. One can display group membership as one sees fit in a context or situation (Glazer & Moynihan, 1970; Husband, 1994; Padilla, 1985). At the group level, pluralism refers to sustained ethnic differentiation and heterogeneity, implying practice of one culture while participating in the majority society (Subervi-Velez, 1986).

Mass media studies of acculturation and Latinos have tended to focus on English-language versus Spanish-language media use, and indicated that language of media used related to acculturation level or ethnic identity (Jeffres & Hur, 1981; Johnson, 1996; Korzenny et al., 1983; Riggins, 1992; Rios, 1993; Shoemaker, Reese, & Danielson, 1985; Shoemaker et al., 1987; Zmud, 1992). This body of research shifted to include Latinos born in the United States as well as immigrants.

A fourth phase of Latinos and media, clustered around the millennium, has connected Latinos and media with broader issues of identity (e.g., Tanno, 2000; Rios, 2000). Latinos in the millennium have evolved from immigrants to second-, third-, and fourth-generation citizens participating in mainstream institutions, while carving out identities that include not only ethnicity (e.g., Latino), but gendered ethnicity (e.g., Latina) and other complexities. These studies include situational aspects of identity and identification of "otherness" in construction of self (Supriya, 1999).

ETHNIC MEDIA FUNCTIONS

As just mentioned, the tendency of recent studies has been pluralism-oriented, but most theoretical models of ethnic media functions recognize assimilation and pluralism functions. The following have been delineated as key pluralistic functions of ethnic media: to preserve and transmit native culture and identity by maintaining the language and promoting ethnic pride; to establish a minority news agenda; to announce community events and cover minority social activities (including minority business advertising); to promote the group's political/social interests and motivate them to be socially and politically active; to serve as collective expressions of anger at injustices; and to provide comfort and respite from negative images in general market media (Constantakis-Valdes, 1992; Downing, 1992; Fox, 1996; Gutierrez, 1977; Huntzicker, 1995; Riggins, 1992; Subervi-Velez, 1994). Others include symbolic empowerment (Riggins, 1992) and unification of subgroups (Flores, 1997; Fox, 1996; Husband, 1994; Rodriguez, 1997).

Assimilation functions of ethnic media are: serving as instruments of social control; maintaining the dominant languages of the host society; maintaining the dominant ideology; borrowing general market media genres; and socializing to "the modern" (Constantakis-Valdes, 1992; Gutierrez, 1977; Riggins, 1992).

In summary, models of ethnic media functions have concentrated on pluralism and assimilation functions. Researchers posit that although ethnicity is not media-created, it may be media-bolstered. Rios argues that more emphasis should be placed on the function of "preservation and fortification of their ethnicity and culture" (Rios, 2000, pp. 105–106), function of ethnic media, rather than on the acculturation functions. Studies that have done so (Johnson, 2000; Rios, 2000; Rios & Gaines, 1998) have tended to focus on text and/or genre, rather than images.

IDENTITY, SKIN COLOR, SELF-IMAGE

Communication researchers have analyzed media's role in identity creation (Gergen, 1991; Merelman, 1995; Turow, 1997). In particular, the way female readers use magazines to construct self-identity and socialize to society norms has received attention (Brown, White, & Nikopoulou, 1993; Ferguson, 1983; McCracken, 1993; Simonds, 1996; Wolf, 1991). One contributor in self-construction is the perception of one's physical self.

Communication research has supported the effect of the media on body image perceptions among U.S. women (Botta, 1999; David & Johnson, 1998; Harrison & Cantor, 1997; Myers & Biocca, 1992). Body image is defined as the evaluation of one's own body and related feelings or attitudes about one's evaluation. One of the emerging themes from this research is that the media set unrealistic standards of attractiveness, which result in body image dissatisfaction, particularly among young women. Like elsewhere in the world, U.S. and Latin American societies place a higher value on the physical presentation of women than they do on men. Moreover, media critics and some women's groups have argued that globalization and multinational advertising tend to glamorize the Eurocentric notion of beauty and attractiveness, which leaves women from other cultures with an ideal of beauty and attractiveness that is far from reality.

A few studies of body image have been conducted with multicultural groups in the United States. Altabe (1998) found that African Americans, in particular, view light skin color as desirable because of stereotyped beliefs. In reporting both their own ideals and general cultural ideals, Caucasian and Latino respondents were less likely to mention light skin, compared to Asian Americans and African Americans. Ideal traits listed by Latinas were large breasts, long hair, tallness, thinness, and dark or darker skin. In another body image study, Striegel-Moore et al. (1995) concluded that skin color might be more important than thinness to African Americans (compared to Anglo Americans) but Latinas were not included in their sample.

Studies of African Americans and skin color have found that color extremes (very white or very black) in skin color are least preferable, and that women are more color conscious than males (Robinson & Ward, 1995). Lighter-skinned features have been associated with socioeconomic advantages (Keith & Herring, 1991; Seltzer & Smith, 1991). Robinson and Ward (1995) found that self-esteem among students who self-reported darker skin was lower than among those who reported lighter or in-between skin color.

Content analyses of skin color in mass media are few, and they usually focus on African Americans rather than Latinos. Researchers have found that blacks in advertisements are lighter-skinned than in editorial photographs (Keenan, 1996); black women are lighter than black men (Keenan, 1996); and media targeted to African Americans also feature blacks who are light-skinned (Leslie, 1995). As Latinos are highly underrepresented in general market media editorial/entertainment content (Dixon & Linz, 2000) and in advertising (Bowen & Schmid, 1997; Taylor & Bang, 1997), skin color among Latinos has been a difficult variable to study. Given the paucity of research in this area, in this chapter we tackle the issue of skin color in Latina editorial images.

LATINAS AND LATINA MAGAZINES

There are 11 million Latinas in the United States and 5 million Latinas aged 16 or over in the U.S. workforce (Byerly & Deardorff, 1995). Latino/Latina purchasing power in the United States is $348 billion, which suggests that the "Latino market" is an attractive group for magazine advertisers (Nuiry, 1997).

Editorial Televisa publishes, either solely or via agreements with other magazine publishers, most of the major Spanish-language women's magazines distributed in the United States (Caitlin, 1997). Titles include *Cosmo en Espanol*, *Vanidades*, and *Cristina*. However, upstart publications in the United States have targeted second- and third-generation Latinas who don't necessarily read Spanish. The trade press reports that the new publications and major advertisers are marketing to upscale, educated, acculturated Latinas (Ballon, 1997; Beam, 1996; Fest, 1997; Gremillion, 1996).

The magazines *Latina Style* and *Latina* are in English but frequently use Spanish phrases, not unlike the code-switching that occurs between Latinos and Anglos in cities like San Diego or Santa Fe.[1] Bilingual magazines include *Estylo*, *Moderna,* and *Latina Bride*. *Moderna* was published by *Hispanic* magazine in Austin, Texas and had been issued since 1997. It is no longer published, but was included in this study's data collection.

HISPANICS AND RACE IN THE UNITED STATES

U.S. Census data from 1990 report 52% of Hispanics identifying as white, 3% as black, 1% as Asian or Pacific Islander, fewer than 1% American Indian, and 43% as "other race."[2] These self-reported identities lead us to believe that in representing Latinas in the United States, media should be portraying a variety of body images.

MASS MEDIA AND SELF-IMAGE

Whether in these Latina magazines or in general market media, body images of models or persons in editorial coverage are selected by editors and/or photo editors, given the options available (e.g., celebrity photos submitted by public relations practitioners). Follow-up treatments (e.g., airbrushing, digitized changes) are the consequences of gatekeeper choices. So considering news and feature photographs separately from advertising photographs is useful. Unlike portrayals in advertising, for which businesses could be blamed, editorial photographs are directly indicative of the decision processes of media workers.

Given the literature on Latinas, race and identity, the role of media in acculturation and pluralism, and the impact of media on personal identity and ethnic identity, the following research questions were developed for nonadvertising women's photographs in Latina publications:

RQ1: What range of skin colors is found in Latina magazines distributed in the United States?

RQ2: How do individual magazines portray Latina skin color in nonadvertising photographs?

RQ3: Does skin color of women portrayed in nonadvertising photographs differ between Spanish-language and English-language/bilingual publications?

RQ4: Are there differences in skin color between fashion magazines and other general interest magazines for U.S. Latinas?

METHOD

The intent was to include all magazines targeted to Latinas in at least major markets of the United States. To be included in the sampling frame, magazines had to have a U.S. circulation of at least 20,000 and be available on newsstands or via subscription in the United States (Whisler, Nuiry, & McHugh, 1997). If a reader was required to write to Mexico or Spain for a subscription, for instance, the publication was not included. Regional publications and organization-specific publications were excluded, resulting in 13 magazine titles.

The sampling period was July 1997 through June 1998. Magazine publishing schedules ranged from biweekly to quarterly, so the sampling frame was comprised of each of the four quarterly magazines during the period, plus a randomly selected issue from each quarter for the nine titles published monthly or biweekly

(Riffe, Lacy, & Fico, 1998). The quarterly *Latina Bride* did not begin publication until the winter of 1998, so only three issues were coded. This resulted in 51 magazine issues.

A pretest of three magazines with different origins, language, and length was conducted to determine an appropriate procedure for selection of images to code. Based on the time needed to code each magazine and the desire for a manageable sample size, every other female editorial image at least one inch square was selected for coding. All advertising was excluded, as were illustrations. Both individual and group photos were selected, with every other woman coded in a group photo. In order to be included, a woman's body had to be visible at least to the waist. This resulted in 1,579 non-advertising images.

MEASURES

The pretest indicated that the magazines did not portray the range of skin colors we initially had conceived. So, this study's skin color choices have less range and smaller intervals than scales that would be constructed for use in a study of Latinas in the general U.S. population. After a pretest, a 5-point Likert scale was operationalized. The Likert scale categories for skin color were 1 for fair-skinned, 2 for light brown, 3 for medium brown, 4 for dark brown and 5 for black-skinned. In order to maintain coder consistency, photo samples of each of the five measures were used by the coder along with the code sheet. One student coder analyzed all of the images.

When a random sample of seven percent of the images from the 13 magazines was double-coded by the student coder and one of the other authors, intercoder reliability was 80%. There was no pattern in the differences between coders. During the interreliability coding, the coders also used the photo samples.

RESULTS

Twenty-seven percent of the models had pale white skin, 57% had beige skin, 12% had medium brown skin, 3% had dark brown skin, and fewer than 1% had black skin. To put it more bluntly, out of 1,579 women's photos, 8 women were black-skinned, and more than 1,300 were light-skinned.

Our second research question queried how average skin color differed by magazine ($X^2 = 171.7$, 48 df, $p < .000$). Table 12.1 shows the results of the analysis. The third research question grouped magazines by language to determine whether there were differences. We thought that being part of a "minority" culture in the United States might skew skin color toward an Anglo American look. However, bilingual and English-language magazines originating in the United States featured more darker-skinned women than Spanish-language titles published in Miami, Mexico, or Spain. A chi-square analysis of group differences yielded $X^2 = 47.7$, 4 df, $p < .000$. For example, 29% of Spanish-language magazine images were white, compared to 17% of English-language/bilingual magazine photos. Conversely, 14% of Spanish-language photos were medium brown, dark brown, or

Table 12.1
Skin Color in Magazines Targeted to U.S. Latinas

| Magazine | White | Skin Color | | | |
		Light Brown	Medium Brown	Dark Brown	Black
Buenhogar	2.1	4.8	3.7	9.6	12.5
Cosmopolitan en Español	8.0	13.3	4.7	11.5	--
Cristina la Revista	5.7	10.7	18.9	9.6	--
Elle en Español	14.4	10.6	12.6	13.5	25.0
Estylo	2.6	4.2	8.4	1.9	--
Harper's Bazaar	8.3	7.6	4.2	1.9	12.5
Latina	1.7	5.1	4.2	--	--
Latina Bride	0.7	3.0	7.9	3.8	--
Latina Style	1.7	2.1	5.3	3.8	--
Marie Claire en Español	11.6	11.4	6.3	15.4	25.0
Moderna	5.7	6.0	10.0	7.7	--
Vanidades	15.3	8.5	3.7	5.8	--
Vogue en Español	22.4	12.8	10.0	15.4	25.0
TOTAL	100.0	100.0	100.0	100.0	100.0

n = 1,579.

black, compared with 25% of English language/bilingual magazine images. Fashion magazines had the highest percentages of light-skinned women. A comparison of the images in fashion magazines versus general women's feature magazines yielded a significant difference ($X^2 = 26.3$, 4 df, $p < .000$). In these groupings the differences were not quite as dramatic. For instance, five of the eight black women were in fashion magazines, although 88% of fashion magazine women were fair or light brown-skinned, compared with 81% of feature magazine women. We hypothesize that this may be due to the emphasis on "exotic" photos in fashion photography and dramatic posturing, which would provide an acceptable genre for darker-skinned women, much like entertainment and sports have been acceptable forums for people of color.

DISCUSSION

Perceptions about skin color run the gamut from the primitive notion that dark skin is inferior, to more subtle prejudices that offer advantages to people with lighter skin. Although the ideal would be that the color of a person's skin should have no bearing on social judgments about that person, this ideal is far from the reality.

Skin color has certain advantages in our society. From fairy tales, such as Snow White, fairness is emphasized as an inherited attribute that is equated with affluence, beauty, and success. In real life too, sometimes fairness of skin provides subtle advantages, whereas darker skins tones carry negative stereotypes and even stigma in some extreme cases. In some subcultures, the politics of skin color is open and unabashed, where dark skin is equated with lower class, less intelligence, and an overall liability, particularly for women. For example, in some subcultures in South India, parents worry about the skin tone of their daughters because women with darker skin tones are less likely to be sought after by grooms in an arranged marriage system.

Although there has been a significant push toward education and sensitization about the corrosiveness of color and racial stereotypes, the United States is not immune to the politics of color. Oppressive stereotypes, which are openly applied in some parts of the world, take on various manifestations in the United States.

Functions of Ethnic Media

The findings support some assimilation and pluralism functions of ethnic media models. The editorial images serve an assimilation function in that the diversity of representations is limited. These results do not differ from analyses of African American images in news and entertainment media (both in general market and in African American media) that show light-skinned ideals. Brown-skinned readers who look to Latina magazines for "women like me" could experience body image dissatisfaction, a dysfunctional outcome of media supposedly more functional than general market media.

The data suggest that Latina media serve a symbolic role in creating a panraza[3] identity by presenting dominant images of the ideal Latina—but that ideal is someone light-skinned. This may fulfill the ethnic media function of preserving and transmitting ethnic pride, but only in a partial manner. It raises the question of whether these ethnic publications, unintentionally and unwittingly, are creating their own visual projections of symbolic media racism.

Media Responsibility and the Social Construction of Reality

Within the scope of this chapter, the question is, "What can the ethnic media do about it?" After all, the media are cultural artifacts that represent society and are vulnerable to the same weaknesses and prejudices that we see around us. To examine the role of media within this context, it is important to review the marketing and social responsibility functions of the media.

By the marketing model, media products, including ethnic magazines, are products configured specifically for target markets (Gutierrez, 1987; Turow, 1997). Like advertising, the editorial content is also crafted carefully to fulfill the demands of the target audience. This model of media consumerism is inevitable in a free market economy. However, the media are empowered with the role of social construction of reality and with it a social responsibility function. Women's fashion and feature magazines have groups of loyal readers who look to these magazines for help and advice on issues from beauty care, to relationships to financial investments. There is empirical evidence that suggests that some women turn to magazines to help alleviate feelings of inadequacy or low self-esteem stemming from physical appearance. Therefore, the construction of social reality offered by the media plays a very important part in people's lives, especially the reality offered by ethnic media. The ethnic media serve as the bridge that keeps the ties alive between the geographically distant native culture and the reader.

As part of this social responsibility function, media professionals should be sensitized to the core value of diversity and plurality. One of the mechanisms for infusing diversity in the media has been the recruitment of journalists, editors, photographers, and newsroom professionals from diverse cultures. The findings from this study suggest that representation of various ethnic groups in the business is not enough. Despite the representation of ethnicity on the editorial staff in Latina magazines, the range of representation of skin color was fairly limited. While this is could be attributed to the systemic biases in the dominant culture, the lack of pluralism can be alleviated to some extent with more aggressive professional training.

Transfer of Professionalism

The media industry around the world is strongly influenced by the transfer of professionalism from the West, particularly the United States and the United Kingdom. This is not surprising given that global popular culture is shaped in large part by U.S. media exports. The transfer of media professionalism is one such export with considerable impact on production values. For example, most magazines and television programs around the world are created with comparable American media products as templates. (Ethnic media scholars refer to this "borrowing general market media genres" as an assimilation function.) The glossy finish, vivid images, and professional look of media programs are copied by media from different countries.

While some could argue that the transfer of professionalism is a manifestation of cultural dominance, it could also be used to transfer professional values of social responsibility. Our data indicate that Spanish-language and bilingual magazines produced in the United States represented more diversity in color, compared to Spanish-language magazines produced abroad. This is a noteworthy finding because it reinforces our argument that more emphasis on diversity training could have an impact on representation of pluralistic norms and ideas in media content. It is possible that training and sensitization through education and other social channels had some role in diversity represented in American-produced ethnic magazines. Perhaps, with more emphasis on the social responsibility function, magazine producers abroad could be sensitized to the importance of diversity and over time this could have a cumulative effect on content.

Fashion versus Feature Magazines

Often, fashion magazines and advertising are blamed for the unrealistic norms of beauty and attractiveness presented in the media. While this cannot be disputed, the findings from this content analysis indicate that even in nonadvertising images, lighter-skinned people are featured more frequently and prominently. This finding brings into focus two popular notions that advertising and fashion magazines are primary culprits when it comes to lack of pluralistic representation.

After examining only images from editorial content, it seems fairly obvious that editors and production staff are no more color-blind than advertising professionals. More disturbing is the trend that feature magazines are significantly better than fashion magazines in representing diversity. Clearly fashion models are there to sell the elusive and the ephemeral concept of beauty. But one would expect feature magazines to be more sensitive to diversity in color. It was somewhat disappointing to see that in the conscious choices made about visual editorial content, there was still a serious dearth of skin-color representation.

NOTES

1. Since this study was conducted, *Latina* has featured more articles in both languages, attaining a more bilingual profile.

2. In particular, this study focuses on skin-color diversity. U.S. Census data from 1990 report 52% of Hispanics identifying as white, 3% as black, 1% as Asian or Pacific Islander, fewer than 1% American Indian, and 43% as "other race." Hispanics in the latter category may perceive themselves as mixed race, as members of indigenous groups not listed by the U.S. Census, or in other ways. Of course, Hispanics may reject the concept of race, preferring to focus on ranges of appearances among ethnic groups, as this study does. U.S. Census data are only partially applicable to this study, as many of the magazines in the sample are distributed in the United States as well as elsewhere in the Americas.

3. Panraza, or pan-Hispanic, refers to unity across a number of different Latino cultures, such as Mexican American, Puerto Rican, or Cuban American.

REFERENCES

Altabe, M. (1998). Ethnicity and body image: Quantitative and qualitative analysis. *International Journal of Eating Disorders,* 23 (2), 153–159.

Ballon, M. (September, 1997). Start-up mambos to beat of booming market. *Inc, 19,* 23.

Beam, C. (September 1, 1996). The Latina link in two languages. *Folio: The Magazine for Magazine Management,* 25, 23–24.

Berry, J. W. (1980). Acculturation as varieties of adaptation. In A. M. Padilla (Ed.), *Acculturation: Theory, models and some new findings* (pp. 9–25). Boulder, CO: Westview.

Botta, R. A. (1999). Television images and adolescent girls' body image disturbance. *Journal of Communication,* 49 (2), 22–41.

Bowen, L., & Schmid, J. (1997). Minority presence and portrayal in mainstream magazine advertising: An update. *Journalism & Mass Communication Quarterly,* 74 (1), 134–146.

Brown, J., White, A. B., & Nikopoulou, L. (1993). Disinterest, intrigue, resistance: Early adolescent girls' use of sexual media content. In B. S. Greenberg, J. D. Brown, & N. Buerkelll-Rothfuss (Eds.), *Media, sex, and the adolescent* (pp. 177–195). Cresskill, NJ: Hampton Press.

Byerly, E., & Deardorff, K. (July, 1995). *Bureau of the Census, current population reports: National and state population estimates 1990–1994* (Online). Retrieved October 5, 1998 from the World Wide Web: http://www.census.gov/prod/1/pop/p25–1127.pdf.

Caitlin, K. (November 15, 1997). A Spanish "sleeping giant" looks northward. *Folio: The Magazine for Magazine Management,* 26 (15), 14–15.

Chabram-Dernersesian, A. (1997). On the social construction of whiteness within selected Chicana/o discourses. In R. Frankenberg (Ed.), *Displacing whiteness: Essays in social and cultural criticism* (pp. 107–164). Durham, NC: Duke University Press.

Chen, G., & Starosta, W. J. (1998). *Foundations of intercultural communication.* Boston: Allyn and Bacon.

Constantakis-Valdes, P. (1992). Toward a theory of "immigrant"and "ethnic" media: The case of Spanish-language television. Paper presented at the annual convention of the International Communication Association, Miami, FL.

David, P., & Johnson, M. A. (1998). The role of self in third-person effects about body image. *Journal of Communication,* 48 (4), 37–58.

Dixon, T. L., & Linz, D. (2000). Overrepresentation and underrepresentation of African Americans and Latinos as lawbreakers on television news. *Journal of Communication,* 50 (2), 131–154.

Downing, J.D.H. (1992). Spanish-language media in the greater New York region during the 1980s. In S. H. Riggins (Ed.), *Ethnic minority media: An international perspective* (pp. 256–275). Newbury Park, CA: Sage.

Entman, R. M., & Book, C. L. (1999). Light makes right: Skin color and racial hierarchy in television advertising. In R. Anderson & L. Strate (Eds.), *Critical studies in media commercialism.* New York: Oxford University Press.

Fest, G. (October 27, 1997). Speaking the language. *Adweek, 38,* 25–30.

Ferguson, M. (1983. *Forever feminine: Women's magazines and the cult of femininity.* London: Heinemann.

Flores, J. (1997). The Latino imaginary: Dimensions of community and identity. In F. R. Aparicio & S. Chavez-Silverman (Eds.), *Tropicalizations: Transcultural representations of Latinidad* (pp. 183–193). Hanover, NH: University Press of New England.

Fox, G. (1996). *Hispanic nation: Culture, politics, and the constructing of identity.* Secaucus, NJ: Birch Lane Press.

Gergen, K. J. (1991). *The saturated self: Dilemnas of identity in contemporary life.* New York: Basic Books.

Glazer, N., & Moynihan, D. P. (1970) *Beyond the melting pot.* 2nd ed. Cambridge, MA: M.I.T. Press.

Gordon, M. M. (1964). *Assimilation in American life.* New York: Oxford University Press

Gremillion, J. (June 10, 1996). Young, gifted, & "Latina." *Mediaweek,* 6, 34.

Gudykunst, W. B., & Kim, Y. Y. (1997). *Communicating with strangers: An approach to intercultural communication.* 3rd ed. New York: McGraw-Hill.

Gutierrez, F. (1977). Spanish-language media in America: Background, resources, history. *Journalism History,* 4 (2), 34–41.

Gutierrez, F. (1987). Marketing the news in Third World America. *Gannett Center Journal,* 1, 88–96.

Harrison, K., & Cantor, J. (1997). The relationship between media consumption and eating disorders. *Journal of Communication,* 47 (1), 40–67.

Huntzicker, W. E. (1995). Chinese-American newspapers. In F. Hutton and B. S. Reed (Eds.), *Outsiders in 19th-century press history: Multicultural perspectives* (pp. 71–92). Bowling Green, OH: Bowling Green State University Popular Press.

Husband, C. (1994). General introduction: Ethnicity and media democratization within the nation-state. In C. Husband (Ed.), *A richer vision: The development of ethnic minority media in Western democracies* (pp. 1–19). Paris: The United Nations Educational, Scientific, and Cultural Organization.

Jeffres, L. W., & Hur, K. K. (1981). Communication channels within ethnic groups. *International Journal of Intercultural Relations,* 5 (2), 115–132.

Johnson, M. A. (1996). Latinas and television in the United States: Relationships among genre identification, acculturation, and acculturation stress. *Howard Journal of Communications,* 7 (4), 289–313.

Johnson, M. A. (2000). How ethnic are U.S. ethnic media: The case of Latina magazines. *Mass Communication & Society,* 3 (2/3), 229–248.

Keenan, K. L. (1996). Skin tones and physical features of blacks in magazine advertisements. *Journalism & Mass Communication Quarterly,* 73 (4), 905–912.

Keith, V. M., & Herring, C. (1991). Skin tone and stratification in the black community. *American Journal of Sociology,* 97, 760–778.

Kim, Y. Y. (1988). *Communication and cross-cultural adaptation: An integrative theory.* Clevedon, England: Multilingual Matters.

Korzenny, F., Neuendorf, K., Burgoon, M., Burgoon, J. K., & Greenberg, B. S. (1983). Cultural identification as a predictor of content preferences of Hispanics. *Journalism Quarterly,* 60 (2), 329–333.

Leslie, M. (1995). Slow fade to?: Advertising in *Ebony* magazine, 1957–1989. *Journalism & Mass Communication Quarterly,* 72, 426–435.

McCracken, E. (1993). *Decoding women's magazines: From* Mademoiselle *to* Ms. New York: St. Martin's Press.

Merelman, R. M. (1995). *Representing black culture: Racial conflict and cultural politics in the United States.* New York: Routledge.

Myers, P. N., Jr., & Biocca, F. (1992). The elastic body image: The effect of television advertising and programming on body image distortions in young women. *Journal of Communication,* 42 (3), 108–133.

Nuiry, O. E. (1997). Cashing in on Latinas. *Latina Style,* 3 (4), 23–33.

Oboler, S. (1995). *Ethnic lables, Latino lives: Identity and the politics of (re)presentation in the United States.* Minneapolis: University of Minnesota Press.

Padilla, F. M. (1985). *Latino ethnic consciousness: The case of Mexican Americans and Puerto Ricans in Chicago.* Notre Dame, IN: University of Notre Dame Press.

Park, R. E. (1922). *The immigrant press and its control.* Westport, CT: Greenwood Press (reprinting, 1970).

Riffe, D., Lacy, S., & Fico, F. G. (1998). *Analyzing media messages: Using quantitative content analysis in research.* Mahwah, NJ: Lawrence Erlbaum.

Riggins, S. H. (1992). The promise and limits of ethnic minority media. In S. H. Riggins (Ed.), *Ethnic minority media: An international perspective* (pp. 276–288). Newbury Park, CA: Sage.

Rios, D. I. (1993). Mexican American audiences: A qualitative and quantitative study of ethnic subgroup uses for mass media. Doctoral dissertation, University of Texas, 1993. Ann Arbor, MI: University Microfilms International.

Rios, D. I. (2000). Latino/a experiences with mediated communication. In A. Gonzalez, M. Houston, & V. Chen (Eds.), *Our voices: Essays on culture, ethnicity, and communication*. 3rd ed. (pp. 105–112). Los Angeles: Roxbury.

Rios, D. I., & Gaines, S. O., Jr. (1998). Latino media use for cultural maintenance. *Journalism & Mass Communication Quarterly, 75* (4), 746–761.

Robinson, T. L., & Ward, J. V. (1995). African American adolescents and skin color. *Journal of Black Psychology, 21* (3), 256–274.

Rodriguez, A. (1997). Cultural agendas: The case of Latino-oriented U.S. media. In M. McCombs, D. L. Shaw, & D. Weaver (Eds.), *Communication and democracy: Exploring the intellectual frontiers in agenda-setting theory* (pp. 183–194). Mahwah: NJ: Lawrence Erlbaum.

Seltzer, R., & Smith, R. C. (1991). Color differences in the Afro-American community and the differences they make. *Journal of Black Studies, 21* (3), 279–286.

Shibutani, T., & Kwan, L. (1965). *Ethnic stratification: A comparative approach*. New York: Macmillan.

Shoemaker, P. J., Reese, S. D., & Danielson, W. A. (1985). Spanish language print media use as an indicator of acculturation. *Journalism Quarterly, 62* (4), 734–740.

Shoemaker, P. J., Reese, S. D., Danielson, W. A., & Hsu, K. (1987). Ethnic concentration as a predictor of media use. *Journalism Quarterly, 64* (3), 593–597.

Simonds, W. (1996) All-consuming selves: Self-help literature and women's identities. In D. Grodin & T. R. Lindlof (Eds.), *Constructing the self in a mediated world* (pp. 15–29). Thousand Oaks, CA: Sage.

Striegel-Moore, R. H., Schreiber, G. B., Pike, K. M., Wilfley, D. E., & Rodin, J. (1995). Drive for thinness in black and white preadolescent girls. *International Journal of Eating Disorders, 18* (1), 59–69.

Subervi-Velez, F. A. (1986). The mass media and ethnic assimilation and pluralism: A review and research proposal with special focus on Hispanics. *Communication Research 13* (1), 71–96.

Subervi-Velez, F. A. (1994). Mass communication and Hispanics. In F. Padilla (Ed.), *Handbook of Hispanic cultures in the United States: Sociology* (pp. 304–357), N. Kanellos & C. Esteva-Fabregat (Eds.). Houston: Arte Publico Press.

Supriya, K. E. (1999). White difference: Cultural constructions of white identity. In T. K. Nakayama & J. N. Martin (Eds.), *Whiteness: The communication of social identity* (pp. 129–148). Thousand Oaks, CA: Sage.

Tanno, D. (2000). Names, narratives, and the evolution of ethnic identity. In A. Gonzalez, M. Houston, & V. Chen (Eds.), *Our voices: Essays in culture, ethnicity, and communication*. 3rd ed. (pp. 25–28). Los Angeles: Roxbury.

Taylor, C. R., & Bang, H. (1997). Portrayals of Latinos in magazine advertising. *Journalism & Mass Communication Quarterly, 74* (2), 285–303.

Turow, J. (1997). *Breaking up America: Advertisers and the new media world*. Chicago: University of Chicago Press.

Whisler, K., Nuiry, O., & McHugh, S. R. (1997). *The 1997 national Hispanic media directory*. Carlsbad, CA: WPR Publishing.

Wolf, N. (1991). *The beauty myth*. New York: Anchor Books.

Zmud, J. P. (1992). *Ethnic identity, language, and mass communication: An empirical investigation of assimilation among U.S. Hispanics*. Doctoral dissertation, University of Southern California, Los Angeles.

Part IV: Education and Community Relations

Chapter 13

School-Home Communication for Latino and African American Families: Informed Reflections

A. Y. "Fred" Ramirez

INTRODUCTION

When asked to discuss the one area that gets them upset with schools (McEwan, 1998), parents stated "communication." Parents feel frustrated, annoyed, over-whelmed, and angry when school personnel, and specifically teachers, fail to com-municate with them concerning changes in school policies, educational programs, or their children's instruction. During an investigation on parental involvement (Ramirez, 1999a) I found that when teachers did communicate with parents, the letters and telephone calls were often concerning negative student behavior, a stu-dent failing a course, or some other negative information. How many of us, as chil-dren, remember a parent walking onto the school campus during hours of operation? What thoughts did we have? When I asked this question to my preservice teachers (students preparing to become teachers) in a course in the School of Education, most responded that "the kid must be in trouble."

Communication, whether by phone or by letter, that is negative in tone or that contains negative information is commonplace. How school personnel interact with families can be as important as the school curriculum itself. Communication that takes place between the school and ethnic communities, in particular within Latino and African American communities, is a process that merits continued ex-amination. This chapter looks at school-home communication patterns, focusing on Latino and African American families. Based on my experiences as a high school teacher in public and private schools, and a researcher looking at par-ent-school relationships, I will discuss the challenges of effective school-home communication and recommend ways that schools and families can work toward mutual understanding.

As a teacher educator and supervisor of preservice students in schools, in the Midwest and on the west coast, I have had the pleasure to meet many administrators and teachers who are "in the trenches." As a former high school teacher in parochial and urban public schools, I have also had the opportunity to work with some of the finer teachers in the country. There were times as a teacher that I felt that parents wanted to be involved in areas where they were not "competent," such as curriculum committees. I felt that parents needed to participate in areas such as "Back-to-School Night" so that I, as a teacher, could communicate with them about their child. As a graduate student, years later, when I began to research parental involvement in schools, I found one issue was in serious need of investigation—school-home communication. Teachers often neglect to communicate consistently with their students' parents (Ramirez, 1999a), or don't communicate at all. Not only are many parents excluded from communication within schools, but also low-socioeconomic parents are often excluded from communication pathways due to stereotypes and prejudice that teacher and staffs hold toward the parents (Ramirez, 1999b). It was at this point that I started to reflect upon my teaching, and how I did or did not communicate with parents. I felt I sometimes negated my students, their parents, and my community by not effectively communicating with them. Although I did communicate in positive ways (making positive phone calls about student performance), I realized many of my parents did not receive the positive feedback that they were entitled to.

The information, insights, and analyses that I will be sharing come from professional experiences as an elementary substitute and high school teacher, researcher, and teacher educator. The people interviewed for this piece are parents from the Midwest and on the west coast, along with professional educators from these areas as well. The information presented in this chapter includes data from my dissertation, "Teachers' attitudes toward Parents and Parental Involvement at the High School Level"; additional personal interviews, and my own experiences as a high school teacher. All names have been changed. We will begin the discussion of school-home communication by looking at personal reflections and perceptions, then issues in multicultural education, and conclude with recommendations to improve school-home communication.

PERCEPTIONS

While cultivating our nature as human beings, we engage in the act of perceiving our surroundings based on previous experiences. Our perceptions are not based on passive, objective, or neutral processes. Rather, every perception is an active process. Human beings distinguish between important and unimportant items. As humans we tend to perceive certain situations and people actively and clearly, while other situations are perceived to be partially or fully ignored. This is important to understand if we are to research communication patterns between schools and home in ethnic communities. Often, we fail to focus on the many perceptions teachers have toward parents (Ramirez, 1999a). In my experience with schools, perceptions toward families and students are predetermined before the student walks into the classroom on the first day of class. My colleagues would discuss students and their parents in negative and often harsh tones within the faculty lounge. Comments such as, "you know, if those parents [African American parents] would only listen, it would make my job easier" and "don't they [Latino parents] know this is America, and they should learn English so I can speak to them" were common.

With some parents that I interviewed, many felt that their children's teachers had perceived that they (the parents) were "uncaring" based on previous relationships the teachers had with other parents of color. Imelda, a Latina mother stated, "before I went to meet the teacher, her attitude toward me was so negative that I didn't want to go back and talk to her during Open House." Another parent commented, "I mean, why would I want to go to my child's school when all I hear is that black parents don't care about education?" Perceptions have caused parents and teachers to miscommunicate, thereby, creating an atmosphere of antagonism. However, these perceptions could be altered if teachers develop multicultural understanding and communication skills (Nieto, 1992).

When teachers are better able to understand the community that they teach in, their teaching may become more enjoyable. Steve, a high school science teacher who was working in an urban Latino school stated, "when I finally found out how to say something in Spanish to my non-English speaking parents, their eyes widened and they smiled. . . . I knew then that I made a connection and I needed to learn more." Steve went on to say, "I told them that I was *embarazada* or *embarrassed,* for my Spanish was not as fluent as I wanted it to be . . . they laughed. What I told them was that I was *pregnant* and not *embarrassed*. My parents and I still laugh about that." Steve went on to make the comment that his trying to communicate with them went further in creating stronger school-home connections than anything else he had tried.

LANGUAGE AND CULTURE

Language use by teachers and students as well as language policies are volatile, especially in the state of California where bilingual instruction is permitted only with a parent's written permission. Standardization, assessments, and standardized testing have contributed to teachers teaching toward the test they are administering. "Teaching toward the test" occurs because many teachers fear for their jobs from principals; many principals fear for their jobs from superintendents; and many superintendents fear for their jobs from school boards. Parents are asked by the schools to teach their children more English skills within the home, but many Spanish-speaking Latino families do not have the resources or skills to assist in the development of the English language for their children (personal communication, Office of Bilingual Education-Los Angeles Unified School District, January 2000). Nonetheless, schools do need to be in contact with parents to determine how to assess fluency in the children's native and second language. At times, this is more difficult due to teacher's lack of training in this area of assessment.

As I began to research and interview the school community on limited English proficient (LEP) students, I found teachers and parents willing to address the topic of school-home communication. Grace, a fifth grade teacher commented that she wanted her students to speak only English at school (even during recess) for she "didn't know what the students were saying about her." Her policy resulted in negative commentary from her parents. Grace said that parents transferred their children to other schools. Grace felt the students needed to speak only English so they could learn the language, and felt the parents did not want their children to learn English if they placed their children in other schools as a reaction to her mandate. Parents felt that if their children could speak in Spanish, and learn English, then they would become bilingual and have more opportunities than themselves.

Mary, a Latina woman from Guatemala commented that teachers "persuaded" her younger daughter to forgo bilingual education, and be immersed in English-only classrooms. Although the woman's two older sons went through bilingual education and were succeeding at a major university, the daughter struggled to learn one language fluently after her sophomore year of high school. The role that the mother has played in the development of her daughter's language included trusting her teachers' judgments. Now, the mother is looked upon as "troublesome" because of her insistence in allowing her daughter to be placed in bilingual education.

One question we need to ask ourselves as teachers and citizens is whether we in the school community need to learn the languages represented among our communities. This may prove difficult because there may be over 70 languages represented in simply one district. However, by educating ourselves in one language, and learning greetings in others, we would be better able to communicate with families. Steve, the teacher who stated he was "pregnant," would agree.

One student teacher of mine named Stacey, who was teaching at the elementary school level, discussed how she communicated with parents: "Yes, I write letters home in Spanish so my parents will have all the information." Upon further review, Stacey was not fluent in Spanish, nor did she obtain a fluent speaker in Spanish to help her write the letters. She stated, "Oh I just do my best (she had three years of high school Spanish), I mean, they can't read anyway." Other students commented that although they were willing to work in districts with large populations of Spanish speakers, they did not want to obtain a credential in second-language learning, nor did they wish to learn Spanish. The students were also willing to forgo their student teaching semester to obtain a job before their skills as a teacher were mastered. Although I would discuss the difficulty of teaching without student teaching (something I did myself), and teaching second-language learners, many of my student teachers felt that if students just learned English everything would be fine. The following message has become quite clear in many developing teachers: "I may not know everything there is to know about teaching, but I'm going to teach you without the skills it takes to assist you to succeed." This is unfortunate for many schools that are facing teacher shortages since they will have to take student teachers who have not completed their credentials and who do not possess the skills in teaching LEP students.

For students from bilingual-speaking homes, researchers found that there are overall cognitive advantages to learning two languages (Baker, 1996). Teachers who acquire a second language in Spanish increase their ability to communicate with students, and students' families. Overall, they create stronger school-home partnerships. Teachers would also be better able to assist students if they learned how to teach LEP students.

The expectation that schools have regarding communicating with families is different from what families desire from the schools. Schools from the Midwest to the west coast would like parents to attend Open House or Back-to-School nights. However, school personnel do not realize that parents come from cultures that believe it is not appropriate for parents to visit their children's school. The idea of setting foot onto school grounds is a foreign idea in many cultures. Although teachers would like parents to attend Open House, the hidden curriculum (teachers lack of interest in including certain parents) of the school prevents parents from attending (Ramirez, 1999a). In one predominately Latino community, Robert desires to work in a district 30 miles from his home. His reason is simple. He stated, "I love working in Santa Lucia, for the parents never show up for anything, and they never question my teaching." A catch-22 is interjected for parents in this community. If you never show up to events such as Open House, then you are seen as "uncaring." If you do show up and start to ask questions, then you are looked upon with suspicion.

I found there was a dilemma for parents in the research project I conducted on teachers and their attitudes toward parents and parental involvement at the high school level (Ramirez, 1999a). Teachers felt that if parents did not attend Open House, then they did not care about their children's education and performance. When parents were interviewed, a different picture emerged. Parents who did not attend Open House were those who were unable to get time off from work to attend the Wednesday or Thursday night Open House. Also, there were daycare issues and transportation difficulties that parents faced. Some parents also confessed that their children needed to work to supplement the family income. Parents felt the schools did not listen to their needs as parents, since many of them wanted to participate at their children's schools, but were unable to do so. Teacher school-home communication is critical to ensure positive student improvement.

The communication pattern among the teachers was such that only 5% of their students' families were contacted during the school year (Ramirez, 1999b).

In a recent interview, Sheneekra Williams, a Title I administrator, stated, "I am in contact with many of the principals and vice-principals in this district. Honestly, I would be surprised if Title I schools[1] are in compliance regarding parents . . . rarely do the schools communicate or involve parents" (personal communication, January 2000). When asked about urban ethnic communities, she started to laugh. She stated, "black families need to push harder than other families just to see the teachers! Then, the parent is labeled as being a troublemaker. I would like to see more schools communicate better with all of our families." Schools need to realize that parents are a vital component to the improvement of student academic success. When teachers label parents in negative ways, parents may resist participating in their children's education.

MULTICULTURAL EDUCATION AND COMMUNICATION

The interaction between families and schools is unique. Schools face the challenges of considering many ethnicities and cultures that are represented within their schools. Parents and caregivers need to familiarize themselves with school expectations, which is that their children are ready to learn, and are knowledgeable about the school culture. All people involved in the education of youth depend on one another for information. Parents and caregivers need to communicate with the school about their children, and schools must communicate with parents to ensure that academic and social advances within each child are enhanced. However, due to research and personal experience in my life, I ask whether schools are too "educentric"; or are educators willing to learn from parents and families outside of the academic community?

A sad issue to address is what I wish to call, "educentrism." In the area of multicultural education, "ethnocentrism" refers to the idea that one's own ethnicity and ethnic perspective is the main point of reference. In education, and especially in the field of parents and schools, schools and teachers often believe that their (teachers, administrators) way of educating should not be challenged or amended and is above the comprehension of students, visitors, and especially parents. The idea of educentrism needs to be explored especially with regard to how this perspective impacts engagement with parents from a variety of backgrounds. In developing communication between the school and home, teachers and administrators need to understand that a person is made up of a variety of layers, like an onion. The outer layer can be made up of what is seen on the surface like language, food, clothing styles, etc. The second layer can be values that the person shares with others, along with norms. Values represent a person's definition of what is good and bad, and norms are what people perceive as right and wrong among people. By looking at this explanation, we can understand that communication between schools and diverse homes can be difficult if the senders of information (school personnel) do not convey or describe in detail what their cultural communication entails.

Advocates for diminishing the role of multicultural education fail to recognize how communicative patterns differ from culture to culture. When this is understood in the context of communicating with families, schools are better able to understand the cultural relevancy of education upon a student's life. In an interview I undertook with an African American mother, she told her son (who was going to school for the first time), "Now don't go causing any troubles in school." Upon further questioning, the mother felt that the school was a place where her son may experience troubles because of her experience with school as a student. It was her perception that children of color often get singled out for discipline problems, although many of the nonblack children around her son could be just as disruptive.

This mother's description paralleled the feelings of many African American parents and their ideas and feelings about schools.

Effective school-home communication is vital for the health of a school. Unfortunately traditional communication between schools and parents has been during Open House, teacher-parent conferences, and sporting events. Often the communication is ineffective and deals with disciplinary circumstances (Ramirez, 1999b). To better facilitate communication, schools need first to recognize that there is a problem with communication. Then they should pursue a personal connection of involvement with the parents, which includes communicating with them by using positive phone calls home; sending notes and letters to the families in their native language; refraining from using verbose language or speaking down to parents; and having a person on site who could translate for the parents and teachers. This demonstration by school personnel will empower parents. If schools question their existing communication patterns, and recognize that within ethnic groups there is diversity within the group, then their school-home communication would improve.

Parents develop perceptions of the school from their specific historical-cultural experiences. Educators would improve communication if they understood that language barriers, difficulties in adapting to a new society, and socioeconomic differences between teachers and parents all contribute to ineffective communication. Therefore, if educators wish to understand how messages are understood, they need to realize that different people and cultural groups communicate in different ways. By doing this, educators would support self-efficacy among parents and promote better communication. In other words, empowerment is the key in communication with families.

Alvarez et al. (1994) suggest a heterogeneous group of policymakers to improve school-home communication. This group should include a diverse makeup of parents, ethnic groups, and socioeconomic groups. I would suggest that the group also include parents that have not felt comfortable participating in past events, single parents, and parents who do not speak English well.

By including a translator at Open House, or other school-related functions for second-language speakers, parents would feel more free to express themselves and would become more active in their children's school. Also, by asking for parent volunteers to translate school documents, parents would feel empowered. School personnel should take note that computer translators often do not translate documentation or colloquialisms properly. Therefore, a school would need a knowledgeable person at Open House, and a knowledgeable person who is able to correct school literature before it is delivered to the homes.

For African Americans, I suggest that enhancing self-efficacy is key. School administrators need to provide avenues for parents to become empowered in their children's school, and feel that the school is working for the best interest of the child. By lowering the amount of tension between school and home, positive results in communication would be established. As mentioned earlier, many teachers and administrators communicate in a manner and style in which they are accustomed. Also, many groups and individuals have manners of expression that are unique. Furthermore, in any new project concerning culture and ethnic groups, educators need to be careful not to stereotype any groups or individuals they encounter.

In education we need to be aware of stereotyping that may be present in traditional multicultural education courses. In a graduate course that I enrolled in, the professor asked if I spoke Spanish. When I said no, she stated, "Oh that is too bad, you could be a great spokesperson for your people." This comment came from the resident multiculturalist. Because multicultural courses have been taught by using single-group studies in the past (Ramirez, Autry, & Morton, 2000), her experience with Latinos was limited.

In a teacher education program in California, a professor delivered a handout during a multicultural course to students that described African Americans and Latinos. The handout described blacks as being religious and living in urban environments. These "urban blacks" are also more heterogeneous, stress "personal uniqueness and style," and have strong family ties. This handout also goes on to state that when they express emotion it is genuine, which may tie in with their acceptance of handicapped children. "If one of the many [teenaged] single parents . . . disciplines their children, it is usually strict but done out of love. Whether urban blacks are single parents or not, children are often raised by extended family members. Which may be problematic, for the urban black is often impoverished."

This handout included Cubans, Mexicans, Puerto Ricans, Argentineans, Chileans, and so on, as part of the "Hispanic" culture. According to the handout, the strong individual Hispanic loves the arts and honors their family and traditions. However, they are not punctual for gatherings, which doesn't matter for they are a laboring people who are less educated than whites. They stay close to where they live, and also have an extended family that includes godparents. When they get married, they intermarry with whites, and the family becomes the center of the individual's life. Although children are included in family gatherings, let's hope the children do not have disabilities for it will be looked upon as an illness. When in the community, they work together and are accountable for everyone's well-being and honor, except when it comes to males and females. You see in the Hispanic world, states the handout, there is a double standard placed between males and females. Specific roles are predicated on your gender.

How many people or cultures have these traits as part of their families? Lists such as these only pigeonhole families and maintain stereotypes differentiating one family from another. I regret this list not only because of the stereotypes that may be generated with students and their families, but also because there is no room for individuals who are multiethnic. In society, many people have married outside of their culture and ethnicity. If we agree that Hispanics marry with whites (as the list includes), then their offspring would include not just one, but many ethnic possibilities. How, then, would the teacher communicate with a student's family if that student has a parent who is Latino, and another that has French, Irish, or German ancestry, or, as my children are represented, Irish, Filipino, French, Latino, and "American" ancestry?

Researchers and educators also minimize the diverseness within ethnic groups. A recent migrant from the city of Juarez, Mexico is probably different than a recent migrant from a small town such as San Juan de los Lagos, Jalisco Mexico. Although people may come from the same country, they may communicate in different ways. For example, whether educated or not, there are often regional biases that northern Mexicans have with one another. As well, Puerto Ricans, people from Honduras, and Guatemala, all have distinctive characteristics. A commonality that recent immigrants from Latin American countries may share is the Spanish language, although there are still many regional differences.

TEACHER EDUCATION

Excellent teachers have to be excellent communicators as well as fine technicians. This is why quality school-home communication is needed. The difficulty with examining quality communication is that teacher education programs do not always demand that students complete public speaking or some other communication courses. The result is what Leary (1957) calls *Dominance-Submission,* where one person is controlling the communication without allowing the other person to contribute. Although Wubbels, Levy, and Brekelmans (1997) found that good teachers who are dominant contribute to student achievement, Ramirez (1999a, b) found that schools control the level and amount of communication between the school and the home. Often, the teacher (Dominant) is the person who is controlling the communication within the classroom and the parent (Submissive) is subordinate while listening. Often, this style of school-home communication develops into ineffective communication between parents and the school. Leary also suggests a *Cooperation-Opposition* dimension where levels of cooperation are present between people. Wubbels, Levy, and Brekelmans (1997) found that good teachers need to have both dominant and cooperative understandings of their students. They need to set standards, yet be able to understand the needs of their students in a controlled environment that allows for measures of freedom for students.

Gordon (1997) reports that beginning teachers need to develop a sense of *Social Insight,* as well as "withitness" to maximize classroom learning. Social Insight involves learning about the students' (1) verbal language, (2) nonverbal communication, (3) culture, (4) world view, (5) behavioral style, (6) values, (7) methods of reasoning, and (8) cultural and ethnic identification (p. 56). Withitness means taking what is learned by Social Insight, and instructing in a manner that expresses a familiarity with the students' culture and background. Should a teacher be "with it," theoretically mutual respect can be formed between the school and home. By including this training within teacher education, the teacher becomes aware of what is meaningful in the students' lives. The socially insightful and "with it" teacher uses cultural information effectively. Then, the teacher will be better able to communicate with parents about his or her student, and the students' education.

Gordon proposes how to gain social insight and "withitness." To do this, teachers need to (1) expose themselves to adolescent culture, (2) affirm students' interests, (3) relate content to students' outside interests, (4) know the students and (5) share their humanity with their students. These social insights may improve school-home partnerships and communication. In one course that I teach, students are asked to visit different cultural museums and gather information that they would use as a teacher. Many students immediately tend to think of "subject matter" material like visiting the bookstore and reading a book on Japanese American life or The Holocaust. Although my history and English teachers find these books useful, many of my other subject area students need assistance to understand that interviewing Japanese American docents who were interned during World War II, or a Holocaust survivor also brings breadth to their understanding of cultures.

Communication is key when developing social insight and withitness. By communicating with family members in a non-educational arena, more information would be gained by teachers to build the necessary blocks to provide for a less stressful teaching and learning environment for the teacher and the students. Some schools offer Back-to-School nights on Saturdays instead of during the week, and the atmosphere includes potluck suppers, skits, and presentations from teachers and students.

HOME VISITS

Home visits, although not new, contribute to the funds of knowledge from households for teachers and schools (Gonzalez et al., 1995; Nieto, 1992). With the information that home visits would generate, schools would be better able to communicate with the homes and the families. Home visits would also establish reciprocity, for the schools would receive more willing and involved parents. These parents would understand the school culture. Should a family be unable to attend school functions, the home visit would enable teachers to inform parents about school events, their children's progress, and other information. However, in order to produce home visits that would ensure the best for both school personnel and families, the teachers need to enter the home as learners.

As part of a teacher preparation course that I teach, students are asked to interview parents in their homes in pairs. Before the students interview the parents, they are asked about their attitudes toward parents from the perspective of a future teacher. Most comments have negative connotations such as this from one preservice teacher: "I don't mind if parents wish to get involved. I would just hope that they don't back their children all the time if I phone home regarding a problem."

Teachers need to understand that parents will defend their children. As a high school teacher, the first phone call I made was always positive. A brief introduction of myself followed by a positive comment about their child surprised many parents. They were surprised because they were used to negative phone calls from school personnel. I learned that if later I needed to make a negative phone call, the parents were less defensive and more receptive toward my comments.

When asked about phoning home, the student teacher acknowledged that she would only have time to contact parents whose children were doing poorly or were in trouble. Most of the students felt apprehensive regarding the prospect. When asked why, many students responded that it was "too obtrusive" to enter a parent's home, or made comments such as, "Why do we need to do this?"

The student teachers had different views on parents and parental involvement after the exercise. Many stated they learned from the parents, and wanted to make home visits a part of their teaching. Although we discussed the feasibility of going to every student's home if they had over 150 students, we were able to generate ideas about how to incorporate the visits into their curriculum. One suggestion was to only visit those parents with whom they were unable to make some other contact. From the exercise the student teachers learned that parents did care for their children (there were comments to the contrary when parents did not attend Open House), and were knowledgeable about curriculum, school, and (national) education policy. Parents desired to be asked about their opinions on their child's school, and were very inviting toward school personnel. The student teachers also discovered that parents might have daycare, work, or transportation problems on Open House night.

The student teachers learned that ethnography could be used as a tool to learn about families and the lives of their students. Many were able to look within urban families' lives (Latino and African American) for the first time, and realize that many of them (my students with urban parents) had shared experiences. Student teachers were unable to address all the needs of the parents, but felt comfortable about contacting the parents and asking for follow-up interviews with them.

Observations by the student teachers in my multicultural education course parallel what Jones and Velez (1997) suggest in communicating with Latino families and what Nieto (1992) suggests in communicating with ethnic families. Jones and Velez in particular identify a "sociocultural capital" (ethnic families have valuable educational information about their families to share with others) that is apparent in Latino families. The preservice students in their observations recognized that in Latino and African American families, many family members were concerned about the well-being of the child in school. Many of the students in my class felt that the schools were not "challenging" enough to meet the needs and demands that the interviewed parents requested. The parents believed the educational system "took them [the parents] for granted," for the parents would do anything the school wanted. But they were never asked to do anything, and were only contacted if their child was doing poorly academically or was disruptive. For the parents whose children were doing well, rarely was communication delivered from the school. Harry (1992) mentions that many ethnic families defer trust to the schools unconditionally, but if the schools do not reciprocate this trust, then the trust may be lost from the parents. Like Harry in her observations of ethnic families, my students did not find the trust that is often present from families to schools. Often the parents cited "no communication" from the school as the reason for the lack of trust from the parents to the school.

CONCLUSION

So what do schools need to do to promote open and productive dialogue between the school and home? From my experiences as a teacher and researcher, I suggest that schools and teachers need to recognize that parents communicate in a variety of ways. If teachers were able to recognize and begin to ask questions regarding communication patterns within their school community, then they would be better able to communicate in ways that would benefit the school, the parents, the students, and themselves. Chambers (1998) suggests a change of attitude, behavior, and communication from schools. I believe families would also need to become more familiar with the school and how the school communicates.

Ways to increase positive school-home communication would be to hold off-campus meetings between teachers and parents so both parties understand the needs of one another concerning the education of the student. Also, informal gatherings (e.g., Saturday "family day") would allow parents and teachers to meet without the pressure of discussing school-related matters. Although all of this would need to be developed in order to create a more positive relationship between the school and home, it is communication that contributes to a first impression. Teachers and schools need to be aware that communication by way of letters and phone calls reaches a limited amount of parents or guardians. In the United States, 24% of the nation is not literate past the fourth-grade level (Ramirez, 1999a). Most teachers communicate at a much higher level than their constituents, and families may or may not have phones, or their current phone number may be unavailable to the teacher (Ramirez, 1999a, b). As a teacher, I found it difficult to find the time to call all my parents. However, when I scheduled phone calls during my class preparation period (an off-period to create lesson plans, and grade papers), I was able to make phone calls to all of my 165 parents within three weeks. The phone call took two minutes, and was positive in nature. I found that as a teacher, I was able to say something positive about every student in my class (some teachers may find this amusing, for we often only think of the negative part of a student). The parents appreciated the effort, and my students learned that I contacted parents for positive reasons. Not only did this make relationships with my parents better, but my students also suggested that I contact their parents when they did well in my class.

Communicating with parents is an issue that intimidates many teachers. When a student needs to be disciplined, the teacher often calls home, and lets the parent know that their child needed to be disciplined. The communication process that is being delivered from the school to the home is often negative. However, this does not need to be the case. Teacher education programs, community agencies, families, and individuals need to take the time to explore how to communicate in more positive forms to promote parental involvement for student success. Also, teachers need to develop how to communicate in multicultural settings (Nieto, 1992). As mentioned previously, this does not mean learning a second, third, or fourth language, although learning a second language would be beneficial. It means recognizing that different groups and people communicate in different ways. Finding ways to communicate with second language learners is important. For example, a bilingual parent volunteer could translate and make home phone calls to non-English-speaking parents. Effective communication allows greater partnerships between the school and home, and creates a brighter environment for students.

In conclusion, writing and examining communication between the school and home reminds me of the movie *The Breakfast Club* (1985). There is a scene where the vice-principal is telling the janitor that the "kids have turned" on him. In reply, the janitor tells the vice-principal, "the kids haven't changed, you have . . . you got into teaching because you thought it would be easy with summer off. When you found out it was work, it really bummed you out" (my paraphrase). There are many aspects to successful teaching. To teach well is to effectively interact with students. Part of the interaction involves supportive and effective communication with parents. When this kind of communication occurs, parents become teachers' allies, and, in my experience, student academic performance improves. As teachers and parents, academic improvement among our students/children is our goal. It starts and ends with communication.

NOTE

1. Title I is a national program, which gives resources to low-income and/or low-achieving schools. Parental involvement is one criterion for receiving funds.

REFERENCES

Alvarez, D. S., Hofstetter, C. R., Donovan, M. C., & Huie, C. (1994). Patterns of communication in racial/ethnic context: The case of an urban public high school. *Urban Education, 29* (2), 134–149.

Baker, C. (1996). *Foundations of bilingual education and bilingualism.* Bristol, PA: Multilingual Matters Ltd.

Chambers, C. (1998). How customer-friendly is your school? *Educational Leadership,* 56 (2), 33–35.

Dunn, R. (1997). The goals and track record of multicultural education. *Educational Leadership,* 54, (7), 74–77.

Duran, R. P. (1983). *Hispanics' education and background: Predictors of college achievement.* New York: College Entrance Examination Board.

Gonzalez, N., Moll, L. C., Tenery, M. F., Rivera, A., Rendon, P., Gonzalez, R., & Amanti, C. (1995). Funds of knowledge for teaching in Latino households. *Urban Education* 29 (4), 443–470.

Gordon, R. L. (1997). How novice teachers can succeed with adolescents. *Educational Leadership,* (54) 7, 56–58.

Harry, B. (1992). *Cultural diversity, families, and the special education system: Communication and empowerment.* New York: Teachers College Press.

Hidalgo, N. M., Siu, S. F., Bright, J. A., Swap, S. M., & Epstein, J. L. (1995). Research on families, schools, and communities: A multicultural perspective. In J. A Banks, & C. A. McGee Banks (Eds.), *Handbook of research on multicultural education* (pp. 498–524) New York: Macmillan.

Jones, T. G., & Velez, W. (1997) Effects of Latino parent involvement on academic achievement. Paper presented at the Annual Meeting of the American Educational Research Association, (Chicago, March 24–28).

Leary, T. (1957). *An interpersonal diagnosis of personality.* New York: Ronald Press Company.

McEwan, E. K. (1998). *How to deal with parents who are angry, troubled, afraid, or just plain crazy.* Thousand Oaks, CA: Sage.

Nieto, S. (1992). *Affirming diversity: The sociopolitical context of multicultural education.* White Plains, NY: Longman.

Quiroz, B., Greenfield, P. M., & Altchech, M. (1999). Bridging cultures with parent-teacher conferences. *Educational Leadership,* 56, (7), 68–70.

Ramirez, A. Y. (1999a). Teachers' attitudes toward parents and parental involvement in high schools. Dissertation, Indiana University, Bloomington.

Ramirez, A. Y. (1999b). Survey on teachers' attitudes regarding parents and parental involvement. *The School Community Journal,* 9, (2), 21–39.

Ramirez, A.Y., Autry, M., & Morton, M. L. (2000). Different backgrounds, same results: Teacher educators teaching a pre-service culture course. *The Multicultural Journal,* 7, (4), 2–9.

Wubbels, T., Levy, J., & Brekelmans, M. (1997). Paying attention to relationships. *Educational Leadership,* 54, (7), 82–86.

Chapter 14

Why Can't We "Conversate"?: Silencing and Alienation of Latinos and African Americans in School Settings

Xae Alicia Reyes

INTRODUCTION

She rolled her eyes and gestured with her hands as she described her experiences with schools and teachers. She was passionate and optimistic about her future. Olive-skinned, petite, her hair pulled back in a tight bun, the seventeen-year-old Latina spoke of her job with Planned Parenthood where she counseled many women about birth control. The connections she made between her personal growth and her interactions with one of her teachers were very powerful and the audience at the Ivy League school were in awe of her. All but one, the one who had only listened to her use of non-standard English as she stated that "in our class, we 'conversate' with the teacher and that has helped me in my work with adults." When the panel session was over, most of the people in the room were very complimentary. Many were responding to the empowerment projected by the students in the panel. These students embraced the opportunity to develop voice and break their silence on how their lives and their educational processes are affected by teachers' interactions with them, in and outside of classrooms. The one person who was critical of the students' use of non-standard English, a retired English teacher, was hired by the school subsequently, to teach the students oral communication skills. (April 1997)

In the days that followed this presentation, a group of faculty from both the high school where the students were enrolled and the college partnered with the school, were discussing the use of non-standard English by our student. Some of us felt that the critical issue in this event was the fact that these inner-city students who seldom have opportunities to be heard by an elite group of educators, which in this case included national and international speakers, had been strong and articulate;

They gave voice to scores of other students who are silenced and disregarded. One English teacher argued that using standard English for presentations was essential. She argued that the high school students needed to understand that you must not "wear pajamas to the prom." The analogy was very eloquent. None of us could disagree, but many of us were unhappy with the validation of the criticism lodged by the retired English teacher mentioned earlier. We understood that students needed to have a sense of when one language repertoire should be chosen over another. That, we felt, was a legitimate goal of English instruction. What was not comforting for us was that somehow, in recognizing the value of form over content, after the fact, students would feel that their message was both unimportant and that it had been lost in the midst of the debate.

In revisiting the process through which students learned the appropriate repertoire for different situations we are reminded of Gee's (1990) description of the role of an English teacher: "the English teacher is not teaching English grammar or even 'language' . . . but rather teaching a set of discourse practices, oral and written, connected with the standard dialect of English" (p.67). He states further that "the language and literacy equation are forms of socialization, in this case socialization into mainstream ways of taking meaning and of making sense of experience."

The statements I have just cited will illuminate my discussion of the discourses used by educators, in overt and covert ways, to pass judgment on students. These judgments often disallow and/or dismiss students' voices in the learning and teaching dialogues in academic settings at all levels, kindergarten through college, in the United States. In this chapter, I will discuss communication patterns and their contexts as they affect the lives of students.

The existence or not of parallel cultural capital and life experiences among teachers and students often dictates the unwritten rules of participation and access. Those students whose cultural capital matches that of their teachers are oftentimes, not by coincidence, the ones who succeed academically and socially in the school setting. These consequences are a result of the lack of what Freire (1970) calls "emancipatory literacy." Students need to know that different kinds of texts call for different types of background knowledge and require different skills to be read meaningfully (Gee, 1990). The same argument can be extended to different "contexts." The discussion of these "contexts" and their implications will be the focus of much of this chapter.

Students need to "crack" the codes required to communicate successfully in different academic and nonacademic settings. It is important that teachers help students master the corresponding codes by explaining clearly the repercussions and social consequences of making the wrong choices. In some cases, choosing the wrong code in a given setting can lead to exclusion in the job market, social settings, academic settings and so on that will prove significant to a student's future opportunities.

CONTEXT AND DISCOURSES

My observations in numerous Northeastern schools (K–12) as a teacher, teacher educator and researcher, have provided data that reflect the importance of choosing the appropriate linguistic code to communicate successfully and to "fit" into a variety of contexts. In many of the schools I have observed, the student leadership, parent involvement, and social life of the school are notable in the cases where the students are in advanced placement (AP) and are honor students (H). The parent leadership is usually made up of the parents of those very same students. The social agenda of the school is defined by the interests and concerns of these two groups—those of the high-achieving students and their parents. In other words, the voices of a majority of students and parents, in the middle range where most of the Latino and African American populations in urban schools are situated, are neither heard nor represented in most of these organizations. In one school in a suburban setting with an increasingly diverse population, the School Improvement Team (SIT), included parents, students, and teachers. Some were teachers whose own high-achieving children attended the school, some were parents who were teachers in other schools, and some members were the high-achieving students. Other active parents were connected to the school in various ways. Some were involved in city government/ politics and business and others were related to or had been classmates of some of the teachers at the school.

What is difficult to accept is that this cycle of access to power is difficult to break. In his book *Social Linguistics and Literacies*, Gee speaks of standard/dominant "cultural models" in society. He states that the mastery of these are the basis on which "choices about exclusion and inclusions" are made (p. 90). According to Gee, the key factor in understanding the impact of these dynamics rests with teachers, because the "cultural models of a student's own home culture can conflict seriously with those of mainstream culture." This has been documented by the work of Heath (1983) and Trueba (1989). Teachers must "focus the student's attention on the relevant aspects of experience that will make the system, the network of cultural models, begin to gel" (p. 91). Mastery of the forms and understanding of their contexts is what would determine access and success for students and for their families as well.

The secret of privileged relationships based on the mastery of the mainstream cultural models may be based on the lack of congruence between teacher education of a homogeneous teacher corps and the changing demographics of our student population in schools throughout the United States. Therefore, according to Gee, it is the role of the teacher to research language and culture and to observe and learn from her/his students. Teacher education programs are emphasizing the teacher knowledge of students through intensified fieldwork and reading of authentic research. Interactions with diverse students and in diverse communities create understandings and feelings of comfort among teachers that will increase the acceptance of students and enhance their learning opportunities in classrooms.

TEACHERS AS FACILITATORS OF SUCCESSFUL DISCOURSES

In order to access success within the educational system and eventually in U.S. society, teachers must find ways to create the necessary opportunities for students of color, particularly Latinos and African Americans, to develop voice. These opportunities are embedded in the interactions that the students' families sustain in the community, the interactions with school staff, administrators, teachers and other students. Many of our schools in urban settings have become segregated through processes of immigration, job and housing trends, and the burgeoning opportunities provided to those who have accessed financial privilege and social mobility. Teachers, and other educational staff in urban centers continue to be white while their students are increasingly black and brown.

Many, if not all, of our teachers and administrators have little to no insider knowledge about the languages and cultures of the new student populations they are serving. For the longest time, the norm has been to reinforce the language of the dominant group, in this case: standard English. The privileging of standard English has been detrimental to student teacher communication and to parent interactions with staff, because it has placed both students and their parents in a subordinate position vis a vis the school system. This subordination creates the silencing and alienation that is subsequently interpreted by teachers and school authorities as lack of interest and caring by parents and students of color.

Among the many factors that contribute to the subordinate status assigned to the speakers of nonstandard English, especially blacks and Latinos, we can identify the biased, stereotypical portrayals of these groups in the popular media. I would agree that stereotyped character images and speech patterns are engraved in our subconscious minds in pervasive ways. Hence, the mere mention of the "Gonzalez" surname conjures the image of a small rat named Speedy Gonzalez and makes us think of inauthentic Mexican food at Taco Bell, switchbladed gangs in the film, *West Side Story*, and, more recently, of over-sexualized images of Jennifer Lopez and Ricky Martin. Stereotypes with regard to the black community are just as pervasive. The media has exploited images of Mammy, Sambo, and other, now jaded, stereotypes, as well as images of sports figures and music celebrities such as Dennis Rodman and Puff Daddy. News reports on blacks and Latinos emphasizing their dropout rates and their majority status in jails, continue to feed the negative views of these groups held by mainstream society without questioning the roots of the problems. The lack of more powerful nonmedia-related representations of blacks and Latinos in mainstream memory and in school textbooks, maintains the subordinate status of these populations in the national public discourse and influences interactions between mainstream and non-mainstream individuals and groups. These interactions have become institutionalized; that is, they are practices that are sanctioned by both the educational system and mainstream society.

Teaching against the grain is what many schools of education across the nation are encouraging their preservice teachers to do. Teachers must challenge existing social practices in order to allow equal access to education to *all* students. They must find ways to foster their participation and development of voice in the educational process. Eventually, they must rid our schools of the practices that relegate some students to secondary/subordinate status.

The inclusive teacher described by the student in the vignette mentioned at the beginning of this chapter was doing just that. She challenged the paradigm of teacher-centered classrooms by creating a dialogue in her classes and moving

away from the teacher-centered authoritarian model. At the same time she validated students' experiences by inviting and including these in her discussions and
used them to supplement the knowledge she shared in the classroom. The students'
language was monitored, but not silenced or corrected in ways that may have limited or stifled their expressions. The teacher modeled by using standard English in
her own discourse and discussed the impact of not using standard English in specific contexts emphasizing distinctions between formal and informal contexts.
Perhaps the teacher needed to delve into a deeper discussion of cultural and linguistic hegemony and its relationship to sociopolitical and economic conditions as
an important aspect of this discourse, which is often omitted in classrooms.

I reviewed some of the behaviors, and both verbal and nonverbal communication styles that affect the dynamics among teachers and schools; I saw patterns that
included failure to greet parents and students of color in the same way that mainstream and known parents were greeted. I have made this observation in many
school settings, where I have questioned the lack of courtesy of some staff who
rendered certain parents invisible by shifting eye contact to more familiar parents.
While working in school settings, I have noticed repeatedly that the "hellos' and
"good mornings" are missing from the discourse when Anglo teachers and staff
deal with nonwhite parents. These greetings are notably present when faculty and
staff interact with parents and visitors who are ethnically and culturally similar to
them or are known to have a certain status in the community. I have repeatedly witnessed how the front office staff has lowered their gaze when they hear an accent
or see a person of color. These same staff members react with very defensive tones
when addressed by parent visitors who are non-Anglo. All of these behaviors create an unwelcoming atmosphere for Latino and African American parents, and
eventually affect the students' sense of belonging and feeling welcome in the
school. When discussing these issues in parent involvement workshops, I encourage parents to persevere and to seek out advocates and supporters when visiting
schools.

Once, while sitting in on a parent-teacher conference at a predominantly African
American school where I was a participant observer, I glanced over to the board
and read:

It's ask, not axe
It's you, not yous

I remembered my conversation with some parents in the hallway about black
English. I also remembered media portrayals, and pieces of authentic African
American literature. I thought of the children going home and correcting their el-
ders, and the tone of superiority in which the statements were written by the Anglo
teacher in the classroom. I discussed the issue with some of the parents and was not
surprised when they stated: "I want my child to speak 'properly.'" Sadly, the parents had internalized the notion that their home language was "wrong."

The discourses of teachers that omit a discussion of the context in which one
language variety is assigned a superior status over another are short of negligent. A

subjective, judgmental stance adopted by teachers reinforces a status of subordination of parents and students and alienates both parties from the dominant discourse
that is rewarded by the school. But even worse than that, it contributes to alienating
students through silencing and repressing their voices (Christensen, 1994).

I have encouraged school systems to address the social behaviors of the staff
and urged them to be more in tune with appropriate public relations skills. In
one of my entries when doing fieldwork, a student of color shared that he lost
respect for his high school teacher once he heard her tell a co-worker "Ugh,
here comes that woman" and she was referring to his mother. Many thought-
less remarks are this blatant and contribute to placing many of our students at
risk. Language and gestures, verbal and nonverbal can convey loaded messages that define our relationships.

DISCUSSING LANGUAGE IN TEACHER EDUCATION

The discussions of language usage, the hegemony of standard English over
other varieties, and the assignment of the lowest rungs on the totem pole to Latino
and black English, are not easy discussions to sustain in classrooms dominated by
white faces. Such is the case with most teacher education programs still dominated
by young white females. With this reality in mind, one has to make a bigger effort
to expand the understanding of these concepts among those who have been privileged by circumstances. Language hegemony, is not, and has never been, an issue
to discuss and or consider; it has been taken for granted. Since most of the teacher
education students have not moved beyond their boundaries, beyond the sheltered
environments of suburban or smaller-town existences, my discussions of these issues seem unnecessary and questionable.

The privilege of owning the valued cultural capital, in this case the dominant
language and culture valued by teachers and schools, goes unnoticed when it is
part of one's heritage, reinforced through one's environment and rewarded by society's institutions, including schools. It is hard to imagine tensions and exclusion
from participation in democratic processes and educational opportunity when one
has not lived similar experiences. The charge to teacher educators is to create the
opportunities and experiences needed by preservice teachers to develop a sense of
empathy toward students whose lives are different from their own. They must also
develop critical understanding of the dynamics of schooling and how teaching and
learning are affected by the sociopolitical context. As Lisa Delpit (1995) points
out:

[I]f teachers hope to avoid negatively stereotyping the language patterns of their students, it
is important that they be encouraged to interact with and willingly learn from, knowledgeable members of their students' cultural groups. This can best become a reality if teacher education programs include diverse parents, community members, and faculty among those
who prepare future teachers, and take seriously the need to develop in those teachers the humility required for learning from the surrounding context when entering a culturally different setting. (p. 56)

As teacher educators work to reconstruct the understanding preservice teachers have of language and cultural behaviors, they increase the repertoire of sources such as authentic literature and works by ethnically diverse writers. Empathy is also accomplished by exposing students to urban experiences through field placements in urban settings. Both of these activities can be extremely effective if they are woven into reflective dialogues and introspections that allow preservice teachers to see the difference between their life experiences and those of their students.

DIALOGUES OF EMPOWERMENT

The multiple dimensions of the learning context present a challenge to educators that has never been greater. On one hand, we have the changing demographics, and on the other, we have a nation competing to maintain a leadership role in world markets. In spite of this, many teacher education students are still convinced that monolingualism and cultural ethnocentrism can be maintained as the paradigm for this country. In addition to this, technological advances have made the world smaller and mass communication links the world simultaneously to share events that often change the world.

As we engage in the discourses of schools and other social institutions, we need to understand the complexity of the term *discourse*. Giroux (1997) stated that "discourse can be recognized as a form of cultural production linking agency and structure through public and private representations that are concretely organized and structured within schools" (p. 135). He goes on to discuss that one must discover the relationship of the discourse to power in schools, and teachers who are committed to social reconstruction must design the strategies to make schools democratic public spheres. These strategies could well be framed in dialogues of empowerment. The dialogues that validate students' culture and languages and create opportunities for success are based on knowledge of our students gleaned through interaction with the students and their communities. This is the beginning of the empowerment process.

Whether it is a different language, such as Spanish, or a variety of English such as Spanglish or black English, the layers of relationships and hierarchies are embedded in the language choices we make. Those choices, deliberate or involuntary, may determine our inclusion or exclusion from participation in a given setting. Some styles are more accepted and expected within schools or as Noel (2000) puts it, certain styles are "privileged" (p. 13).

The understanding of the dynamics of language is an important lesson to learn but the way to "teach" about the linguistic codes to choose in a given moment, depending on context and goals of the participants. This is a critical part of teaching. Delpit (1995) suggests a series of activities that show appreciation for linguistic diversity in the classroom. These include allowing students opportunities to use the new code (standard English) in a non threatening, real, communicative context, and performing role plays using standard English while not under the threat of correction (p. 53). According to Delpit, "forcing speakers to monitor their language for rules while speaking, typically produces silence" and that "correction may also affect students' attitudes toward their teachers" (p. 51). Nieto (2000) stresses that "language diversity needs to be placed within a sociopolitical context to understand why speaking a language other than English is not itself a handicap . . . it can be a great asset to learning" (p. 188).

One other recommendation would be for all teachers to understand the processes of second language acquisition so that they could better understand the needs of their students and plan and construct lessons that would consider these aspects of learning. This is where the "humility" mentioned earlier by Delpit becomes very important. Teachers need to be willing to recognize that there is much that they can learn from their students, and from the students' parents and their communities.

OVERSTEPPING OUR BOUNDARIES

In our quest for equity in educational opportunities we often "buy into" the dominant discourses and somehow convince ourselves and our students that owning the dominant discourse or cultural model will result in successful participation in mainstream society. This is one of the pitfalls of our social stratification. As we characterize discourses as successful and unsuccessful and allow our students to experience the consequences of their choices to prove our point, we are inadvertently perpetuating the hegemony of one language repertoire over another. This is also where language could become stagnant as it loses its flexibility to incorporate new expressions that reflect the experiences of those who continue to be conspicuously absent from the dominant discourse.

Perhaps the clearest example of these language tensions is evident in the proliferation of "underground hip hop." Through this medium and in conjunction with electronic communication, many of our urban youth whose discourses are dismissed in our classrooms have felt validated. They respond cybernetically to each other's conceptualizations of life, love, music, and a myriad of relevant concerns. Their understandings seem not to matter in the mainstream forums of schools, communities, and even sometimes in their own homes. As teachers and parents, we often focus on language choices and fail to listen to the messages and concerns they try to communicate. As long as we continue to exclude these voices, we maintain the status quo. In the process, we dismiss these students' views and disallow contributions that may challenge paradigms of social justice as conceived by dominant society.

It has long been a concern of progressive teacher educators to harness and channel the voices of students so that all possible perspectives are represented in the classroom and hence a more democratic environment prevails. This approach is needed to create a more inclusive atmosphere in classrooms that will eventually extend itself to greater society. If we continue to silence some discourses in favor of those that are aligned with the discourses of the dominant culture, we are perpetuating the social patterns that grant a higher status to the home cultures of some groups over those of the others. As Gee puts it "some of the values of mainstream culture are complicit with the oppression of some students' home cultures . . . black, Hispanic and many students from third world cultures" (p. 90). As daunting as this challenge seems, it is necessary to provide spaces for the non-mainstream discourses to flourish and intersect with the dominant discourse in order to move forward toward a more equitable society. This agenda is only possible in an educational framework of social reconstructivism.

SUMMARY

The alienation of black and brown students in the school system is possible because of the discourse patterns that dominate our classrooms. Teachers are instrumental in producing the changes necessary to validate discourses and voices of those that have traditionally been silenced. For this to happen, there needs to be an acknowledgment of a hegemonic structure in our schools and classrooms that mirrors the social stratification in the greater society. There also needs to be an acknowledgment of the role that schools have played in the perpetuation of these structures. Students in our schools must be made aware of the consequences of their choices of repertoires in terms of exclusion and inclusion into privilege and success. This awareness must be a part of the learning experience in our schools without devaluing the home languages and cultural patterns of non-mainstream students.

The challenges presented by the variety of goals mentioned earlier must be made clear in the process of educating teachers for a fair and equitable society. No amount of "book" knowledge can provide the totality of insights needed by teachers to relate to their students' realities. The increasing diversity among our students requires a more experiential approach to teacher education. It is important that our preservice teachers acquire first-hand knowledge through lived experiences within the cultural environments of their students. This can be accomplished through travel, field placements, and the study of authentic literature and research.

The other side of the educational context to reflect on is that we must consider an ideological stance that allows for the questioning of the assignment of superior status to some discourses, language varieties, and cultural models over others. We might serve social justice in a better way if we were to allow a more inclusive and participatory model of discourse in our classrooms. This is possibly the most complex of the goals of progressive, social reconstructivist education. On one hand, we must educate our students to succeed in the mainstream world by understanding and adopting the norms, styles, and attributes of the dominant discourse, while on the other we must challenge the very concept of dominance of a discourse vis-à-vis the exclusion of other discourses that have not been heard. How does a teacher balance these two goals? How do we validate voices that have been traditionally silenced, while we teach our students the strategies and styles of the "winning" dominant discourse?

There is no amount of teacher education that can address the true changes needed in our preservice and inservice educators. The true changes that need to occur are embedded in attitudes and beliefs about the "other." These attitudes and beliefs are reinforced by the literature, stereotypes, and the generally uncontested mainstream discourse. The key approaches to address the problems presented here are a combination of inquiry and exposure to the otherwise silenced discourses. The inquiry into mainstream cultural models should ask who is represented and who made the choices as to what constitutes valued knowledge and cultural behaviors. This would fall under the need for political education and social justice inquiry by students in schools (Apple, 1995). In an earlier text, Apple clearly outlined an agenda for teachers who are to embark on this social reconstructive agenda by questioning whose interests schools are to serve (p. 153) and further stating:

Those who engage in critical scholarship in education should have constant and close ties to the real world of teachers, students and parents . . . and they need to be closely connected to feminist groups, people of color, and those teachers and curriculum workers who are now struggling . . . for gains that have been made in democratizing education and to make certain that our schools and the curricular and teaching practices within them are responsive in race, gender, and class terms. (p. 204)

We must make a special effort to make and find connections between students' home lives and discourse patterns in order to validate their voices within the classroom dialogues. This requires knowledge of our students and of their home cultures. It also calls for an analysis of the discontinuities between the dominant discourse and the subordinate discourse in order to build the necessary bridges to create inclusive atmospheres in our schools and classrooms to invite participation of all students. This means there must be a willingness to acknowledge privileged status by our mainstream teachers, students, and community members. A commitment to engage in an honest critique of power structures in and outside of schools is extremely important in this effort to avoid alienating any of our students.

REFERENCES

Apple, M. (1995). *Education and power.* New York: Routledge

Apple, M. (1986). *Teachers and texts: A political economy of class and gender relations in education.* New York: Routledge & Kegan Paul.

Christensen, L. (1994). *Whose standard? Teaching standard English: Rethinking our classrooms.* Milwaukee: Rethinking Schools Ltd.

Delpit, L. (1995). *Other people's children: Cultural conflict in the classroom.* New York: The New Press.

Freire, P. (1970). *Pedagogy of the oppressed.* New York: Seabury Press.

Gee, J. P. (1990). *Social linguistics and literacies: Ideologies and discourses.* London: The Falmer Press.

Gee, J. P. (1999). *An Introduction to discourse analysis: Theory and method.* New York: Routledge.

Giroux, H. (1997). *Pedagogy and the politics of hope.* Boulder, CO: Westview Press.

Heath, S. B. (1983). *Ways with words: Language, life and work in communities and classrooms.* Cambridge: Cambridge University Press.

Nieto, S. (2000). *Affirming diversity: The sociopolitical context of multicultural education.* 3rd ed. New York: Longman.

Noel, J. (2000). *Developing multicultural educators.* New York: Longman.

Trueba, H. (1989). *Raising silent voices: Educating linguistic minorities for the 20th century.* Cambridge: Newbury House.

Chapter 15

Latino and African American Relations in Academia: A Case Study of Solidarity between Faculty of Color

Daryl M. Rowe and Reyna Garcia Ramos

INTRODUCTION

Recently, changes in the demographics of this country have become more notice-able as the faces of our American society look increasingly multicultural (Nieto, 2000). It is presumed to be inevitable that conflicts will arise between those who feel that they are somehow being displaced by a new "foreign" group (Campbell, 2000). Two such groups that have had a history of conflict in the United States are African Americans and Latinos. Although little has been done to systematically explore this tension, it has now become more common to ask questions about its roots. Given unequal access to education opportunities and the increase of racial diversity, interaction between these two groups has been painful at times. The po-larization of segments of society has sometimes created violent outbursts that have devastated communities and cities (Campbell, 2000).

LATINO AND AFRICAN AMERICAN RELATIONS

Historically, Latinos and African Americans share a common mistreatment by whites in the United States. Each group has suffered from residential and job dis-crimination, educational neglect, economic restrictions, and racialized violence (Hraba, 1994). According to Hraba, the tension between African Americans and Latinos varies according to which ethnic group is being examined and the era dur-ing which the examination occurs. For example, while tension has existed between African Americans and Puerto Ricans, the struggle has been more recent and cen-tered on competition for jobs, political influence and public education (bilingual education). Each of these flashpoints seem to reflect the impress of the racialized worldview in the United States that stratifies opportunities based on race or ethnic group affiliation (Smedley, 1999). Similarly, tension between Cuban Americans and African Americans is recent and centers on job competition and language usage (bilingual education), primarily in southern Florida. In terms of Mexican and African American tension, initially there was little tension because the widespread use of Mexican labor occurred in the Southwest, where few African Americans originally settled; Latinos faced little competition from other ethnic groups. However, as more and more African Americans settle in California, the opportunities for competition in both residential choices and jobs have increased. Thus, conflict between African Americans and Latinos seems to emerge more from economic competition and racism, as reflected by labor repression, occupational stratification, and dual-wage systems between whites and both Latinos and African Americans (Hraba, 1994).

Although there appear to be anecdotal impressions that considerable tension exists between Latinos and African Americans, the published literature is noticeably scarce about this theorized conflict. A computer search of literature indexed through The ERIC Database (1992–2000/03) yielded a total of eight sources identified. African American and Latino and violence, racial tension and conflict were the keywords used in the search. Of the 11 articles identified only three directly addressed African American and Latino relations (Williams, 1996; Akinyela, 1997; Piatt, 1997). Williams explores African American and Latino relationships, with particular emphasis on strategies for enhancing cooperation and eliminating barriers. Most of the work contained within presents the parallel dimensions of struggle African Americans and Latinos manage in their quest for empowerment and improvement.

Akinyela's (1997) work focuses more directly on conflicts between African American and Latino communities. He uses a cultural democracy frame to conceptualize his ideas. Cultural democracy is defined as an operational framework that actively seeks to include the experiences, ideas, and practices of ethnic and language diverse family members, practitioners, academics, and lay workers in family support policy implementation, program development, and service delivery. The critical aspect of this frame is the rescue and reclamation of the voices or perspectives of Latinos and African Americans to examine the phenomenon of cultural diversity within the family support movement. Its design is to significantly impact the decision-making influence and unequal power held by persons of color in the national family support movement, by renegotiating power and equity in American society. Akinyela suggests that tension between African Americans and Latinos can be understood through family support and policy issues.

Piatt (1997) suggests that although Latinos and African Americans share common experiences and reactions to racism and discrimination, there is an undercurrent of tension influencing much of their interaction and creating barriers to more effective coalition building. Furthermore, given the changing demographics in the United States, there is a greater need to resolve this underlying tension to insure movement on a broader human rights level for either and both groups. Piatt's comments effectively capture the focus of this chapter, namely to advocate for more solidarity and respect between and among African Americans and Latinos.

Unfortunately, a more lasting area of conflict between African American and Latinos exists within the gang elements of both communities. However Phillips's (1999) anthropological study of gangs and graffiti use in south central Los Angeles provides insight that runs counter to the notions of indiscriminant or rampant conflict between African Americans and Latinos. Her position is that violence between African American and Latino gangs shift periodically based on different neighborhood-specific transgressions, but that the majority of conflict occurs more within same-ethnic groups versus between them: "Cross-ethnic warfare shifts with local events and has not yet been stigmatized" (p. 170). Her qualitative research contradicts the cross ethnic violence that "many have predicted" (p. 343). She contextualized the potential of systemic conflict as resulting from both the loss of demographic footing within historic African American neighborhoods and the statistical numbers advantage of Chicano gangs (they outnumber all other gang types in Los Angeles). Nonetheless, based on her fieldwork, she catalogued four styles of interaction, the majority of which seemed to paint a more hopeful picture regarding black/brown relations.

The first style is a race-based dislike where the conflict extends beyond specific transgressors to all African Americans or Latinos. The tensions in this style tend toward more global cross-ethnic hatred. The second and more common style reflects negotiated relationships emerging out of specific events and not widespread racial conflict. Thus, there are alternating periods of harmony or animosity dependent on whether sufficient respect is accorded to the rules of particular gangs. The third style is characterized by more harmonious cooperation and a degree of satisfaction with the level of relationship. Lastly, there are some rare instances of Latinos and African Americans being members of the same gangs. Phillips concludes that the considerable majority of Los Angeles African American and Latino gangs get along—they trade, support/defend each other, and engage in illicit business jointly—while maintaining their distinct ethnic/racial identities.

CRITICAL RACE THEORY

Given the focus of this text and the paucity of literature uncovered regarding issues that serve to separate African Americans and Latinos, it is important to understand Latino/African American relations within a broader social and political analysis. According to Delgado (1995), critical race theory serves as a framework for analyzing a variety of issues related to race in the United States, and can provide an adequate method for examining the perception of strained relations between African Americans and Latinos. Critical race theory is an eclectic system of thought emerging out of civil rights law that posits a need for a more comprehensive challenge to understanding race-related concerns. The overarching theme is that movement toward more equitable distribution of power among America's ethnic/racial groups has been unnecessarily belabored; and that customary strategies for addressing the resistant strains of racism have increasingly led to limited results.

Delgado identifies a number of assumptions that uphold much of the thinking of critical race theorists, as follows. First, critical race theorists see racism as the normative condition underlying the social structure in the U.S, not the atypical, peculiar system of beliefs held by a few that many presume. As such, an understanding of racism must be overlaid on any analysis exploring interracial or interethnic tension. Because of the pervasive existence of race-based identifications and racism—preferences for or against persons based on their presumed phenotypic characteristics (see Smedley, 1999 for a fuller discussion)—the focus in discussions of race-based phenomena tend to only capture more extreme sorts of injustices, not the everyday, "business-as-usual forms of racism" (p. xiv) embedded throughout the social fabric of American society. It is this common, rooted degree of racism that can impact African American and Latino relationships because of an occasionally superficial struggle among themselves for a delimited piece of the social-political pie.

Second, critical race theorists assume that there is a need to analyze the prevailing presuppositions, rules, and practices of this society in order to develop new perspectives regarding racial issues. Specifically, they argue the necessity of using more person-centered forms of expression—storytelling, autobiography, and myth deconstruction—as methods for reconstructing a social reality that is centered in the life experiences of those racial/ethnic groups that have been historically disenfranchised. Such methods of social commentary authorize the unique perspectives of those whose voices have been disregarded, dismissed, and discounted. It is from this viewpoint that we write this chapter; critically examining our experiences as African American and Latino faculty involved in building an effective coalition within an academic institution that still maintains a very parochial position regarding ethnic/racial diversity.

Third, critical race theorists assume that interest-convergence operates throughout U.S. society in race-related issues. Interest-convergence means that powerful whites only tend to support the concerns of persons of color when our concerns converge with the interests of the powerful. This perspective will be highlighted through a discussion of various diversity-enhancement activities at the university, as a whole, and within our specific departments. The emphasis on diversity or multiculturalism within university communities provides a clear example of interest-convergence, and how well-intended goals often become subverted to the interests of the powerful.

Finally, critical race theorists place an emphasis on the specific details of the lives of people of color, as the basis for energizing conceptual frameworks. For our purposes, we will describe the unique sets of pressures evident in the university climate that seek to maximize competitiveness and minimize effective coalition building among ethnic faculty, and our strategies for managing those influences, such that we understand the context of institutional racism underlying our personal academic careers.

Unfortunately, the majority of the presumptions underlying the discussion of African American/Latino conflict have been shortsighted in both scope and vision. In addition to the problems within the society for addressing the needs of African Americans and Latinos, the conflict thesis has been decontextualized (Rowe, 1998). Those who favor conflict or tension arguments fail to adequately consider the historical context out of which these issues emerge. For example: (1) the colonial domination and targeted genocide of native American Indians (Smedley, 1999); (2) the exploitative use of migrant labor forces from Mexico and Central and South America (Hraba, 1994); (3) participation in the depopulation and enslavement of millions of Africans; and (4) coordinated systems of disenfranchisement of African Americans through Reconstruction, Jim Crow, and segregation (Asante, 1999). In short, the well-documented manipulation of America's racial/ethnic groups for the benefit of the Anglo power structure. The net result is that these situations, which have occurred over generations, have led to pervasive and continuing distortions of economic, social, political, philosophical, religious, and psychological structures and ideas that African Americans and Latinos have of themselves and of each other (Asante, 1999).

For the greater part of this nation's history, the attainment of freedom, self-determination, and equality has been reserved to a small segment of the U.S. population: northern and western Europeans (Rowe, 1998). Those populations have had ascribed privilege as a result of the persistent and multifaceted systems of oppression heaped upon African Americans and Latinos. All facets of the social system have been mobilized to produce a society that both the privileged and oppressed experience: Interethnic tension is merely one aspect of this complex social system.

Unfortunately, up to now, there has been a failure to adequately define the philosophical assumptions and a reluctance to address the broader issues that provide the context for understanding African American and Latino tension. Instead, most of the work has adhered to the underlying Eurocentric cultural assumptions regarding privilege, power and order in the United States.

Thus, the need to consider racism as the normative belief system overarching U.S. social structure is critical as a point of departure in discussing African American and Latino tension. It is from this understanding that a fuller analysis emerges; one that challenges the idea that Latinos and African Americans must compete with each other for a minority share of power and access to resources.

CENTERING OUR STORY

In this context, the purpose of this chapter is to shed new light on the antithesis of this debate and conflict and to demonstrate the solidarity that has been formed between an African American faculty member and a Latino faculty member in a private academic institution of higher education. It exemplifies how an alliance has been forged among the Latino, the African American, and other faculty of color to persevere in an environment that does not value diversity and even further strives to openly maintain homogeneity of culture. The context for this work environment exists within one of the most diverse cities in this nation—Los Angeles,

California. A region that in 1990 had 3,485,398 people living within its city boundaries of which 39% were Latinos, 37% Caucasian, 13% African and 9% Asians (U.S. Census Bureau, 1990). Los Angeles is the center of trade with Pacific Rim countries and as such serves as a "principal global cultural center" (City of Los Angeles, 2000). The Los Angeles metropolitan region has achieved a new ethnic and cultural diversity since its international airport serves as the new "Ellis Island" for immigration into the United States (City of Los Angeles, 2000). That such a parochial approach to ethnic diversity can be adhered to in such a culturally rich environment speaks to both the subtle and blatant efforts to stifle multiple voices.

Within the Los Angeles City boundaries there are several public and private colleges and universities that include the University of California at Los Angeles, University of Southern California, California State University at Los Angeles, California State University at Northridge, Occidental College, and Loyola Marymount University. There are also seven community colleges within the city limits (City of Los Angeles, 2000). The greater Los Angeles basin is also home to more public and private colleges and universities. One is a mid-sized private Christian university. It is this institution and the larger community backdrop that have framed the analyses contained in this chapter.

A PRIVATE CHRISTIAN INSTITUTION

This work is based on the experiences of two faculty who have come to rely and depend on each other in order to succeed within the work environment. The institution is a mid-sized university offering bachelor's, master's, and doctoral degrees across a wide range of disciplines. The entire university enrolls approximately 8,000 full-time and part-time students, with a full-time faculty of more than 300 professors and scholars. Established during the depression era in Southern California, this institution was primarily a small, undergraduate liberal arts college. In the 1970s, with the addition of professional schools, the college became a university. The most distinctive feature of the institution is its commitment to academic excellence in the context of "Christian values" (Seaver Catalogue, 2000).

It has an undergraduate program that enrolls approximately 3,000 students, and professional programs that enroll approximately 5000 students a year. The professional schools include a school of law, a school of public policy, a school of business and a school of psychology and education. Although the institution professes the promotion of unity and community across its various schools, it is often difficult, at best, due to diverse schedules, disciplines, research interests and geographic locations.

The school of psychology and education enrolls approximately 1,500 students with four educational centers that encompass three counties. This post-baccalaureate school offers an array of master's degrees and doctoral degrees in psychology and education. The school's administration includes a dean of the school and associate deans for each division. Currently the school has 51 full time faculty on tenure track, nontenure track, and visiting. Within this setting there are six faculty of color, three African Americans, two Asians, and a Latina, five of which are tenure track.

CHALLENGES FOR FACULTY OF COLOR

A body of literature attests to the fact that faculty of color have experienced difficulty when integrating themselves into academia. It becomes evident that such an account would be true considering the work by Colby and Foote (1995), which finds that 90% of the total faculty at two-and four-year public and private colleges are white. This same study found that the highest percentage of faculty of color are employed at public four-year institutions (12.6%) while the lowest percentage of faculty of color are employed at private two-year colleges (2.6%) in the United States (Colby & Foote, 1995). These findings are even more alarming considering that these data represent a disproportionate representation of faculty of color in predominantly black colleges and universities and two-year institutions (Alexander-Snow & Johnson, 1998). This indicates that faculty of color at four-year predominantly white institutions are virtually nonexistent. As the number of faculty of color slowly rises at institutions of higher education across the country, questions about proper mentoring and support remain unanswered.

While some attention has been focused on how institutions of higher education adapt strategies for the recruitment, retention, and graduation of students of color at both undergraduate and professional schools, limited work has examined how faculty of color fare in predominantly white institutions (Holcomb-McCoy, 1999). Even though students and faculty of color face similar issues, it is the faculty of color who are most at-risk of severe marginalization at predominantly white institutions (Alexander-Snow & Johnson, 1998). This should come as no surprise, since research has suggested that faculty of color have had to "overcome" racism in order to attain promotion and tenure (Baez, 1998). Whether individual or institutional, the literature indicates that there are real threats to the successful survival of faculty of color. Therefore, the need to examine the impact of homogeneity of culture, predominantly white male culture, in institutions of higher education becomes paramount.

EUROCENTRISM

Briefly stated, Eurocentrism reflects the system of cultural thought that projects the representations of the lifestyles, values, and behaviors of persons of Euro-American ancestry as normal or prototypical for human functioning; that is, as the normative criteria against which all other humans are judged (Shohat & Stam, 1994; Asante, 1999). In so doing, it normalizes the power relations that have evolved out of the specific histories of Western European practices of colonialism and imperialism (Smedley, 1999). It codifies its values and biases such that persons of European descent construe meritocracy to reflect being in charge, and persons of color—specifically Latinos and African Americans—are presumed to be less deserving of their just rewards, except as proffered by special programs. The discussion of culture, then, is useful for delineating the power and pervasiveness of culture generally, and the pervasiveness of a particular cultural system, Eurocentrism, on the understanding of African American and Latino conflict (Rowe & Grills, 1996), generally, and the particular pressures on faculty of color.

The problem is structural in nature. Proponents of a conflict thesis for African American and Latino relations begin their analyses from the standpoint of Western-trained social scientists, adhering to the fundamental assumptions inherent in existing power relations, and simply attempting to apply their acquired knowledge to brown/black struggles (cf. Said, 1978). Rarely are there attempts to understand these struggles from the perspectives of concerted, although sometimes misguided, attempts at empowerment by either Latinos or African Americans.

On the contrary, legitimacy is generally granted to the existing sociopolitical systems and power relationships for comprehending a Latino and African American struggle for human rights. As a result, the representations (in other words, the tension or conflict analyses) are less illustrative of the particular manifestations of struggle out of which the differences of opinion and strategy emerge, but simply re-presentations of existing notions about what is considered legitimate behavior in this society for Latinos and African Americans. Thus, for instance, in terms of our experiences, as faculty of color, there was little expectation from our colleagues that we would develop such a supportive coalition, nor seek to alter the hiring practices and policy initiatives at the institution. A more typical expectation appears to have been that we would struggle as isolates or undercut the other's progress. The major problem with those presumptions is that they presume the constancy of Eurocentric power, while advocating that non-European power is transient, fleeting, and can only come at the expense of other persons of color (Asante, 1999). They minimize the common sociopolitical history within African American and Latino communities of cultural oppression (Hraba, 1994) and they discount legitimate attempts at enfranchisement by both Latinos and African Americans.

Institutions of higher education are microcosms of what exist in our society. Often it is these same institutions that have further perpetuated societal norms, including racist stereotypes (Alexander-Snow & Johnson, 1998). In examining the culture of institutions it is easy to see that the predominantly white environments can impact the performance of faculty of color. Haymes (1995) tells us that to understand this concept we need to understand the power structures in society:

One reason for this is that white wealth and power control the electronic media. In other words, this power exerts much influence over the production of popular culture and how we interpret racial difference, particularly as it relates to multiculturalism. The significance of this situation is that mainstream white culture plays a pivotal role in the formation of our cultural identities and therefore how we see ourselves in relationship to others. Its influence is not only in terms of how we think, but also how we construct our fears, pleasures, desires, and dreams. (p. 105)

If we are all influenced by dominant structures, then faculty of color are just as susceptible. Often as the "only" minority faculty in the department, faculty of color find themselves struggling to understand the culture of the institution. Questions about how to "make it" are often framed within what can best be described as "unfriendly" environments. Learning the rules of the game becomes significant and at times comes too late for pivotal benchmarks such as promotion and tenure. Alexander-Snow and Johnson (1998) tell us that faculty of color often report having to face social and cultural isolation, devaluation of their scholarship, and are perceived as a threat to status quo by their white colleagues. Even when institutions set out to understand the severe underrepresentation of faculty of color at their institutions, it comes at a price of further isolating the few faculty of color that do exist within the departments. One African American female faculty (Holcomb-McCoy, 1999) describes a highly emotional and painful experience at a faculty retreat that was to focus on race in academia:

Although the retreat was emotional for me, it was only the beginning of the "unmasking" process. Writing this paper was the second step. It has caused me to replay the retreat over and over again in my head and to critique faculty dynamics, especially between faculty-of-color and White faculty. By processing the retreat experience with other colleagues, I have examined more closely the anger and fear within me. I constantly evaluate and re-evaluate my career as a black academic. Each day, I ask myself, "Did I feel devalued today?" "Did I feel appreciated for my uniqueness?" Although my goal is not to be dependent on my White colleagues for validation, academia is a symbol of "Whiteness" and to this end, my future in academia is unfortunately based upon how well I fit into the White higher education environment. (p. 11)

Thus, it becomes virtually impossible for many faculty of color to "make it" from the onset. It is also clear that the people who are different from the mainstream would gravitate toward each other for support, validation of work, and common interest. This is our story.

ESTABLISHING SOLIDARITY

It is not difficult to see how faculty of color at this private institution of higher education have come to know and rely on each other closely given the "whiteness" of the institution. In the school of psychology and education there are only five faculty of color on tenure-track positions out of 30 tenure-track positions across both divisions. Along gender lines there is an African American male, an African American female, two Asian women, and a Latina. Four are based in one division; one is based in the other. Within the past six years, there have only been three faculty of color in the school until the recent appointments during the 1999–2000 academic year. When this work was conceived, only one faculty of color was tenured.

The culture of the institution is not unlike many institutions of higher education across the country. What makes this setting unique is the close ties to a Christian church that is patriarchal in its roots. The institution openly promotes its religious orientation with faculty and students. Although students and faculty come from many faiths, it is clear that there is a distinct orientation toward one guiding philosophy. Since institutions reflect a culture of their own (Rowe, 1987), it would be correct to state that the institutional culture is clearly defined as one of a prevailing faith. While the school of psychology and education are geographically separated from the "main" undergraduate campus, this distance can be both positive and negative.

Distance from the undergraduate campus has allowed the school to develop on its own culture, and as such, develop a separate culture. In many respects it is an environment where faculty and administration are able to explore wider avenues. This means that the members of the faculty and the administration represent a wider array of faiths and ethnic and cultural backgrounds. It also means that often a "higher" authority intercedes when it comes to making decisions about the direction of the school (i.e., faculty tenure decisions, the selection of a new dean, and institutional funding for the school).

Both the authors joined the institution within one year of each other. One came from another institution of higher education, while the other joined the faculty upon completion of a doctoral program. While each were based in different divisions, both gravitated toward each other instantly. Within the division, there is an overt attempt to present the faculty within the school as a "family" that engages in activities together. The initiation of the two faculty of color into membership of the "family" was presented in this context. This orientation is further perpetuated by the larger university culture that affirms its commitment to its religious affiliation. These two attributes have created a psychologically "dysfunctional family."

When the two faculty joined the institution their offices were next to each other. The other faculty of color joked that this was the "faculty of color corridor" in the building. Although said jokingly, it was indeed a factual comment that faculty of color were all within close proximity to each other on one side of the building. Both faculty were brought on board to fulfill a need, which is to teach courses in cross-cultural training, multicultural education, and second-language teaching. Both faculty were told that they were coming on board to fulfill this role, and both faculty are often reminded of their prescribed role. The faculty member in education was repeatedly reminded through other faculty, staff, and administration that he/she "had been hired to teach those classes," thus limiting the opportunities to teach other courses. Given these roles with limited institutional support, it is not unexpected to find that students also see faculty of color and the courses they teach as "marginal" and "not relevant" to their entire program. Thus, the decisions to recruit faculty of color reflect interest-convergence, such that these faculty of color positions afford the university reprieve from negative sanctions since regional or national accrediting bodies judge that the university is addressing its diversity concerns.

In an effort to initiate discussion regarding the low number of faculty of color, a meeting was held by the dean with the faculty of color in the fall of 1998. It brought six members of the faculty, only four were in tenure track-positions. The discussion was opened with, "I want to know what the concerns of faculty of color are." This immediately opened suspicions in the minds of those present in the room. Why now? What for? Who is interested? What will you do with the information?

The dean's comment at the end of the session was, "I had no idea!" Which further disillusioned the faculty of color on board, because we knew that little would be done to change any of the concerns shared during that session. The information presented was too much for an institution to follow-up on or to do anything about. This was the only meeting the dean had in her nine years of service in that position.

There have been several methods used to influence policy by the faculty of color. In addition to strategic planning and lobbying for specific committee work—seeking appointments to the rank, tenure and promotions, sabbatical, faculty search, curriculum, and teaching committees—we have been active in faculty governance. When we arrived at the institution, the governance system was considered somewhat perfunctory and obligatory in terms of impacting institutional policy initiatives. We became active members and then advocated a broadening of the focus of the governance organization, so that it became more active in establishing new initiatives with the dean, and maintained a more active interface with the rest of the broader university. As a result of these efforts we created opportunities for supporting each other, our own ethnic communities, and broader cultural initiatives within the context of our faculty responsibilities. Thus, we did not have to engage in extra work to accomplish our own support and survival.

In addition, one of us initiated a faculty committee, including the relevant associate dean as a member, to provide an ongoing forum to address diversity issues. This is open to staff, students, and faculty. The purposes are to promote awareness; provide a mechanism for information dissemination regarding committee actions; and to provide an opportunity to discuss specific issues related to cultural diversity. Brief articles have been written about the goals and interests of the committee and placed into university publications to insure that the community recognized our long-term commitment to these issues. A needs assessment was conducted regarding faculty exercises, discussion formats, readings and/or approaches for addressing cultural issues in their classes. Funds are being sought to obtain release time for faculty and research assistants to develop a clearinghouse or resource library for helping faculty integrate cultural issues more fully. Continuing education workshops have been conducted for all faculty to continue movement on integrating more fully issues of culture and ethnicity into the curricula.

Finally, while both faculty have now been granted tenure, one of them has been overlooked for administrative positions within the school. Although different explanations have been offered as to why that faculty member has been overlooked for these positions, it should be noted that at least in one case, the administrative position was granted to a visiting faculty member.

CONCLUSIONS

While there have been changes that have come about from a concerted effort by both faculty to recruit and retain underrepresented faculty of color, the culture remains the same. As a team, the faculty of color has been able to influence the hiring practices of the school and exert some influence on the manner in which institutional decisions are made. In the process, a very solid coalition has been established between the faculty of color—a coalition grounded in an understanding that racism still is the normative condition pervading our institution, even if it is a benignly neglectful disregard. We understand that interest-convergence predominates in the institution decision-making process, such that unless our interests converge with the stated interests of the institution, we end up being mere bugs on the windshield of institutional functioning. Last, we are committed to giving voice to our personal and collective experiences, with sufficient detail to serve to locate us in an authentic struggle for human rights. We refuse to attenuate the tension between us; we argue that the tension will necessarily dissipate when understood from the context of Eurocentric dominance.

As we remove the veil of shortsighted thinking and truly begin the process of understanding inter-ethnic relations, in all of their cultural manifestations, the positivistic methods must give way to, at minimum, contextualist epistemologies and at best, altogether new paradigms (Rowe, 1998). Paradigms for understanding human behavior are shaped by the wisdom, indeed the inherent legitimacy, of the worldviews of various cultural groups. True multiculturalism can only occur when distinct cultural groups can coexist in relative peace and cooperation. They then can decide when and how to blend their cultural assumptions and worldviews. Thus, our challenge—yours and mine—is to rescue and reclaim more authentic conceptions of human interaction, use them to delineate features of functioning, and then develop methods of coalition building that reflect those conceptions.

The reflections contained in this chapter have been a healing process for both faculty members. The fact that this topic is being addressed at this point and time reflects the security that both faculty now share after receiving tenure. This security has granted both of us a chance to voice our concerns and needs in a much more open forum. Writing this chapter has also brought legitimacy to all the informal discussions between us. This process has brought both of us closer and created a unified force across the two divisions. Although our story may be similar to the experiences of others, it is hoped that this work will begin to draw out the voices of those who have gone unheard and those who have been silenced.

REFERENCES

Akinyela, M. (1997). Culture and power in practice: Cultural democracy and the family support movement. Best Practices Project Commissioned Paper III. Chicago: Family Resource Coalition.

Alexander-Snow, M. & Johnson, B. (1998). Faculty of color and role performance. Paper presented at the Annual Meeting of the Association for the Study of Higher Education, Miami.

Asante, M. K. (1999). *The painful demise of eurocentrism: An afrocentric response to critics*. Trenton, NJ: Africa World Press.

Baez, B. (1998). Negotiating and resisting racism: How faculty of color construct promotion and tenure. Georgia State University. (ERIC Document Reproduction Service No. ED 430 420).

Campbell, D. E. (1996). *Choosing democracy: A practical guide to multicultural education*. Englewood Cliffs, NJ: Prentice-Hall.

City of Los Angeles (2000). Office of administrative and research services. Economic and demographic information. 2000 City of Los Angeles economic & demographic information. http://www.lacity.org/oars/econdemo.htm.

CNN.com U.S. News (2000). Census figures show dramatic growth in Asian, Hispanic polupations. http://www.cnn.com/2000/US/08/30/minority.population/index.html.

Colby, A. & Foote, E. (1995). Creating and maintaining a diverse faculty. *Eric Digest*, ED386261. Eric Clearinghouse for Community Colleges, Los Angeles.

Delgado, R. (1995). *Critical race theory: The cutting edge.* Philadelphia: Temple University Press.

Haymes, S. (1995). White culture and the politics of racial difference: Implications for multiculturalism. In *Multicultural education, critical pedagogy, and politics of difference,* (Eds.) C. Sleeter and P. McClaren, pp. 105–128. Albany: State University of New York Press.

Holcomb-McCoy, C. (1999). Understanding "whiteness" in academia: A black woman's perspective. Paper presented at the Annual Meeting of the American Educational Research Association, Montreal, Canada.

Hraba, J. (1994). *American ethnicity.* 2nd ed. Itasca, IL: F. E. Peacock Publishers.

Nieto, S. (2000). *Affirming diversity: The sociopolitical context of multicultural education.* 3rd ed. White Plains, NY: Longman.

Phillips, S. A. (1999). Wallbangin': Graffiti and gangs in L.A. Chicago: The University of Chicago Press.

Rowe, D. (1987). Problem solving for institutional cross-cultural issues. Unpublished manuscript. Pepperdine University, Culver City, CA.

Rowe, D. M. Rethinking multiculturalism: Diversity in psychology. Keynote address presented at the California Association for Counseling and Development's Black Caucus' Regional Conference, Los Angeles, CA, February 1998.

Rowe, D. M., & Grills, C. N. Eurocentric foundations of psychology: Implications for the future. Paper presented at the National Council for Schools of Professional Psychology, Orlando, Florida, January 1996.

Said, E. W. (1978). *Orientalism.* New York: Random House.

Seaver Catalogue. (2000). Pepperdine University http://www.pepperdine.edu/seaver/Catalog/catalog00/ Malibu, CA.

Shipman, P. (1994). *The evolution of racism: Human differences and the use and abuse of science.* New York: Simon & Schuster.

Shohat, E., & Stam, R. *Unthinking Eurocentrism: Multiculturalism and the media.* New York: Routledge.

Smedley, A. (1999). *Race in North America: Origin and evolution of a Worldview.* 2nd ed. Boulder, CO: Westview.

U.S. Census Bureau (1990). Demographics for Los Angeles, CA. http://venus.census.gov/cdrom/lookup/968199083.

U.S. Census Bureau (2000). County population estimates. http://www.census.gov/population/www/estimates/countypop.html.

Chapter 16

Blackout, Brownout, or Both?: The Dynamics of Ethnic-Oriented Media Advocacy

Kenton T. Wilkinson

INTRODUCTION

As the editors and other contributors to this volume have noted, the increasing diversity of the U.S. population is contemporaneous with greater emphasis on media industries and their products as sites of contestation for power. This chapter explores minority advocacy organizations' struggles to increase and improve on-screen representations as well as off-screen employment of their constituent populations in the U.S. film and television industries. While most advocacy actions during the twentieth century involved racial or ethnic groups acting on their own, a "brownout" of network television in September 1999 included a variety of minority advocacy organizations, with African American and Latino groups foremost among them. Since it appears that more such collaborative efforts will—and in my opinion should—be forthcoming in the twenty-first century, a clearer understanding of past developments and future prospects is needed. This chapter represents a first step in that direction.

The collaborative media advocacy is important for several reasons. First, notwithstanding their differences, African Americans and Latinos share numerous political, economic and social/cultural interests and concerns in common (Jennings, 1994). Mainstream media coverage of the groups tends to focus either on issues dividing them such as competition for jobs and political power, or mutual problems such as crime, poverty and low educational achievement. Few are the reports on positive attributes held in common or successful collaboration in confronting the shared obstacles to upward mobility (Piatt 1997; Romer et al., 1998). Second, by speaking in a unified voice, African Americans, Latinos and other minority groups emphasize the cross-ethnic nature of their media-related challenges and render themselves less prone to "divide and conquer" attitudes and political attacks. Third, by and large Hollywood has taken neither the social influence of its cultural production nor the concerns of minority groups seriously enough. Persistent monitoring and well-executed action by a diverse coalition has greater chances for success than sporadic, isolated efforts by separate advocacy organizations. Finally, as their numbers grow, so too will the economic influence of African Americans, Latinos and other minority groups. Ethnic consumers should be prudent in wielding (not yielding) their power at the box office, in television ratings, and in purchasing advertisers' goods and services. While difficult to organize and execute, brownouts and boycotts are among few options for consumers to flex their collective muscles in the marketplace. Having such power at their disposal is a recent development in the longer history of negative representation of African Americans and Latinos in mainstream U.S. audiovisual media.

PRE-BROWNOUT ADVOCACY EFFORTS

Past actions by African American and Latino advocacy organizations have included coalitions of organizations advocating for the same population, but cross-ethnic alliances are a more recent phenomenon. A review of past advocacy efforts will reveal that despite remarkable transformations in communication industries, markets and technologies during the twentieth century, the challenges facing organizations, like their goals and methods, have changed very little. My discussion begins with the oldest and best-known African American advocacy group, then turns to Latino organizations.

African American Efforts

Only six years after its founding in 1909 the National Association for the Advancement of Colored People (NAACP) protested the depiction of African Americans in D. W. Griffith's racist epic, *The Birth of a Nation*. The group lobbied, unsuccessfully, to have the film censored or banned in advance of its opening in New York. Particularly troublesome were the ill consequences of glorifying the Ku Klux Klan's lawless terrorism, portraying black men as sexual aggressors against white women, and depicting blacks in general as willing participants in a benign, paternalistic slave system (Guerrero, 1993:13). In 1939 the NAACP joined the (more radical) National Negro Congress in advocating for non-stereotypical portrayals of African Americans in another epic film that achieved national prominence even before its release, *Gone with the Wind*. In this case the producer, David O. Selznick, was persuaded to drop from the novel or cut from the film potentially offensive elements such as references to the Ku Klux Klan and militant blacks. Selznick commented, "we have to be awfully careful that the Negroes come out decidedly on the right side of the ledger" (Cripps, 1983:140). Although isolated criticisms appeared in the press and occasional protesters picketed premieres, the careful attention to representations and the presence of a black advisor on the set mitigated many of the NAACP's initial concerns.

Earlier, in 1931, some African Americans protested the popular radio program, *Amos 'n' Andy* through local chapters of the NAACP. The program followed the foibles of the lead characters, their kin and associates all of whom had migrated from the South to a northern city. The most offensive characters were Kingfish, a conniving, double-dealing lodge leader and Algonquin J. Calhoun, a bumbling, linguistically challenged lawyer whose characterization seemed to mock black professionals. The fact that the lead roles and many of the supporting characters were spoken by two white men, Charles Correll and Freeman Gosden, deepened concerns about racial stereotyping. But not everyone agreed that the show was harmful. Some black listeners commented that the show accurately depicted the speech and other characteristics of Southern blacks while others found it so entertaining as to offset the negative representations. Ely (1991:5) captures the dichotomous nature of black responses to the program in describing Correll and Gosden's appearance at a parade and picnic hosted by one black newspaper, *The Defender* of Chicago, while at the same time another paper, Pittsburgh's *Courier*, was collecting signatures to petition the show's cancellation. The *Courier's* protest was assisted by a handful of NAACP chapters and other organizations, but failed to garner sufficient influence to force the cancellation of a very popular program. Two decades would pass before the issue was revisited as *Amos 'n' Andy* made its television debut.

In the late 1940s, African American performers saw television as a promising new medium—talent was in demand since some radio and film artists were initially reluctant to perform in the new medium, black celebrities appeared on inaugural shows, and blacks hoped to secure better roles than other media had afforded them (MacDonald, 1983:2). The prospects dimmed in 1951 when CBS began broadcasting its televised version of *Amos 'n' Andy*, in which black performers interpreted the characters previously spoken by white men. In a major public relations blunder, CBS held previews for the press only a few days before the annual meeting of the NAACP in Atlanta, then aired the first episode while the convention met. This enabled the NAACP leadership to organize a collective viewing of the show which, as Melvin Ely points out, had the delegates "reinforcing each other's negative responses and influencing the views of members who might otherwise not have reacted or even tuned in" (1991:213). The delegates agreed to pressure television stations and sponsors to cancel the program and, if necessary, to organize a boycott of the sponsoring company's products. An excerpt from one of the letters circulated to NAACP youth councils and college chapters stated that *Amos 'n' Andy*, "depict[s] the Negro and other minority groups in a stereotyped and derogatory manner," and "tend[s] to strengthen the conclusion among uninformed or prejudiced people that Negroes and other minorities are inferior, lazy, dumb and dishonest" (Herbert L. Wright, July 19, 1951, quoted in Ely, 1991:7). Those comments could apply equally to the radio program, and some members of the black leadership questioned why the NAACP took such strong exception to the TV version after ignoring the radio program for many years. Roy Wilkins, an NAACP national administrator who in 1930 had defended the radio program as "clean fun from beginning to end" (Ely, 1991:171), explained the problem with television:

The visual impact is infinitely worse than the radio version . . . the television brings these people to life—they are no longer merely voices and they say to millions of white Americans who know nothing about Negroes, and to millions of white children who are learning about life, that this is the way Negroes are. (Ely, 1991:215–216)

While many blacks may have agreed with Wilkins's arguments and appreciated the NAACP's efforts, a large number also enjoyed the program. Ely documents letters to editors, news reports and survey data indicating mixed opinions on the harmfulness of portrayals and whether they warranted protests and boycotts. This hampered the NAACP's ability to call for a general boycott of the program's sponsor, Schenley Distillers, and it relied instead on a word-of-mouth boycott and the activities of local chapters. For its part, Schenley called on the American Jewish Committee, for which it was an important benefactor, to control the damage and mediate between the NAACP and CBS.

The professional and economic interests of African American performers were—and continue to be—another source of dissension. Entertainers and their representatives in Los Angeles and New York complained that the NAACP was meddling in an industry it did not understand, and the New York Coordinating Council for Negro Performers organized to oppose the NAACP's protest and boycott (Ely, 1991:218). As for CBS, its blunder in debuting during the NAACP convention a program that made liberal use of the same stereotypes criticized in the radio program reflected a gross insensitivity to—or lack of concern for—its own social influence and public opinion regarding the burgeoning television industry. As my discussion of the brownout will reveal, this problem continues to plague the industry following the civil rights, black power, and brown power movements of the 1960s and 1970s. Hollywood's unfortunate response to the *Amos 'n' Andy* problem was to avoid potential conflicts by whitewashing programs. Lichter and Amundsun, (1997:59) point out that until the mid-1960s "black characters didn't even show up in the backgrounds of early shows . . . [they] were simply not a part of the early prime time world." Although the mid-1960s to the late 1990s saw a gradual increase in the number of blacks on screen, the trend did not include Latinos or other minority groups.

Latino Efforts

Latinos' efforts to address negative representations in the media and inadequate levels of employment have been more isolated and sporadic than the African American endeavors, but began in the same period. While space constraints limit this discussion to Mexican American images and advocacy, the reader is reminded that other Latino subgroups have actively monitored media images and pushed for increased employment of Latinos, and also that the 1999 brownout was a pan-Latino effort. The advent of moving pictures did little to dispel many Americans' negative preconceptions of Mexicans and Mexican Americans derived from pulp dime novels, distorted views of the Mexican-American War, and fanciful popular histories of the West. The so-called "greaser" films of the silent era perpetuated negative images by depicting Mexican men as villains who "robbed, murdered, plundered, raped, cheated, gambled, lied and displayed virtually every vice that could be shown on the screen" and women as jealous vixens who were enamored of Anglo American men. (Woll, 1977:7) The films provoked disdain and protestations from Mexican and Mexican American audience members and journalists, but no major efforts to organize against them emerged until 1922 when the government of Mexico banned the importation of *all* films produced by any studio that portrayed Mexico and its citizens in a derogatory manner (Limon, 1973; Delpar, 1984).

The Mexican government's ban, like the NAACP's protest of *Birth of a Nation* seven years earlier, confronted an industry so ingrained with the racism and ethnic prejudice of the period that epithets such as "coon" and "greaser" were routinely included in film titles, title cards and promotions (Keller, 1994:13–14). While blasé about its social influence, Hollywood, then as now, was sensitive to its economic interests, and made a conciliatory response to Mexico's ban. The Motion Pictures Producers and Distributors of America acted immediately to smooth ruffled feathers in Washington as well as Mexico City, and its Production Code of 1930 stated that in Hollywood-produced films, "the history, institutions, prominent people and citizenry of other nations shall be represented fairly" (Delpar, 1984:40). So as to avoid conflicts, film producers began basing stories in South American countries, especially Argentina and Brazil, or in fictional countries with Latin-sounding names (Woll, 1977). World War II and the Cold War shifted Hollywood production toward soldier stories and "Good Neighbor" films, which many Latin Americans took for what they were, propaganda. The first sustained effort to address representation problems emerged in the late 1960s when offensive images in advertising were challenged by U.S. Latinos who had begun to organize and mobilize on a number of political, economic, and social fronts.

The most notorious and enduring stereotype was the Frito Bandito created in 1967 for the Frito Lay Company. The pot-bellied, mustached, and sombreroed cartoon character was armed with six guns he wielded freely to satisfy his craving for corn chips. "Frito" frequently sang, over the airwaves and in heavily accented English, of his love for the snacks. In print media, this text accompanied his image: "He loves cronchy [*sic*] Fritos corn chips so much he'll stop at nothing to get yours. What's more, he's cunning, clever—and sneaky!" (Nuiry, 1996:26). In a study that the Mexican American Anti-Defamation Committee adopted as its position paper in protesting "Frito," Thomas Martinez (1969:3) described the advertising campaign as "a very effective prejudicial form of anti-locution—effective in terms of making the out-group appear inferior, and the in-group superior." While the anti-defamation committee and other groups applied sufficient pressure on Frito Lay to close the campaign in 1970, the image has endured. In 1985 a political cartoonist for the *San Diego Union* newspaper ridiculed a Mexican American

council member who had misused public funds by depicting him as a
Frito-type who wields a Visa card rather than six guns. Public outcry of racism
forced an apology by the newspaper's editor (Acuna, 1985). The newer interactive media have also incorporated stereotypical *bandido* images. In 1999,
some student groups joined the National Conference for Community and Justice in protesting a Fritoesque character in the video game "Toy Story 2." In
order to proceed to the game's next level, a protagonist character (manipulated
by the player) had to kill the *bandido*, an action that the protesters said promoted violence and racism and was potentially damaging, particularly to
young players. The Walt Disney Company, whose ABC television network
was being publicly criticized by Latino groups at the time, agreed to change
the character and reissue the game (Vega, 1999).

As Montgomery (1989:55) points out, a number of Mexican American organizations joined the anti-defamation committee in opposing the original *bandido* and
launched their own media reform campaigns in the late 1960s and early 1970s.
Most of the groups, like "Justicia" which Montgomery profiles, were militant but
also short-lived. A different approach has been taken by "Nosotros," which
formed among Latino actors in Hollywood in 1969 and endured to join the 1999
brownout. As industry insiders, Nosotros representatives have "confronted studio
heads, network heads, producers and writers and urged them to re-evaluate the
problems of stereotypical depictions of Hispanics" (Reyes & Rubie, 1994:24). The
group occasionally joins forces with the National Hispanic Media Coalition
(NHMC), which formed in Los Angeles in 1986, has a dozen chapters nationwide,
and represents the media advocacy interests of some twenty affiliated organizations. The coalition has combined legal tactics such as challenging license renew-
als, petitioning the FCC and applying for broadcast licenses with political
activities like organizing viewer protests and boycotts. While the NHMC has
mainly focused on English-language film and television, some efforts have targeted U.S. Spanish-language broadcasting which is contested terrain for representation, influence and employment among subgroups of Latinos, most notably
Mexican Americans and Cuban Americans (Wilkinson, forthcoming). A principal
legal instrument of the coalition has been the Half-Workforce Parity Rule, which
mandates that the ethnic composition of a broadcast licensee's workforce reflect at
least 50% of the ethnic makeup of the market it serves. (For example, in a city having a population that is 30% African American and 25% Latino, the licensee's employees must be at least 15% African American and 12.5% Latino.) While all
movie studios, radio and television networks are monitored by the NHMC, ABC
television received particular attention during the 1990s. In addition to increased
recruitment and retention of Latinos in upper management and creative positions,
NHMC advocated for Latino-owned companies listed on ABC's vendor roster and
appointment of a vice-president for labor diversity. After ABC failed to meet its
promises, NHMC organized a letter-writing campaign and implemented a boycott
of Disney products and theme parks in 1997. The boycott was called off in March
1998, but the network had only a short reprieve before it became embroiled in a
larger action.

GENESIS OF THE BROWNOUT

Within a year of the NHMC's canceling its boycott against Disney/ABC, the network, together with its principal competitors, faced problems first with individual advocacy organizations, then a multiethnic coalition of groups. The opening shot was fired by the *Los Angeles Times*, which reported in May, 1999 that recent "upfronts"—meetings where networks reveal their fall prime-time series for advertisers—had "not one . . . minority in a leading role" and "few blacks in supporting roles [with] Latinos, Asian Americans, Native Americans and other ethnic groups [are] virtually invisible" (Braxton, 1999). In a situation reminiscent of the *Amos 'n' Andy* premiere, the timing permitted the NAACP leadership to include the issue as an agenda item for its ninetieth annual convention. During his keynote speech in July the NAACP President Kweisi Mfume said:

When the television-viewing public sits down to watch the new prime time shows scheduled for this fall's line-up, they will see a virtual whitewash in programming. This whitewash exists because none of the 26 new shows slated for the fall season have a minority in a leading or starring role. This glaring omission is an outrage and a shameful display by network executives who are either clueless, careless, or both. ("NAACP blasts," 1999)

Later in the speech Mfume vowed, "we know what to do, turn off the tube. We're not going to watch those shows that make us invisible . . . [W]e intend to send a strong, clear signal that the frontier of television must reflect the multiethnic landscape of today's modern American society" (Brand-Williams & Kisha, 1999). Mfume's speech and the prospect of a NAACP-led boycott and/or lawsuit charging network abuse of the public interest sent the networks scurrying to write in minority characters and find talent-of-color for the fall shows. It also engendered significant comment in the press, with many asserting that a boycott was correct in spirit, but misguided in practice. Specific calls for a viewer "tune-out" were not heard until late July when the National Council of La Raza (NCLR) convened in Houston and introduced the newly formed National Latino Media Council (NLMC) which began organizing a brownout for September 12–25, 1999 to coincide with National Latino Heritage Week and the Emmy Awards. The council leadership, which collectively represented many years' experience in monitoring and pressuring mass media industries, expressed frustration with Hollywood's unfulfilled promises to address persisting problems, and called on Latinos to use their power as consumers (about $380 billion annually) to improve their images in the media (Kolker, 1999). Numerous statements to the press condemned the paucity of Latinos in off-screen as well as on-screen positions, and claimed that economic pressure was the only way to get through to Hollywood. Thus the brownout would be the first volley in a longer campaign against the networks; other tactics would include legal action and—following the NAACP's lead—purchasing shares in the networks to gain access to shareholder meetings. In a gesture that reflected the NCLR's concern for media representations and access, and perhaps its eagerness to align with the NAACP, one of the convention's keynote speakers was William Kennard, then chief commissioner of the Federal Communications Commission, and the first African American to head that agency. While most of his remarks focused on the government's e-rate program to bring computer and internet technology to underprivileged schools, Kennard supported the NCLR's protest by stating:

And perhaps when those who own and run America's networks look more like America, so will their shows. America needs TV shows that reflect the diversity that we see in our own neighborhoods, not programs that distort the reality of America. . . . Remember "I Spy"? I remember how important it was in my family to finally see an African American [Bill Cosby] in a starring role on network television. Thirty years later, we are still waiting for network television to fully reflect what America really looks like. (Kennard, 1999)

The commissioner's recollection of *I Spy* reflects a shared concern among media advocates representing a variety of population groups: lack of representation causes minorities to devalue or even deprecate their own group and may foster low self-esteem, especially among children (Martinez, 1969; Skyhawk, 1999). This threat is particularly acute at a time when electronic media occupy increasing amounts of people's time, and the U.S. population becomes racially and ethnically diverse.

The 1999 summer convention season continued as the Rainbow/PUSH Coalition convened in early August, endorsed the NAACP's condemnation of the networks, and met with industry representatives to discuss the business side of broadcasting, including ways to encourage greater access by minority business owners ("Rainbow/PUSH coalition," 1999). In the wake of the NAACP and NCLR resolutions the Reverend Jesse Jackson, Sr. emphasized the common challenges faced by African Americans and Latinos,

In this type of medium there are five different types of stereotypes that emerge—Blacks and browns are projected as less important than we are, less hardworking than we are, less universal than we are, less patriotic and more violent. . . . So, we challenge the networks, because there is simply a need for them to display our contributions in the building of America. ("Rainbow/PUSH coalition," 1999)

In spite of their shared concerns, common calls-to-arms, and the significant press coverage of their shared interests, the advocacy groups' first joint public appearance was at a September 10 press conference held just two days before the brownout was to begin. The timing and limited press coverage of the meeting likely reflected strains among the coalition's membership that were to surface later.

REACTIONS TO THE BROWNOUT

Reactions to the advocacy organizations' call for a brownout not only reveal editorial and public opinion on the issue, but also lend insight into the difficulties of securing broad public support for collective action. The contrasting opinions and comments that appeared in mainstream and ethnic/independent publications reflect the challenges to political pluralism in the twenty-first century. Press reports on how network management and creative talent reacted to the brownout suggest the daunting prospects of confronting Hollywood's access to, and influence in, the news media.

Much commentary in the mainstream press affirmed the issue's legitimacy, but criticized the organizers' tactics. The general argument was that rather than pressure the networks, the brownout should target advertisers who foot the bill for television and give insufficient weight to the purchasing power of black and Latino consumers (estimated at $500 billion and $380 billion respectively) (Chavez, 1999; Maxwell, 1999). Some questioned the logic of improving the representativeness of prime time television programming when blacks already spend more time watching television than do other ethnic or racial groups, and Latinos have the highest high school dropout rate (Walker, 1999). Others argued that many black viewers had migrated to cable channels, and Latinos had their own Spanish-language networks. Some commentators seized the opportunity to attack the NAACP for a misguided agenda in pursuing media representation and employment rather than more pressing concerns such as family issues, crime and incarceration rates, public school education, teen pregnancy and computer literacy (Walker, 1999).

Commentary in the minority and independent press supported the notion that media representations strongly influence minorities' self-perceptions as well as mainstream viewers' understanding of minorities, but not all agreed that proportional representation in the population should be mirrored on screen. Such a proposal sounded too much like quotas, a controversial subject that most advocacy leaders were careful to avoid. A recurring comment was that boycotts and other economic actions is the only pressure Hollywood would respond to, and some encouraged continued pressure after the boycott ended (Gonzalez & Rodriguez, 1999; Perez, 1999). There were also calls to extend the brownout beyond prime time entertainment programming to television news and other genres as well as other media like radio and print (Reynolds, 1999). Several editorials challenged the aforementioned argument that Latinos have their own media—in Spanish—by arguing that many Latinos prefer English-language television, and much of the programming, especially *telenovelas* contain racist themes and do not reflect U.S. Latino interests or experience (Miranda, 1999; Vazquez, 1999). As one might expect, commentary in the minority and independent press was more supportive of the brownout and less critical of the advocacy organizations and their leadership than was the mainstream press.

Given the close relationship between Hollywood and the press, it is not surprising that the television industry's responses to the brownout received ample coverage. The fact that members of the Television Critics Association were touring Los Angeles in July, 1999 certainly added to the volume of the reports. As Virginia Rohan of *The Record* (Hackensack, NJ) points out, at each gathering of the critics "one theme or controversy inevitably develops, intensifies, and envelops the gathering—making for nice dramatic dispatches from the Hollywood front"; for this gathering, the "virtual whitewash" and network responses were the hot issue (1999:Y1). Many articles reported the networks' responses, in word and deed, as they scrambled to include more minority characters—especially African Americans, but also Latinos and Asian Americans—in new prime time series. Doug Herzog, president of Fox Entertainment highlighted one concern in responding to the advocacy groups' complaints: "We don't want to fall into the trap of casting minority actors just to fill a quota . . . that kind of tokenism is insulting" (Pennington, 1999). The producer Tom Fontana, whose shows have included multi-ethnic casts like those of *St. Elsewhere* and *Homicide: Life on the Streets*, concurred, "if a character isn't organic to a series since its inception, kind of slapping a character on later is the worst kind of tokenism" (Rohan, 1999). Such afterthoughts also reduce the likelihood that minority characters will be central to the stories, well-developed, or multidimensional. Other explanations for the paucity of minority lead characters included the rush to get programs funded, produced, and aired that causes diversity issues to be overlooked, and Hollywood's tendency to play it safe by casting young white actors in comfortable urban settings. "Playing it safe" means the networks deliver to advertisers the demographic groups they seek, and in the late 1990s young whites were the principal target.

With so many television writers attending the critics association meetings, some industry representatives could not pass up the opportunity to plug upcoming shows. CBS garnered ample mention of its "City of Angels" series that is set at an urban county hospital and features a mostly minority cast. The network's president and CEO, Leslie Moonves got substantial coverage when he challenged the whiteout charge and asserted that 12 of 19 CBS series featured minority characters in a primary role; he was careful to name the programs, actors, and actresses. It should be noted that Moonves affirmed the industry's responsibility to reflect diversity in its programs, and made greater efforts than others to hear and address complaints, yet his comments before reporters must be interpreted in light of public relations and promotion as well as the interests of network management (Stafford, 1999). The writer and producer Lee Goldberg, whose show *Martial Law* (on CBS) stars an African American and two Asian Americans in lead roles, also took issue with the protests arguing that while new prime time series may have been "whitewashed,"

If you look at all of television, then the NAACP attack is an acute case of tunnel vision. If you look at daytime, cable, syndication, public television and even returning shows, there's incredible diversity. I don't think it's right to castigate an entire industry based on one area of programming that's lily white. (Dawidziak & Feran, 1999)

Other networks were less vocal and proactive than CBS even when they had reason to brag. The *New York Times* reported that UPN's black sitcom *Moesha* met the advocacy organizations' standards but was poorly promoted, even on its home network (Mifflin, 1999). If the advocacy organizations were to identify positive shows and explain their merits to the public, it might encourage similar productions in the future as well as deflect criticism that the advocates only highlight Hollywood's failures and inadequacies, not its successes. In 1999 the negativity charge was leveled at the NAACP by two prominent African American actors,

Arsenio Hall and D. L. Hughley, in a situation reminiscent of the Negro Performers' opposition to the NAACP's protest of *Amos 'n' Andy* in 1951 (Dawidziak
& Feran, 1999).

DISCUSSION AND CONCLUSIONS

Following the September brownout, which did not noticeably impact audience
ratings, there was little reporting on the issue until early 2000 when the NAACP
and the four major networks announced agreements to address representation and
employment problems. Leaders of other groups in the multiethnic coalition criticized Kweisi Mfume for not inviting their participation and for neglecting their
specific concerns in negotiating agreements (Kuczynski, 2000). The exclusion
weakened the prospects for future coordination among coalition organizations and
appeared to confirm a critical observation by Guy Aoki, the president of Media
Action Network for Asian Americans, who wrote, " 'minorities' do not equal
'blacks only.' They also include Hispanic, Asian, Arab and Native Americans"
(1999:3). The difficulties of one organization acting on behalf of other groups with
distinct memberships, goals and methods are hardly unique to this case, but are especially sensitive given the identity issues at play and the history of intergroup
competition among U.S. minorities. For example, in joining the coalition the
NCLR had to look beyond its own research which documented the steady improvement in representation of African Americans on television in the 1970s
through 1990s even as Latino images remained stagnant and stereotyped in the
rare instances when they did appear (1994, 1997). The feeling that black colleagues had mishandled their interests must have been disheartening for all coalition leaders, but doubly so for the Latinos.

The foregoing historical review showed that the NAACP began its media advocacy efforts a half-century before the first sustained endeavors by Latinos and
other minority groups. This fact certainly contributes to the NAACP's high profile
in the reporting and addressing the whitewash problem, but there are other factors
that can only be mentioned here yet merit further exploration in the future. As Guy
Aoki's comment suggests, much of the discourse on race, bias and inequality in the
United States has been set in the bipolar oppositions of black versus white. This is
a significant obstruction when considered in light of the fact that television and
other electronic media are becoming key forums for social discourse and power
struggles in contemporary society. Lichter and Amundsun (1997:68) argue that
Latinos and other non-black people of color have been little more than spectators:

Unfortunately, Hispanics have never played a significant role in television's debate over
race relations. When television has explored discrimination, prejudice, or the appropriateness of inter-racial relationships, it has almost always staged them as a black versus white
issue. Whenever racial tensions exist between Latinos and other groups in American society, they have very rarely made it to the small screen.

Thus, despite the efforts of organizations such as Nosotros and the National Hispanic Media Coalition, both of which have been active for years, television tends to depict race relations and other social concerns in monochromic hues. The discourse must become polychromic without diminishing the importance of African American issues or their legitimacy. This study demonstrates that the same holds true for collaborative media advocacy efforts.

This brings me to the topic of public figures and their involvement in media advocacy processes. Familiar names like Kweisi Mfume and Jesse Jackson catch the attention of journalists and the public thereby attracting important awareness to the issue. But multiple organizational as well as personal agendas together with strong allegiances to a particular constituency can limit such luminaries' ability to act effectively on behalf of a broad coalition. In similar fashion, representatives of aggressive organizations, such as the NHMC, may be less willing to take a conciliatory position, even when it is in the best interest of their constituents. In fact a dispute within the NAACP derived largely from a struggle for control, especially over the advocacy agenda and methods. In 1997 the Beverly Hills/Hollywood chapter angered the national office by protesting eight television comedies that it claimed portrayed African Americans as buffoons. The national office objected to the protest's timing—shortly before the NAACP-sponsored Image Awards—control over which it had wrested from the chapter in 1991 (Braxton, 1997). Such internal tensions are inevitable and by no means confined to the NAACP (Wilkinson, forthcoming), but are damaging when reported in the press.

Whether internal to advocacy organizations or shared among the participants in a coalition, tensions may derive from disagreement or misalignment of two closely-related elements: the organizations' agendas and agency. Here I can offer only preliminary comments on complex dynamics which warrant further investigation and discussion. For the advocacy organizations, common agenda issues are what brings them together in the first place. The initial press report (Braxton, 1999) and Kweisi Mfume's speech served as calls-to-arms by posing the whitewash problem as one shared among all people of color. The shared enterprise of pressuring Hollywood to improve representations, employment and influence of minorities had to be reconciled with existing actions and agendas unique to a specific racial or ethnic group. As regards agency, groups pursue differing objectives and methods for promoting change. While some quietly work inside connections (e.g., *Nosotros*), others appeal to public activism through boycotts and demonstrations (e.g., NHMC). The debate over which methods are most effective sometimes airs in public and risks a public perception of "minorities fighting amongst themselves" (Braxton & Breslauer, 1995). While the differences cannot be eliminated, and in fact add strength—through diversity—to a coalition, it is important that the organizations learn from their prior experiences.

The press influences the public agenda through what and how it reports and, of course, has its own agenda. My earlier overview noted differences in mainstream and ethnic/independent press coverage of the brownout. Some commentators used the brownout as a pretext to rail against problems they noted in the broader agenda of an organization—that is they pushed their own agenda in criticizing the organization's. This process is akin to network representatives using coverage of the brownout to promote their programs and stars. The agency issue is especially salient in the case of the television critics association. By seizing on a particular issue or controversy at each meeting the journalists are likely to overemphasize particular stories on the news agenda. Thus public perception of the problem and subsequent actions by stakeholders may be overly influenced by how the stories "spin." Spin is a principal agency function of network management and other Hollywood representatives who strive not only for damage control, but also positive public relations opportunities. In this case, while most executives conceded that a problem exists, some argued the specifics of the complaint and/or emphasized television programs that *do* reflect diversity.

The networks, while probably feeling that they dodged a bullet when the agreements were signed with the NAACP, must understand that the issues and organizations discussed in this chapter will not disappear quietly. There is much to learn not only from the brownout and prior conflicts with media advocacy organizations, but also from past and contemporary successes such as David O. Selznick's adept handling of race issues in making *Gone with the Wind* and the adroit handling of race, ethnicity, and representation issues in the multicultural casts of some television shows. As many commentators pointed out, minority markets have become too large to ignore or offend, and Hollywood must accommodate the new conditions more effectively. The common belief that the way to get Hollywood's attention is through its pocketbook indicates a public image of a money-grubbing, elitist industry having little sensitivity to its public. This need not be the case as the following example demonstrates. Lichter and Amundsun (1997) describe how the producer Norman Lear sacrificed $700,000 in withdrawing a new comedy series, *Mister Dugan*, after negative appraisals by the Congressional Black Congress and the threat of organized opposition to the show. Clearly the industry cannot give ground on every show to which a group objects, but in the twenty-first century it must choose its battles more carefully, and fight them more thoughtfully and responsibly, than it has in the past.

Media advocacy organizations understand that the best way to get Hollywood's attention is through its pocketbook. Determining the specific means of posing short- and long-term threats to the industry's revenue stream and viewer loyalty is more difficult. As communication technologies continue to converge, and industries to consolidate, determining which outlets to target—and how—will become increasingly difficult. Clearly the challenge of persuading viewers that protesting is in their best interest—and is productive—will persist if not expand with further fracturing of audiences through new distribution channels and narrowcasting. We may safely assume that such fracturing will continue to occur along racial and ethnic lines. When considered in conjunction with the aforementioned difficulties in creating and maintaining a united front of media advocates, the obstacles become all the more formidable. The NAACP's plan to establish an office in Hollywood specifically charged with monitoring and addressing representation and employment issues could be a very productive development *if* it encourages the participation as equals of other groups involved in the brownout, and can sidestep the tensions which developed between the Hollywood/Beverly Hills chapter and the national office in the past.

Given the paucity of research on the subject this chapter has addressed, I could add numerous items to the growing list of "topics requiring further study." I will limit myself to one: the public. The study of collective media advocacy offers researchers and policymakers insight into an important area of overlap among communication, political science and ethnic/race studies. The common thread binding those disciplines together is society and its relationship with the media and political process. Our understanding of public interpretation of advocacy efforts and people's willingness—or lack thereof—to participate in collective action opposing the media is vague at best. This despite the fact that the public determines the success of television programs, advertising campaigns and media advocacy efforts. Media industries will continue to study the public within the commercial constraints of their own economic interests. It is up to researchers and activists to discover the complexities of how and why audiences interpret and act upon counter-commercial appeals as they do. We may safely assume that this will be increasingly contested terrain for people of black, brown, and all other hues of humanity in the coming decades.

REFERENCES

Acuna, Armando. (1985, September 21)Martinez lampoon draws Latino protest. *Los Angeles Times* (San Diego County ed.) Pt. 2, p. 3.

Aoki, Guy. (1999, September 6) Counterpunch: TV's definition of "minority" too narrow. *Los Angeles Times* (Record ed.) p. 3.

Brand-Williams, Oralander, & Kisha, Tim. (1999, July 13) NAACP condemns fall TV: Boycott, lawsuit vowed over lack of minority programs. *Detroit News*.

Braxton, Greg. (1999, May 28) A white, white world on TV's fall schedule. *Los Angeles Times* (Record ed.), A1.

Braxton, Greg. (1997, February 22) Rift slows NAACP protest of 8 shows. *Los Angeles Times* (Record ed.) pp. F1, F5.

Braxton, Greg, & Breslauer, Jan. (1995, March 5) Casting the spotlight on TV's brownout. *Los Angeles Times* (Home ed., calendar sec.) p. 8

Cripps, Thomas. (1977) *Slow fade to black: The Negro in American film, 1900–1942*. New York: Oxford University Press.

Cripps, Thomas. (1983) Winds of change: 'Gone with the Wind' and racism as a national issue. In Darden A. Pyron (Ed.) *Recasting: 'Gone with the Wind' in American culture*. pp. 137–152. Miami: University Presses of Florida.

Dawidziak, Mark, & Feran, Tom. (1999, August 15) Is TV's racism black and white or just green? *The Plain Dealer*, p. 1A.

De Leon, Arnoldo. (1983) *They called them greasers: Anglo attitudes toward Mexicans in Texas, 1821–1900*. Austin: University of Texas Press.

Delpar, Helen. (1984, Spring) Goodbye to the "greaser" Mexico, the MPPDA, and derogatory films, 1922–1926, *Journal of Popular Film and Television, 12*(1), 34–41.

Ely, Melvin Patrick. (1991) *The adventures of Amos 'n' Andy: A social history of an American phenomenon*. New York: Free Press.

Gonzalez, Patricia, & Rodriguez, Roberto (1999, September 13) Television brownout protests further whitening of media. *Minorities' Job Bank.* Downloaded on May 20, 2000. http://www.minorities-jb.com/african/civil/archives/brownout0913.htm.

Guerrero, Ed. (1993) *Framing blackness: The African American image in film.* Philadelphia: Temple University Press.

Jennings, James. (Ed.) (1994) *Blacks, Latinos, and Asians in urban America: Status and prospects for politics and activism.* Westport, CT: Praeger.

Keller, Gary D. (1994) *Hispanics and United States film: An overview and handbook.* Tempe, AZ: Bilingual Press/Editorial Bilingüe.

Kennard, William E. (1999, July 28) *Arising tide: La Raza in the new millennium.* Remarks to the National Council of La Raza, Houston, TX. Downloaded on May 19, 2000. http://www.fcc.gov/Speeches/Kennard/spwek926.html

Kolker, Claudia. (1999, July 28) Latino groups urge boycott: Media coalition decries the lack of industry jobs for minorities and the negative portrayals on screen. *Los Angeles Times* (Record ed.), 12

Kuczynski, Alex. (2000, January 8) Following NBC's lead, ABC outlines minority hiring plan. *New York Times* (National ed.) p. A7.

Lamb, Blaine P. (1975, October) The convenient villain: The early cinema views the Mexican-American, *Journal of the West, 14*(4), pp. 75–81.

Lichter, S. Robert, & Amundsun, Daniel R. (1997) Distorted reality: Hispanic characters in TV entertainment. In Clara E. Rodriguez (Ed.) *Latin looks: Images of Latinas and Latinos in U.S. media.* (pp. 57–72) Boulder, CO: Westview.

Limon, Jose E. (1973, Fall) Stereotyping and Chicano resistance: An historical dimension. *Aztlan 4*(2), 257–270.

Lopez, Ana M. (1991) Are all Latins from Manhattan? Hollywood, ethnography, and cultural colonialism. In Lester D. Friedman (Ed.), *Unspeakable images: Ethnicity and the American cinema.* (pp. 404–424) Chicago: University of Illinois Press.

MacDonald, J. Fred. (1983) *Blacks and white TV: Afro-Americans in television since 1948.* Chicago: Nelson-Hall.

Martinez, Thomas M. (1969, Summer) Advertising and racism: The case of the Mexican-American. *El Grito, 3*(4), 3–13.

Mifflin, Lawrie. (1999, September 26) UPN's 'Moesha,' the non-white hit nobody knows. *New York Times* (Late ed.), p. 29.

Miranda, Frank M. (1999, September) Racial bias abounds on ABC. *Chicano.org Editorials.* Editorial column downloaded May 20, 2000. http://chicano.org/imchicano.htm.

Montgomery, Kathryn C. (1989) *Target: Prime time: Advocacy groups and the struggle over entertainment television.* New York: Oxford University Press.

NAACP blasts TV networks fall season whitewash. (1999, July 12) NAACP press release downloaded Nov. 23, 1999. http://www.naacp.org/president/releases/naacp_blasts_tv_networks.htm.

NAACP and ABC television network agree on initiatives to increase opportunities for people of color. (2000, January 7) NAACP press release downloaded June 17, 2000. http://www.naacp.org/president/releases/NAACP%20and%20ABC.htm.

NBC adopts goals and timetables to increase opportunities for people of color. (2000, January 5) NAACP press release downloaded June 17, 2000. http://www.naacp.org/president/releases/NAACP%20Adopts%20Goals.ht.

National Council of La Raza. (1994, August) *Out of the picture: Hispanics in the media, state of Hispanic media 1994.* Washington, DC: NCLR.

National Council of La Raza (1997) Out of the picture: Hispanics in the media. In Clara E. Rodriguez (Ed.) *Latin looks: Images of Latinas and Latinos in U.S. media* (pp. 21–33). Boulder, CO: Westview.

Nuiry, Octavio Emilio. (1996, July 31) Ban the Bandito! *Hispanic* p. 26.

Pennington, Gail. (1999, August 29) Predominant color in the fall television lineup is white. *St. Louis Post-Dispatch*, p. F9.

Perez, Miguel (1999, August) Hispanic TV boycott is an action long overdue. *Minorities' Job Bank.* Downloaded on May 20, 2000. http://www.minoritiesjb.com/hispanic/commentary/archives/tvboycott899.html.

Piatt, Bill. (1997) *Black and brown in America: The case for cooperation.* New York: New York University Press.

Rainbow/Push coalition supports NAACP brownout. (1999, September 9) Minorities' Job Bank article downloaded May 20, 2000. http://www.minorities-jb.com/african/civil/jessebrown0909.html.

Reynolds, Barbara. (September 22, 1999) 'Black-out' should be for all media. *Sacramento Observer*, p. G3.

Reyes, Luis, & Rubie, Peter (1994) *Hispanics in Hollywood: An encyclopedia of film and television.* New York: Garland.

Rodriguez, Clara E. (Ed.) *Latin looks: Images of Latinas and Latinos in U.S. media.* Boulder, CO: Westview.

Rohan, Virginia. (1999, August 1) Affirmative reaction amid cries of 'whitewash.' *The Record* (Hackensack, NJ), p. Y1.

Romer, D. Jamieson, K.H., & De Coteau, N.J. (1998) The treatment of persons of color in local television news: Ethnic blame discourse or realistic group conflict. *Communication Research, 25*, pp. 268–305.

Skyhawk, Sonny. (1999, August 16) Reel Indians: Minorities stand up to television networks. *Indian Country Today (Lakota Times)* p. A5.

Stafford, Laura. (1999,December 8) NAACP takes on the television industry in L.A. *Los Angeles Sentinel*, p. A1.

Turner, Patricia A. (1994) *Ceramic uncles and celluloid mammies: Black images and their influence on culture.* New York: Anchor Books.

Vasquez, Marcherie (1999, August 10) ¡Más latinos en la televisión! *El Diario/La Prensa*, p. 2.

Vega, Miguel (1999, December 10) Protestan por personaje latino en juego: La compañía Walt Disney anuncia que eliminará un segmento del videojuego 'Toy Story 2.' *La Opinión* (Los Angeles) p. 1B

Walker, Lee H. (1999, September 6) Talking politics: An out-of-step NAACP must reclaim its vision. *Crain's Chicago Business*, p. 11).

Wilkinson, Kenton T. (forthcoming) Situational ethnicity and the intra-ethnic struggle for control of U.S. Spanish-language television. *Communication Quarterly* (Special issue: "Identity Negotiation: An Exploration of Racial, Cultural, and Gendered Identities").

Woll, Allen L. (1977) *The Latin image in American film.* Los Angeles: UCLA Latin American Center Publications.

Index

Wright, Herbert L., 219
Wubbels, T., 185

Yu-Wei, H., 94

Zaller, J., 124, 135
Zhang, X., 6
Zinn, M. B., 30

About the Editors and Contributors

ALAN B. ALBARRAN is Professor and Chair of the Department of Radio, Television and Film at the University of North Texas. He is the author of six books, and serves as the Editor of the *Journal of Media Economics*. He has authored numerous articles. He serves on several editorial boards and has lectured and presented workshops in several European countries.

SHARON BRAMLETT-SOLOMON is an Associate Professor in the School of Journalism at Arizona State University. Her research and teaching interests include topics in newspaper reporting, mass communication theory, and race, gender, and media. She has many publications, has held key officer posts in the Association for Education in Journalism and Mass Communication (AEJMC).

META G. CARSTARPHEN is an Associate Professor of Journalism and Mass Communication at the University of Oklahoma. A former magazine editor, she received the "Best Feature" award twice from the American Business Press. She was among the first class of Fellows in the Journalism and Mass Communication Leadership Institute for Diversity (JLID) of AEJMC/ASJMC.

PRABU DAVID is an Associate Professor at the School of Journalism and Communication at Ohio State University. His research is on media andcognition, with a focus on new communication technologies. He also studies the role of media images on body image perceptions.

DAVID DOMKE is an Associate Professor in the Department of Communication at the University of Washington. His research interests include individual values and cognition, media framing and priming, and the interaction of elites and the press in social change. He recently received the University of Washington Distinguished Teaching Award.

ANITA FLEMING-RIFE is an Assistant Professor in the College of Communications at Pennsylvania State University. She was a United Nations Public Information Officer and now teaches on media and the public, and women, minorities, and media. She conducts research on diversity in media and international news. She gained Freedom Forum and Ford Foundation grants.

STANLEY O. GAINES, JR., is a Professor at Brunel University in Uxbridge, Middlesex, United Kingdom. He wrote the book, *Culture, Ethnicity and Personal Relationship Processes* (1997), as well as numerous articles on ethnicity and relationships. He was a Fulbright grantee.

STELLA D. GARCIA-LOPEZ is an Associate Professor of Social and Personality Experimental Psychology at the University of Texas at San Antonio. She teaches courses in attribution, prejudice, relationships, methodology, and personality. Her research includes perception, interpersonal relationships, and social interactions in face-to-face and virtual settings.

NANCY GREER-WILLIAMS is a doctoral student pursuing an interdisciplinary degree at Western Michigan University. Her research interests center on diversity issues, organizations, and educational institutions.

DON HEIDER is an Associate Professor of Journalism at the University of Texas at Austin. He wrote *White News: Why Local News Programs Don't Cover People of Color* (2000), a study of how local newsrooms consistently exclude coverage of people of color. He worked for ten years as a reporter, photographer, producer, and manager in television news.

PRISCILLA HERNANDEZ is a student in the School of Journalism at Arizona State University.

DAWN HUEY-OHLSSON is a Market Researcher for radio stations across the United States.

MELISSA A. JOHNSON is an Associate Professor in the Department of Communication at North Carolina State University. Her research focuses on media, identity, and culture.

JAMES KIWANUKA-TONDO is an Assistant Professor in the Department of Communication at North Carolina State University. He has taught at University of Connecticut and Central Connecticut State University. He was also Head of the

School of Journalism at the Uganda Management Institute. His research focuses on health communication campaigns on AIDS.

CAMILLE KRAEPLIN is a Visiting Professor of Journalism at Southern Methodist University. Her research focuses on mass media and ethnic groups, and public journalism. She worked nearly a decade as a journalist and was an Institute for Journalism Excellence Fellow (ASNE).

KELLEY McCOY is a doctoral candidate in the Department of Communication at the University of Washington. Her research focuses on the relations among news media, race, and ethnicity and public policy, with a particular interest in news coverage of immigration.

A. N. MOHAMED is an Associate Professor at Edinboro University of Pennsylvania. He teaches and conducts research in journalism history and international communication. He was recently awarded a Ford Foundation research grant to study the use of minority sources in the news.

MARK P. ORBE is an Associate Professor of Communication and Diversity at Western Michigan University where he holds joint appointments in the Department of Communication and the Center for Women's Studies. His research interests focus on the inextricable relationship between culture and communication.

FRANK G. PEREZ is an Assistant Professor in the Department of Communication and the Chicano Studies at the University of Texas, El Paso. He is a Research Fellow at the Sam Donaldson Communication Research Center and has published in Chicana/o studies, intercultural communication, and public relations.

A. Y. "FRED" RAMIREZ is an Assistant Professor of Education at California State University, Fullerton. He is in charge of the Placentia-Yorba Linda Professional Development District. His research includes parental involvement, school reform, teacher education, and rethinking multicultural education.

REYNA GARCIA RAMOS is an Associate Professor of Education at the Graduate School of Education and Psychology at Pepperdine University. Her research and teaching interests include the effective instruction of language to ethnic minority students. She publishes on the literacy development of bilingual students and English-language learners.

XAE ALICIA REYES is an Associate Professor in the NEAG School of Education and the Puerto Rican and Latino Studies Institute at the University of Connecticut. She previously taught at Rhode Island College and Brown University. Her research and teaching focus on issues of language, culture and migratory experiences.

DIANA I. RIOS is an Associate Professor in the Department Communication Sciences and the Puerto Rican/Latino Studies Institute (PRLS) at the University of Connecticut. She is Associate Director for PRLS. Her research and teaching includes minorities, women, media effects, cross-cultural communication. She was among the first Fellows of the Journalism and Mass Communication Leadership Institute for Diversity (JLID) of AEJMC/ASJMC.

DARYL M. ROWE is a Professor of Psychology at the Graduate School of Education and Psychology at Pepperdine University. His research and teaching include cross-cultural mental health issues. He consults and publishes on psychological issues affecting African Americans. He holds a national position in the Association of Black Psychologists and is a licensed psychologist.

FEDERICO A. SUBERVI-VELEZ is Professor and Chair of the Department of Communication Studies at Pace University in New York. His expertise is in mass communication and ethnic groups, especially Latinos. His international research focuses on media and diversity in Brazil, and on the media system of Puerto Rico.

MARCOS TORRES is a doctoral student in the Department of Communication at the University of Washington. His research interests include media representations of racial and ethnic groups, with a particular interest in immigration and how immigrants adapt to new cultures.

DON UMPHREY is an Associate Professor in the Temerlin Advertising Institute at Southern Methodist University in Dallas, Texas. His teaching interests include advertising media planning, advanced media planning, and consumer behavior. Umphrey's academic research has centered on television audience studies and theories of social psychology applied to communication.

ANGELA WALKER is a doctoral candidate in Psychology at the University of Connecticut. Her research and teaching interests include race, gender, and the media, intergroup relations, asymmetries of power with communal relationships, stigma, and the social psychology of race and gender.

KIESHA T. WARREN is a Visiting Professor in the Department of Sociology at the University of Akron. She earned her doctorate from Western Michigan University. Her research interests involve criminology, race, ethnicity, gender, and the African American family.

KENTON T. WILKINSON is an Associate Professor in the Department of Communication at the University of Texas at San Antonio. His research interests include cultural-linguistic markets for electronic media, U.S. Spanish-language television, and media advocacy. He is co-editor of *Mass Media and Free Trade: NAFTA and the Cultural Industries* (1996).